Georg Hermann von Meyer

The organs of speech

Georg Hermann von Meyer

The organs of speech

ISBN/EAN: 9783742849021

Manufactured in Europe, USA, Canada, Australia, Japa

Cover: Foto ©Andreas Hilbeck / pixelio.de

Manufactured and distributed by brebook publishing software (www.brebook.com)

Georg Hermann von Meyer

The organs of speech

THE
ORGANS OF SPEECH

AND THEIR APPLICATION IN

THE FORMATION OF ARTICULATE SOUNDS

BY

GEORG HERMANN VON MEYER

PROFESSOR IN ORDINARY OF ANATOMY AT THE UNIVERSITY OF ZÜRICH

WITH FORTY-SEVEN WOODCUTS

LONDON
KEGAN PAUL, TRENCH & CO., 1, PATERNOSTER SQUARE
1883

(*All rights reserved.*)

PREFACE.

The more we become convinced that a true knowledge of the laws which govern the transformation of the elements of speech in the formation of dialects or derivative languages can only be obtained from a study of the physiological laws of the formation of articulate sounds, the more necessary does it become for the philologist to be thoroughly acquainted with the structure and functions of the organs of speech. The ordinary anatomical handbooks are little adapted to this purpose, for much is there discussed at length which is of no use to the philologist, while, on the other hand, points which to him are of considerable importance are only briefly alluded to; in physiological handbooks, also, only a short space is in most cases devoted to this subject.

It is, therefore, my object in the present work to discuss, with special reference to this requirement of the philologist, the structure and functions of the organs of speech.

In explaining the origin of articulate sounds, I have so far departed from the usual method that I have not attempted to arrange physiologically the entire series of sounds employed in the most differing languages, but rather, starting from the structure of the organs of speech, to give a sketch of all possible articulate sounds. I believe I have thus constructed a system in which all known articulate sounds, and all those with which we may hereafter become acquainted, will find a place. Such a sketch could not, of course, be given without reference to existing languages. The object has not been, however, to enter into the field of discussion upon the various modifications of sounds, but merely to bring forward a sufficient number of examples in confirmation of the laws explained, for which purpose the more nearly related European languages are sufficient.

In taking this line, it has been possible to trace the relations and capacity for combination of the various articulate sounds. From this point of view, again, we are enabled to discover the leading characteristics in the manner of the employment of the organs of speech ("accent") from the manner in which words of the original language have changed in the period of transition. I should have had much pleasure in attempting to illustrate this interesting study in the case of a single language, but the scope of the present work rendered such an undertaking impossible. I must, therefore, be contented with referring to this question together with its value in connection with etymology and orthoëpy.

From the great interest which this subject must arouse in all educated people, especially in those engaged in philological studies, and for all musicians, I venture to hope that my work will be welcomed by a large circle of readers; and also that the various new and original interpretations contained in it will be of interest to others of my profession. I trust, therefore, that my work may obtain a friendly and favourable reception.

THE AUTHOR.

ZÜRICH, *November*, 1879.

CONTENTS.

	PAGE
PREFACE	v
INTRODUCTION	1

CHAPTER I.

FORMATION OF THE ORGANS OF SPEECH.

The Production of the Air-Current	5
Importance of the Respiratory Process	6
The Air-Passages	9
The Mechanism of Respiration	10
Strengthening of the Air-Current	17
Survey of the Air-Passages	24
The Larynx	32
The Vocal Chords and their Tension	33
The Vocal Apparatus of the Larynx	35
The Glottis and its Adjusting Cartilages	46
The Superior Cavity of the Larynx	61
Summary	71
The Pharynx	72
The Nasal Cavity	79
The Relation of the Organ of Smell to the Air-Passages	79
Division of the Nasal Cavity into an Air-Passage and an Olfactory Chamber	81
The Bony Framework of the Nasal Cavity	83
The External Nose	92
The Muscles of the Nose	96
Summary	98
The Inner Wall of the Nasal Cavity	100
The Side Chambers of the Nose	107
Individual Variations in the Nasal Cavity	115

CONTENTS.

	PAGE
The Cavity of the Mouth	119
The Teeth	121
The Mechanical Movements of the Cavity of the Mouth	121
The Movement of the Jaws	123
The Lips	129
The Tongue	137
The Hyoid Bone	142
The Pharynx	149
The Soft Palate	156
The Nerves of the Air-Passages	164

CHAPTER II.

THE RELATION BETWEEN THE ORGANS OF SPEECH AND THE FORMATION OF SOUND.

Unusual Forms of the Respiratory Process	173
The Respiratory Noises	181
The Formation of Tone in the Air-Passages	187
The Larynx as an Apparatus for producing Tone	190
Voice and Speech	217
Reciprocal Closure of the Cavities of the Mouth and Nose	220
The Nasal Cavity	230
The Cavity of the Mouth	240
The Superior Cavity of the Larynx and the Pharynx	247

CHAPTER III.

THE FORMATION OF ARTICULATE SOUNDS.

Articulate Sounds	251
The Elements of Articulate Sounds	255
The Vowels	274
The Pure Vowels	275
The Diphthongs	291
The Nasal Vowels	298
The Resonants	
The Consonants	300
The Labials	305
The Dentals	310
The Gutturals	313
The Marginals	315
The Vibrants	318
The Double Consonants	320
Consonants and Resonants	321
L and *N Mouillé*	333
	335
INDEX	345

THE ORGANS OF SPEECH

INTRODUCTION.

The possession of speech has always been considered as a distinctive mark of the human race, and indeed, as far as we can learn from history or ethnography, in no age and in no part of the globe do we meet with a people without a language. Although races are known which in this respect are at a very low standard of development, and which possess a language which is very poor both in its form and in the expression of ideas, they still nevertheless do possess a language, which answers to their humble condition and is sufficient for their different wants.

In fact, the possession of speech cannot be prized too highly, since its possession serves the whole human race as the starting-point towards the acquirement of a progressive development and of civilization; it is the chief means by which the ideas and thoughts of individuals are communicated to their fellows, and the knowledge of one generation transmitted to the next. When, again, we consider that speech is the means by which feelings of every kind are communicated and excited, whether in the various forms of speech or in the higher forms of poetry and song, we shall not hesitate to distinguish language as the centre of the entire mental and intellectual life of man.

If, now, we ask in what this wonderful and priceless gift of the human race consists, and in what manner it is produced, we obtain an answer which gives us a fresh example of the humble means by which in nature the greatest and most important results are obtained.

If we analyze speech, we find that it is nothing more than a combination of separate sounds; that these sounds are noises which are produced by the expired air, with which tones of a musical kind, produced by the same means, can unite as supplementary components.

The power of producing sounds by the current of expired air is by no means a peculiar property of mankind; rather it is possessed in a more or less pronounced form by all vertebrata performing respiration by means of lungs; the noises thus produced being used by them, partly to give expression to their feelings, partly to make communications to each other. What an immense difference between the sounds and the meaning attached to them, in the angry hiss of a snake and the song of a nightingale, in the warning whistle of a marmot and the various accents of the bay of a hound!

But although animals make so much use of their power of producing noise, yet they never attain to human speech; for these sounds have to them no more value than the use made by man of the calls and exclamations —He! Ho! Psh! H'm! The greater use which man can make of his power of producing sounds depends upon the faculty which he possesses of combining sounds into complex sounds, which complex sounds become words used for the expression of certain ideas. But from this view of the characteristics of human speech we are not to conclude that everything included in it is an essentially human property. As far, at least, as the methods of production of these complex sounds (words) go, we find that certain animals—birds, for instance—are able to imitate man in this respect, although to a limited extent.

But although we are quite right in assuming that the talking parrot does not understand the meaning of the words which it has learnt, and undoubtedly connects no meaning with them, we may still ask the question whether, in the combination of sounds which many animals under certain circumstances are able to produce, some conceivable meaning may not be recognized, which allows us to consider them as, at least to a small extent, somewhat analogous to words. The various modulations and combined sounds in the croak of a frog, in the song of a nightingale, and in the nocturnal concert of cats, etc., seem to require such a view; and the probability is increased by the fact that in the legends of all nations an important part is played by wise men, who understand the language of animals.

Even should we conclude to give such an interpretation to the language of animals, we cannot but see that the range of ideas for which it can find expression must be immeasurably smaller than the range of those ideas which human language must and can express, partly by means of the words themselves, and partly by the modification which it gives to these words (declension, conjugation, etc.).

The great variety of the sounds employed in language forces upon us the conclusion, that the possibility of this variety is accounted for by the more or less composite structure of the apparatus employed in their production;

and this to a certain extent is the case. Nevertheless, the groundwork of the structure of this apparatus is simple. It depends upon the fact, that as the air expired from the lungs escapes either through the nasal cavity or through the cavity of the mouth, different sounds are produced by its means dependent upon the path taken by the current of air, and upon voluntary movements of certain structures within the cavity of the mouth. The current of air employed in this manner can either pass out noiselessly through the larynx, or during its passage through the larynx can be thrown into sonant vibration.

How means so simple in their characteristics are able to produce the sounds which form the elements of speech, will be explained in the following pages. For this purpose we must proceed, on the one hand, to examine the structure of the apparatus employed in the production of sound, and on the other to show how with their aid the sounds ordinarily used in speech are produced.

CHAPTER I.

STRUCTURE OF THE ORGANS OF SPEECH.

THE PRODUCTION OF THE AIR-CURRENT.

THE chief condition for the production of articulate sounds is a current of air, modifications of which, produced at will, are perceived as sounds. Such modifications are, *e.g.* streaming through a large cavity or through a narrow slit, sudden interruption of the current or a sudden removal of some obstruction to the current, etc.

Such a current of air is an accessory phenomenon in the process of respiration, in which the air is at regular intervals first drawn into the lungs and then driven out again. The process of respiration is, therefore, carried on by two alternating currents of air, differing in direction, the one going in, the other going out. Both can be employed in the production of sound; nevertheless this, as a rule, only takes place with the expired current. The inspired current is only employed for the production of sound in extraordinary circumstances, either as a make-shift or at times from affectation, or again when the sound is accidental—*e.g.* in the hiccough. On this account, in our subsequent investigations upon the nature of the production of sound, we shall only consider the current of expired air.

But in order that the significance of this air-current, and its differences in strength and rhythm, which are so important for the production of sound, may be correctly understood, it seems necessary that we should first explain the position of the respiratory process among the vital phenomena of the organism.

Importance of the Respiratory Process.

For the success of the different chemical processes which are taking place in the body and are necessary for the maintenance of life, a constant supply of oxygen to all parts of the body is necessary. All highly organized animal forms are on this account provided with special apparatus, by which this supply is maintained. This apparatus is distinguished as the *respiratory apparatus*, or as *respiratory organs*.

The oxygen, which serves for respiration, is either contained in the air or in water, and animals, as a rule, absorb it from either medium, according to the one in which they live. Important exceptions to this rule are certain aquatic mammalia (whales) which breathe atmospheric air directly, although they live in the water.

The absorption of oxygen into the different parts of the body from the surrounding medium takes place partly indirectly, partly directly.

In the direct absorption of oxygen the surrounding medium itself is conveyed in its distribution to all parts of the body, and, according to the nature of the life of the animal, passes through water-channels opening upon the surface of the body, as in the sea-urchin, or through similarly arranged air-passages (tracheæ) as in insects.

This kind of respiration is of no interest for us in connection with our purpose, and is merely mentioned here in order to complete this portion of our subject.

The indirect absorption of oxygen is always connected with the presence of an extensive vascular system, and rests upon the direct supply of oxygen by means of certain organs to the blood which is circulating in these vessels, and its distribution through the body by means of the circulation of the blood. The circulation of the blood, therefore, belongs, strictly speaking, to the respiratory organs, since, as regards its subsequent significance, it plays a part similar to that of the above-mentioned water-passages and tracheæ. Nevertheless it is usual, in animal forms belonging to these classes, to consider as respiratory organs that apparatus only which concerns the transmission of oxygen to the blood.

The respiratory organs in the above-mentioned sense are all formed upon the same plan. They consist of a more or less extended membrane, with which the medium containing the oxygen comes in contact, and which contains in its substance a minute network of capillary vessels. The blood which traverses these capillaries is in this manner only separated from the air or from the water by a very thin partition, through which an exchange by diffusion between both liquids is possible; this results in the blood taking up a small quantity of oxygen from the air or from the water, and consequently evolving carbonic acid gas.

The respiratory organ is, therefore, always a specially organized membranous surface, and the differences noticeable in respiratory organs rest solely upon the differences in its mode of arrangement. In this relation there are, however, only two chief forms to be distinguished. The respiratory organ either consists of a specially organized portion of the outer membrane, which extends as a laminated or ramified process upon the outer surface of the body (gills), or of a cavity of a sacculated or ramified form within the body (lungs). In the lower animals only (*e.g.* snails) is the lung an expansion of the outer membrane; in all higher animals, especially in the three first classes of vertebrata, it takes the form of an expansion of the mucous membrane, commencing with the alimentary canal immediately behind the cavity of the mouth, and spreading out subsequently in the cavity of the trunk.

A peculiar intermediate form is exhibited by fishes, since in the latter the surface of the body, which serves as a respiratory organ (the gills), is provided with narrow openings, which pass outwards from the cavity of the mouth through the substance of the body. It may be laid down as a general rule that water-breathing animals only possess gills, and only air-breathers possess lungs.

The necessary oxygen is supplied to the gills by the flow of the water, which, moreover, is assisted by the rapid movement of the outer surface of the gills. A special apparatus, on the contrary, is requisite for the lungs, which, by its alternating activity, fills them with air and then empties them again.

This is the mechanism which is more or less externally visible, while the peculiar essential process of respiration is not perceived. On this account the succession of movements associated with this process is popularly designated as "breathing," and we distinguish as "inspiration" the movement by which the air is brought into the lungs, and as "expiration" that by which the air is driven out from the lungs again.

The Air-Passages.

We now proceed to describe the working of the mechanism by which the current of air is conducted into the lungs and again expelled from them, and will at present postpone a more exact description of the construction of those spaces which lead to the air-passages strictly so-called. We will confine ourselves to the statement that the back of the nasal cavity and of the cavity of the mouth unite to form a common space (the pharynx), from which the gullet (œsophagus) leads to the stomach on the one hand, and the windpipe (trachea) to the lungs on the other.

The cavity of the windpipe is, therefore, directly connected with the external air by the cavities of the pharynx, the mouth, and the nose; and the current of air created during inspiration finds its way through these cavities into the windpipe, and so into the lungs; and in the same manner the current of air expelled from the lungs passes out again through these cavities. On this account all these cavities may be classed broadly among the air-passages. The important fact, however, must not be overlooked, that between the pharynx and the external air, either the nasal cavity by itself, or the mouth by itself, or the nasal cavity and the mouth together, may serve as passages for the current of air. An important property of these air-passages is that they are always kept open—either from their walls, consisting of solid material, or because they are maintained tightly stretched by some peculiar arrangement. This circumstance is of less importance for the expelled current of air, but of the greatest importance for the inspired current; for it is evident that, if the walls of the air-passages were yielding, they would be compressed by the pressure of the external air, and a clear passage would not be maintained.

The Mechanism of Respiration.

The structure of the lungs themselves is of the very greatest importance to the mechanism of respiration, since the nature of the whole, as well as the properties of its materials, represent in themselves the foundation for the most important part of the respiratory process.

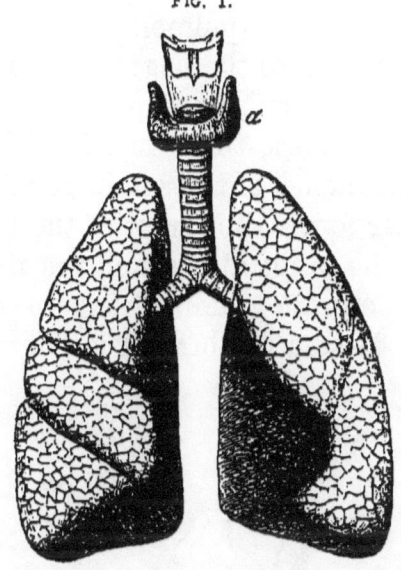

Fig. 1.

Front view of windpipe (trachea) and lungs. Lungs somewhat separated, in order to show the division of the trachea. In the lower inner part of each lung, especially of the left lung, a depression, in which the heart is situated. a, Thyroid gland; above which is the larynx, attached by its three ligaments to the hyoid bone.

The external form of the lungs is that of a rather large soft organ, filling the greater part of the cavity of the chest (thorax), and therefore somewhat approximating to the shape of a cone with the base situated below and a rounded apex directed upwards. It is divided into two entirely separate parts, each of which fills one-half of the cavity of the chest, so that we may distinguish a right and a left lung—a customary distinction. Between the opposing surfaces of each lung rises the windpipe as a simple tube, which is divided, at a point about in the centre of the thoracic cavity, into two branches, one of which leads to each lung. Between the lower divisions of the two lungs, and under the point where the windpipe divides, the heart is situated; from the heart the great tube (pulmonary artery) passes, which conveys the blood, which has to absorb oxygen, into each lung, and from each lung tubes (pulmonary veins) pass to the heart, which bring back to the heart the blood which has been changed by the respiratory process. The point of entrance and exit of these tubes is situated close to the entrance of the branches of the windpipe into each lung, and with the latter forms the "root of the lungs."

The cavity of the lungs into which the air is admitted consists of very minute ramifications of the trachea. The diameter of the smallest branch is $\frac{1}{4}$ mm. ($\frac{1}{100}$ inch),

FIG. 2.

Diagram of an air-cell of the lungs with its surrounding vessels. *a*, Air-cell; *b*, conducting branch of the pulmonary artery; *c*, abducting branch of the pulmonary vein.

and on these branches are placed, lastly, small round-shaped air-cells of $\frac{1}{10} - \frac{1}{3}$ mm. ($\frac{1}{250} - \frac{1}{75}$ inch) diameter, and it is in these air-cells that the transfer of oxygen from the inspired air to the blood takes place, since they are surrounded by a fine network of vessels, and the blood circulating through these vessels is only separated from the air contained in the air-cells by a layer of extremely thin material.

It would not serve our purpose to follow out the structure of the lungs in all its details, and we will therefore limit ourselves to the discussion of those points which are important in a mechanical sense to the current of air during respiration.

In this connection it is first to be noticed, that the solidity of the walls in the trachea mentioned above as characteristic of the air-passages is produced by semi-circular rings of cartilage, and that cartilage is found enclosed in the walls of the trachea as far as its furthest ramification. In the first divisions of the trachea within the lungs, however, this cartilage does not present the regular semicircular form, but, in the finer division of the trachea, the form of small round plates, which are perfectly fitted to keep the cavity of the branches of the trachea open, so that the passage of air may suffer no obstruction.

The most important fact, however, is that in the substance of the windpipe itself and in that of its branches, close under the covering of mucous membrane, there occurs a thick layer of elastic fibres, which run in the direction of the tubes and completely surround the air-cells. This so-called "elastic tissue," to which these fibres belong, is best compared to caoutchouc, since it, like the latter, possesses a considerable expansibility, and, after the expanding force has ceased, an elasticity comes into play which brings it back to its original form and thickness. From the large share of this elastic tissue in the formation of the lungs and from its disposition mentioned above, the lungs may be compared to a branched elastic sac, which can expand upon internal pressure, and upon the cessation of the pressure which had increased its capacity, contracts again in its circumference, and the additional space disappears. The extreme importance of this action for the mechanism of respiration,

Fig. 3.

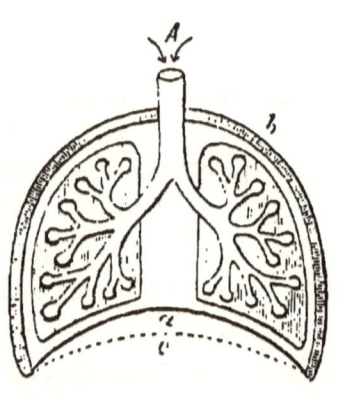

Diagram of the lungs to explain the mechanism of respiration. *A*, Entrance into the branched windpipe; *b*, the breast-bone (sternum) represented as a solid integument; *c*, the diaphragm in its relaxed state (continuous line), and in its contracted state (dotted line); *a*, the space added to the cavity of the thorax by the contraction of the diaphragm.

and also for that part of it which concerns the production of speech, will be explained further on.

The means by which a certain quantity of air can be drawn with such force into the air-space of the lungs, and every part of it enlarged till its sides are in a high state of tension, are provided by the situation of the lungs in the thoracic cavity, and by the mechanism which can be brought into play in the walls of the cavity.

The thoracic cavity is a part of the cavity of the trunk, which is bounded posteriorly by the ribs articulating by moveable joints with the vertebral column, and by the breast-bone, which anteriorly unites the ribs; the lower boundary of the thoracic cavity is formed by the diaphragm.

Regarding for the present the wall of the chest thus formed entirely by the ribs as a fixed and immoveable wall, we may explain most of the phenomena connected with the mechanism of respiration from the action of the diaphragm, after which we shall have no difficulty in adding those modifications which are due to the mobility of the ribs.

The diaphragm is a muscular plate which is attached to the entire lower circumference of the bony framework of the thorax, and so entirely shuts off the thoracic cavity from the abdomen that it only affords a relatively small passage to the œsophagus, and to some of the greater blood-vessels. The pressure of the abdominal viscera produced by the walls of the abdomen and transmitted to the diaphragm, forces the latter upwards, giving it an arched appearance when viewed from below. This gives a convex floor to the thoracic cavity, making it somewhat smaller than we should be led to expect from the size of its bony framework. When the diaphragm is contracted, every diameter of it is shortened, and its convexity consequently diminished. When contracted to its greatest imaginable extent, which is never attained, the diaphragm might present the appearance of a perfectly even plate, and the whole of the arched space which, under ordinary conditions, belongs to the abdominal cavity would then be added to the thoracic cavity. The contraction of the diaphragm thus increases the space within the thoracic cavity by depressing its highly convex floor.

Now, in ordinary quiet breathing, the action upon which the inspiration of the air depends is produced entirely by the contraction of the diaphragm. By this contraction the cavity of the chest is enlarged, and the

STRUCTURE OF THE ORGANS OF SPEECH. 15

action of the diaphragm may therefore be compared to the sucking action of a piston in its cylinder, the air thus sucked in being chiefly the external air, which, entering by the air-passages, is able to fill the enlarged cavity of the chest. But the current of air cannot thus force its way directly into the cavity of the chest, for in following the course of the windpipe it will be lost in the ramifications of the latter and in the air-cells, the closed terminations of those ramifications. Since, however, these air-cells are all provided with elastic walls, they expand when the air enters, and the dimension of the lungs is thus increased so as to fill the additional space within the cavity of the chest.

Inspiration, therefore, is due to the regular activity (contraction) of the diaphragm.

To understand correctly the mechanism of expiration, we must remember that the flattening of the diaphragm, besides enlarging the cavity of the chest, will effect a pressure upon the abdominal viscera, which pressure will be transmitted to the walls of the abdomen. The latter will therefore be forced outwards, and consequently expanded.

Thus the result of the contraction of the diaphragm is a greater or less expansion of the elastic tissue of the lungs by the entering air, and an expansion of the walls of the abdomen by the pressure of the diaphragm upon the abdominal viscera. Let us now see what effect will be produced by the relaxation which is a necessary consequence of this contraction of the diaphragm. The elasticity of the expanded tissue of the lungs will at once be called into play; the walls, namely, of all the cavities within the lungs will contract to the dimensions which they possessed before inspiration, and the superfluous air will thus again be driven out through the air-passages. The lungs will now be smaller than the enlarged cavity of the chest, and the vacuum so produced must, therefore, be filled by the pressure of the external air. This cannot, however, be well effected by the rigid walls of the chest, since they do not yield readily to the pressure of the air. The same result is, however, obtained by the pressure of the air, which acts upon the walls of the abdomen, forcing in the abdominal viscera, which then transmit the pressure to the diaphragm. The diaphragm thus again encroaches upon the cavity of the chest in the arched form of its position when at rest, the cavity itself assuming the smaller dimensions which characterized it before inspiration.

Expiration is, therefore, due to no special muscular activity, but is a phenomenon which is caused merely by the elasticity of the tissue of the lungs and by the pressure of the external air, the parts which had been violently disturbed by inspiration being thus again restored to a state of rest. The last act of respiration before death is, therefore, expiration, and for this reason a depressed abdomen (from the pressure of the external air) is characteristic of a corpse.

The fact, however, must not be overlooked, that the depression of the abdomen during expiration is increased by the elasticity of the expanded abdominal walls, and even further by a slight voluntary contraction of the muscles with which they are provided.

It is now clear why the expired current of air is most suitable for the production of sound in speech, and therefore almost exclusively employed for that purpose. The reason for this is clearly that the entering current of air must be produced by muscular activity, and can only with difficulty be drawn in slowly or for any length of time; the returning current, on the other hand, is involuntary and takes place spontaneously, and only requires to be regulated to form a continuous current of air of sufficient duration for the production of sound.

Strengthening of the Air-Current.

The duplex mechanism just described, which is sufficient for the ordinary requirements of respiration, can be employed in different degrees of activity, so that a single exchange of the air in the lungs is represented by a greater or less quantity of air. The lungs are never completely emptied of all the air which they contain, and never can be, since, as mentioned above, the walls of the air-passages are stiffened throughout their entire length by a cartilaginous layer, which prevents their being ever completely closed; nor are the lungs ever emptied to the extent allowed by the above check to further contraction, even in the strongest forms of expiration to be described directly. This is proved by the fact that after the thoracic cavity of a dead body has been opened, a sound lung contracts to such an extent that it only occupies from one-half to two-thirds of the space which it fully occupied before the opening was made. The lungs, therefore, even when most completely emptied of air, are still in a condition of expansion; from which fact we may draw the following interesting conclusions:—

(1) So much air remains in the lungs, that even in the pause between one expiration and the following inspiration, the essential respiratory process (change of the composition of the blood) undergoes no interruption; (2) this residual air keeps the air-passages always open, so that during inspiration the flow of air inwards can

more readily take place; (3) on this account a certain portion of the elastic contractibility remains in excess, which ensures a powerful action of the elasticity of the lung in expiration.

If, however, only a certain portion of the air contained in the lungs is expelled from them in the ordinary process of quiet respiration, a corresponding quantity only of fresh air is taken in again during inspiration. These facts point to the conclusion that a certain quantity of air is always present in the lungs, and that the respiratory movements only give rise to a partial renewal of this air, to a kind of ventilation which is more complete or more superficial according to the strength of the movements.

There are, however, cases in which a more complete ventilation in the lungs is required; for instance, in those diseases which produce difficulty in breathing, and in the passing condition of "being out of breath," as after violent exercise. Again, a greater current of air is necessary for loud calling, for sustained notes in singing, for the rapid pronunciation of long sentences, etc.; and for this purpose either a more considerable emptying of the quantity of air in the lungs must take place, or a greater quantity of air must be taken in (a deep breath), so that an increased current of air may flow out again.

In all these cases the ordinary gentle ventilation produced by the alternate contraction and relaxation of the diaphragm is not sufficient, and more powerful means are necessary for the greater general enlargement of the thoracic cavity, which is produced by raising the ribs simultaneously with the contraction of the diaphragm, thus increasing the circumference of the thorax. A powerful expiration is similarly produced by drawing down the ribs, which diminishes the circumference of

STRUCTURE OF THE ORGANS OF SPEECH. 19

the thorax. The arrangement of the ribs will explain how these movements can produce the required result.

The ribs are, as is well known, arches of bone, which are attached to that part of the trunk which surrounds the thoracic cavity. Behind they articulate by moveable joints with the vertebral column, and in front are united by means of the sternum, or breast-bone, to which they are all attached, either directly or indirectly. This con-

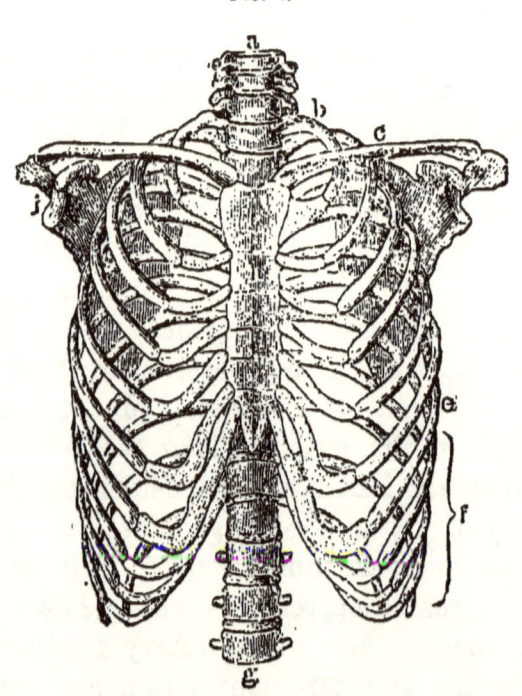

Fig. 4.

Front view of the thoracic cavity. *ag*, Vertebral column ; *h*, sternum ; *bde*, the seven upper ribs which are directly connected with the sternum (true ribs); *f*, the five lower ribs which are not directly connected with the breast-bone ; *c*, collar-bone ; *i*, shoulder-blade.

nection with the breast-bone is only wanting in the lowest ribs (the eleventh and twelfth), which terminate freely in muscular tissue. They are, however, held by this in a fixed position, and have a definite position with regard to the upper ribs. The collection of all the ribs forms, together with the backbone (dorsal vertebræ), to which they are attached, and with the breast-bone, a firm bony framework, the whole of which is called the "thorax," or the "chest." The first is the term used in science, the latter the common name.

The thorax forms firstly a more or less rigid covering for the cavity of the chest, and on the one hand prevents the walls of the chest from sinking in during the contraction of the diaphragm, and on the other hand forces the current of air which has filled the increased space of the thoracic cavity to return by the circuitous, but still the only possible way, which on this account is distinguished as the "air-passages."

On this account we have hitherto taken no further notice of it than to mention it as a rigid wall.

Nevertheless, it contains the needful elements for taking a very active part in the mechanism of inspiration and expiration, and the most powerful mechanism of respiration is shown to be due to its co-operation. Each pair of ribs, together with the intervening portion of the breast-bone, may be regarded as a closed ring articulating behind with the vertebral column. The plane of this ring can be brought into different positions with regard to the vertebral column; it can either be made more horizontal, so that it takes up a position more at right angles to the vertebral column, or it can be depressed so that it in a manner inclines downwards from the vertebral column. In the first case, the portion of the trunk enclosed by the ring will represent an almost circular horizontal section; in the latter case, on the contrary, it will slope from the front backwards. The space enclosed by the ring will, in the first case, be circular, and in the latter case lozenge-shaped. The action of the ribs does not, it is true, attain such

STRUCTURE OF THE ORGANS OF SPEECH. 21

extremes, but the manner of their action proves that their elevation must increase, and their depression diminish the capacity of the thorax.

The position of the ribs when at rest is slightly inclined downwards, so that they can either be raised or depressed; it is therefore evident that, when the occasion for a deep inspiration arises, we can produce it most easily by raising the ribs which form the wall of the chest, and in the same manner a powerful expiration can be produced by drawing the ribs downwards. Respiration is produced by this more or less voluntary elevation and depression of the thorax in the above-mentioned cases of want of breath, and whenever the necessity arises for the creation of a stronger current of air. The same form of respiration is, moreover, adopted in those cases where quiet respiration by the reciprocal action of the diaphragm and the walls of the abdomen is prevented. The commonest example of such a condition is that which is produced by "tight lacing," when the corset compresses the lowest portion of the thorax, and the greater part of the abdominal walls, to such an extent that the free movement of these parts is entirely out of the question. This form of respiration is, therefore, especially striking in public singers, the style of whose dress renders the ordinary quiet mode of breathing impossible, and yet who have frequently to make use of long-continued and powerful currents of air.

There is another interesting point in the mechanism of the elevation of the ribs to which we may briefly allude, a close analysis leading us further than the object of the present work would justify. The greater number of the ribs—all, namely, except the upper two or three—according to the individual, have, in addition to the curvature which they derive from the form of the walls of the trunk, a downward inclination, each rib descending rapidly, and then in a sharply rounded angle again ascending to the point of its contact with the sternum, or, as the case may be, with the preceding rib. At this angle the rib loses its bony character, and becomes cartilaginous, remaining so to its extremity. The cartilage is yielding and elastic, and when the rib is raised, it expands from this angle, increasing in length,

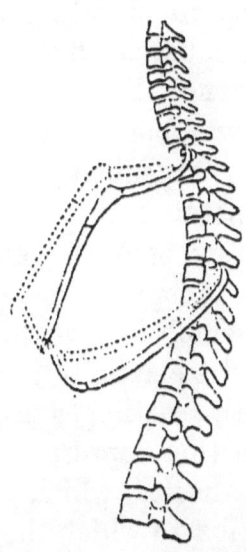

Fig. 5.

Diagrammatic representation of the elevation of the thorax during a deep inspiration. Instead of the entire thorax, the first and seventh ribs only are given, attached both to the sternum and the vertebral column. The continuous lines mark the position of the ribs when at rest; the dotted lines when elevated, showing the tension of the seventh rib.

therefore, and so enlarging the circumference of the thorax. As soon, however, as the muscular activity producing inspiration ceases, the elasticity of the cartilage restores to the angle its former acuteness. Thus, when the mechanism of respiration is carried on by the movement of the ribs, we see that expiration is again to a great extent due to the action of elasticity.

The elevation of the ribs in inspiration is produced

by muscles which descend from the cervical and dorsal vertebræ to the ribs (*scaleni, levatores costarum, serratus posticus superior, serratus posticus inferior*), and by those which pass in the spaces between the ribs from one rib to another (the *intercostal* muscles). The former elevate the ribs from the fixed point of the vertebral column, and the latter draw the lower ribs towards the upper. In cases of excessive want of breath, the muscles which pass from the thorax to the upper extremities are also called into play in elevating the ribs; but in this case the shoulders must be fixed—as, for instance, by resting upon the arm. Such cases are, however, due to disease, healthy subjects only having recourse to a somewhat similar expedient when in excessive want of breath—as, for instance, after rapid running, at which times they will throw back the shoulders so as to be able to take a deeper inspiration.

The depression which follows this elevation of the ribs arises partly from the elasticity of the contiguous parts, partly from that of the cartilages themselves. A stronger expiration by the further depression of the ribs is effected by the abdominal muscles, which by their forcible contraction draw the ribs to which they are attached downwards, and thus contract the thorax; also, however, by the pressure of the abdominal viscera, which forces the diaphragm upwards. The action of the abdominal muscles is reinforced by those parts of the long *erector spinæ* muscle which pass from below to the ribs, and by the *intercostal* muscles, which draw down the upper ribs towards those which have been depressed.

From the above it appears—

(1) That the returning current of air is specially adapted for the formation of sounds, particularly for the rapid succession of sounds necessary for speech,

because its production is not dependent upon any distinct activity.

(2) That it is possible to increase this current of air either by creating a stronger current of air to follow upon a quiet, moderate inspiration, by means of special muscular activity, and so almost emptying the lungs, or by taking a deeper inspiration, and so filling the lungs with a greater volume of air.

Again, from the facts which point to the possibility of the voluntary participation of muscles in both acts of respiration, we may without hesitation assert—

(1) That we are able, by means of certain muscles, to modify the strength and duration of the returning current of air, and thus either to allow it to escape slowly and evenly, as in speech, or to expel it violently, as in a shout.

(2) That it is also in our power to prolong to some extent the act of inspiration, or again, by special muscular activity, to perform it with the greatest rapidity.

(3) That we are, therefore, able to employ for the purpose of speech a current of air of (within certain limits) any volume and strength we please, which may be so regulated, that is, interrupted only by such short inspirations, that it may be regarded as a continuous stream.

Survey of the Air-Passages.

It has already been observed, in the preceding section, that the path followed by the air entering and leaving the lungs is of a somewhat complicated form; but nothing further was said, our only object then being to become acquainted with the mechanism by which the currents of air are formed. We must now, however, endeavour to gain at least a general knowledge of the form of the air-passages.

Now, the alimentary canal must be regarded as the foundation for the structure and arrangement of all organs concerned in the nutriment of the body. Why and how this is necessarily the case with regard to the animal organism we need not here inquire. The mere statement of the fact is sufficient for our present purpose, though we may, in passing, offer the following proof; namely, not only do we meet with a well-developed alimentary canal in those lower forms of the animal kingdom in which other organs of digestion are wanting, but that in the embryonic development of the higher (vertebrate) animals the alimentary canal is the first organ amongst those of digestion to be formed, upon and from which the other organs of this nature are developed.

The alimentary canal commences with the orifice of the mouth, which leads into a spacious cavity situated between the jaws (the *cavity of the mouth*). Here the mechanical division or mastication of the food takes place, to prepare it for solution (digestion) which follows in the stomach. The food thus prepared is then carried to the hindermost portion of the cavity of the mouth, where a descending depression marks the commencement of the œsophagus. Certain muscular actions (swallowing, drinking) then force the food into the œsophagus, down which it is carried, by forces peculiar to that tube, into the stomach.

In the human body the direction of the cavity of the mouth is from the front backwards, and its more backward portion, situated directly above the œsophagus, which descends vertically from it, is cut off from the larger anterior portion by a fold or valve-like structure (the *soft palate*), so that at first sight it might be regarded as a continuation of the œsophagus to the base of the skull. From this peculiarity this portion of the cavity of the mouth is generally regarded as a distinct space, and as such described as the *pharynx;* while the term "cavity of the mouth" is only applied to the space between the soft palate and the orifice of the mouth. A point which we shall presently find of interest is that the food prepared in the cavity of the mouth passes rapidly through the pharynx before falling into the œsophagus. In effecting this an important part is played by the "tongue," a muscular fold lying upon the floor of the cavity of the mouth, the free upper surface (*dorsum*) of which passes as a convex protuberance (root of the tongue) into the anterior wall of the pharynx.

During the embryonic development a small growth appears upon the anterior wall of the pharynx, which afterwards becomes hollow. It continues growing and becomes a tube which divides into a right and a left branch, and each branch continues growing and dividing till it presents at last the appearance of a highly ramified structure. This forms the groundwork of the lungs, which for their completion only require the subdivision of the pulmonary veins and arteries; these vessels unite at an early period with the tube, the growth and ramifications of which they then follow. Thus the lungs arise as an outgrowth, or process of the pharynx. It is evident that this ramifying tube must be the windpipe, dividing at first into two branches, each of which passes to a lung, where it becomes very highly ramified; and since the windpipe originated as a process of the pharynx, it opens into and is immediately connected with the latter. The part adjoining this orifice is termed the *larynx*, and will presently be described as a separate organization.

Now, since the pharynx opens into the cavity of the

mouth, which again, by means of the lips, is in free communication with the external air, it follows that an uninterrupted passage is afforded to the air through the cavity of the mouth to the lungs, and thus inspiration as well as expiration can be effected through the cavity of the mouth. We know, however, that respiration through the open mouth is only resorted to in cases of want of breath, or when a deep inspiration is taken, or, again, as the result of bad habit. In ordinary quiet respiration the mouth is generally closed, and the cavity of the mouth is not employed as an air-passage.

Entrance and exit is, as is well known, afforded to the air employed in respiration by the nose, or rather the *nasal cavity*—a cavity which commences anteriorly with the nostrils, and opens posteriorly freely into the pharynx.

It is interesting to observe that fishes have no nasal cavity, and that in their case the organ of smell, which otherwise is always connected with the nasal cavity, consists merely of folds in the outer integument which are situated above the orifice of the mouth. We first meet with a nasal cavity, in the accepted sense, in the amphibia, while it becomes general with birds and mammals. Its appearance, therefore, in the animal kingdom is simultaneous with respiration by means of lungs, a proof that its structure is more intimately connected with this form of respiration, and that we are therefore justified in regarding it as the true air-passage.

Thus we obtain the curious fact that the air-passage, strictly speaking, commences with the nasal cavity situated above the cavity of the mouth, and that from the nasal cavity it passes into the upper part of the pharynx, then through an orifice in the anterior wall of the pharynx immediately below the cavity of the mouth into the larynx, which marks the commencement of the windpipe, and finally through the windpipe into the lungs. The peculiarity of this arrangement lies in the fact that the air-passage crosses the portion of the alimentary canal formed by the cavity of the mouth, the pharynx, and the œsophagus in such a manner that the pharynx belongs equally to the two passages. It is precisely this peculiarity, however, which makes it possible to employ the returning current of air in the formation of sound and, therefore, for speech. The parts of the cavity of the mouth, and in particular the tongue, by their great mobility can alter the form of the cavity of the mouth in the most varied manner. Every such conformation imparts a peculiar kind of vibration to the current of air which is heard as sound. The possibility of speech is therefore due to the power we possess of voluntarily directing the current of air from the pharynx into the cavity of the mouth, where sound can be produced in the manner described.

It is evident that air and food cannot pass through the pharynx at the same time, as all, moreover, know from experience who have been excited to laughter during the act of swallowing. We should therefore naturally expect to find some arrangement which would keep both passages clear, so that the one process should suffer no inconvenience from the other. Respiration being a continuous process, while swallowing is merely a transitory and quickly executed act, we should conclude beforehand that this arrangement will in its usual form be in favour of the flow of the air; and this we find to be the case. The pharynx, from causes presently to be discussed, is always open. Its walls, indeed, are not composed of such rigid material as the cartilage of the windpipe, but from the manner of their attachment to the bones of the skull and to the hyoid bone, they are held so tense that they cannot collapse, and therefore always form an open cavity. Thus an uninterrupted passage is secured to the air from the nasal cavity through the pharynx into the larynx, and thence through the windpipe into the lungs.

This, however, is not sufficient. We find further that, except during the time of swallowing, the cavity of the mouth and the œsophagus are cut off from free communication with the pharynx. The arrangement for the œsophagus is the simpler of the two. Thus the œsophagus is not to be regarded as simply an open tube down which the food falls by its own weight, for throughout its entire length it is so contracted upon itself as to be perfectly impassable, and special forces are required to force the morsels of food from the pharynx into the œsophagus. Thus the entrance to the œsophagus, viewed from the pharynx, has merely the appearance of a funnel-shaped depression. Showmen in menageries are accustomed to claim this as a striking peculiarity of the crocodile, when they draw attention to the open jaws of this reptile.

The closure of the cavity of the mouth is less simple, being effected by a double system of valves. A broad, crescent-shaped valve, the horns of which, descending laterally, rest upon the root of the tongue, hangs down from the bony plate (the hard palate), dividing the cavity of the mouth from the nasal cavity between the cavity of the mouth and the pharynx. This is the soft palate, or *velum palati*. When at rest it lies immediately upon the highly convex posterior portion of the dorsum of the tongue, and thus closes the cavity of the mouth. When in great thirst the mucous membrane of the cavity of the mouth loses its necessary degree of moisture, the soft palate adheres so firmly to the dorsum of the tongue, that the act of swallowing, by which it is removed, gives rise to a sensation of pain. Thus, in describing a high degree of thirst, we are accustomed to say that the "tongue cleaves to the roof of the mouth." This peculiarity, which we must all have experienced, may be

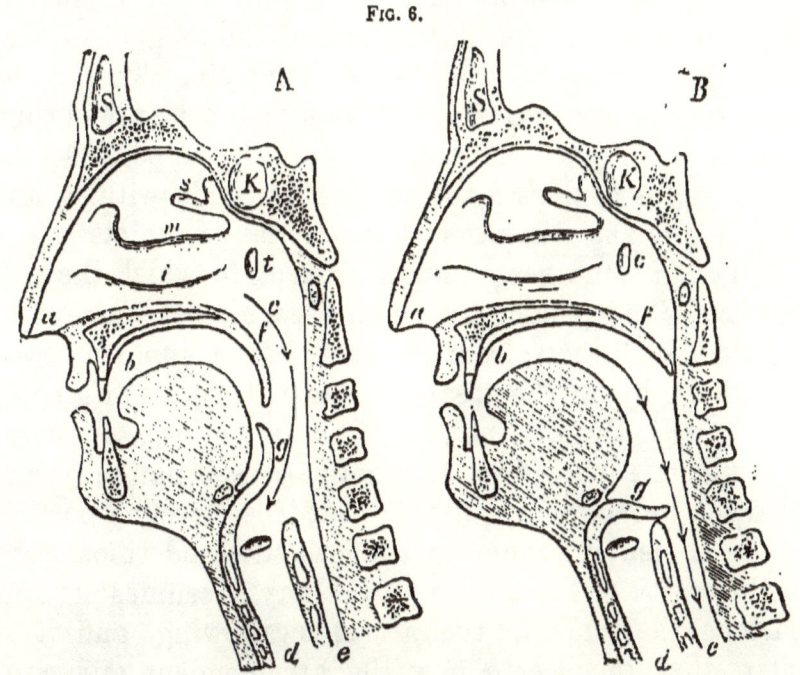

Fig. 6.

A, The pharynx during respiration; the cavity of the mouth shut off by the soft palate and the epiglottis; current of air indicated by arrows.
B, The pharynx during swallowing; the nasal cavity shut off by the soft palate, the windpipe by the epiglottis; course of the food indicated by arrows.
In both figures: *a*, nostril; *b*, cavity of the mouth; *t* in *A*, *c* in *B*, orifice of the Eustachian tube; *d*, windpipe; *e*, œsophagus; *f*, soft palate; *g*, epiglottis; *S*, frontal sinus; *K*, sphenoidal sinus.
In *A*: *s*, superior, *m*, middle, *i*, inferior turbinated bones; *c*, part of the pharynx behind the nasal cavity.

regarded as proving the assertion that the soft palate lies upon the tongue. Opposite the soft palate is situated another valve, which rises as an elastic, rigid plate of a tongue-like form from the upper margin of the entrance to the larynx. This is the *epiglottis;* it lies close to the lowest and most posterior part of the dorsum of the tongue, and runs upward so far as to almost come into contact with the free margin of the soft palate. These two valves, if not absolutely, yet quite sufficiently, shut off the cavity of the mouth from the pharynx, the gap which is left between them being practically closed by the arched position of the dorsum of the tongue, so that the closure may be regarded as complete. This, however, is only the case when the mouth is closed by bringing the lower jaw into contact with the upper. If the lower jaw is depressed the tongue descends with it, and renders the above-mentioned closure less complete.

Having thus seen the full extent to which the air-passage is independent, we might feel almost tempted to regard the pharynx, from the fact of its being connected with it for by far the greater space of time, as originally belonging to the air-passage. There is nothing, however, to support such a view, the entire conformation of the pharynx proving emphatically that it is merely a portion of the alimentary canal, and indeed the hindermost part of the cavity of the mouth. It always resumes its importance as such in the act of swallowing, and it is interesting to observe how the arrangement and conformation of the different parts is then changed. The food which has been masticated in the cavity of the mouth is forced backwards by the pressure of the tongue against the hard palate into the pharynx, and from the latter into the œsophagus. The double system of valves closing the cavity of the mouth gives way; the soft palate is raised, and shuts off the uppermost part of the pharynx from the posterior entrance to the nasal cavity; the epiglottis, on the contrary, is pressed downwards, and covers the entrance to the larynx. Thus during swallowing the continuity of the alimentary canal is preserved by inserting, if not the whole, at any rate the lower half of the pharynx between the cavity of the mouth and the œsophagus, the nasal cavity and the larynx being shut off from the alimentary canal, just as, when in a quiescent position, the cavity of the mouth and the œsophagus are cut off from the windpipe (cf. Fig. 6).

We must defer for the present the examination into the structure of the parts here mentioned, and the importance of their mechanism in connection with the formation of articulate sounds. The above remarks show, however—

(1) That the true air-passage is formed by the nasal cavity, the pharynx, the larynx, and the windpipe.

(2) That the cavity of the mouth is part of the alimentary canal, but that it can, when occasion requires, be also used as an air-passage.

(3) That it always serves this purpose when the returning current of air is employed for speech.

(4) That no inconvenience is caused by the intersection of the air-passage and the alimentary canal, as each passage can be entirely cut off from, and so rendered independent of, the other.

The Larynx.

Having now discussed the creation of the current of air and the passages through which it passes outwards, we must proceed to examine the apparatus, which, situated at the upper extremity of the windpipe, possesses the property of imparting sonant vibrations to the air issuing from the lungs. This apparatus, the *larynx*, is not, however, in constant activity in this respect, but, on the contrary, generally allows the air to pass by without sound; and it is only under certain conditions, the fulfilment of which is dependent upon our will, that it becomes productive of sound. It depends, therefore, entirely upon our will whether the air, which is to be employed in the formation of sound, is with or without tone, in that part of the air-passage in which sound is created, the articulate sound which results owing its character to the choice thus made. We have here, therefore, a means of considerably increasing the number of our elements of speech.

The Vocal Chords and their Tension.

The larynx is the highest portion of the windpipe, which is traversed by the expired air immediately before its entrance into the pharynx. Being in direct communication with the windpipe on the one hand, and with the pharynx on the other, it is in this respect simply a portion of the windpipe; its peculiar significance is due to the fact that it contains an apparatus for the production of tone, towards which the windpipe, as a rule, acts as "porte-vent" ("wind-trunk" of an organ), and the pharynx as "resonance tube." Under certain conditions of rare occurrence this relation may, indeed, be reversed, tone being produced in the larynx by an inspired current of air. The tones produced in the larynx constitute the voice, which stands in a distinct relation to speech. The elements of the latter are only toneless noises; and just as it is possible to make the voice heard without any articulate sound, though it is generally accompanied by the sound of some vowel, so it is equally possible, in whispering, to create articulate sounds without any admixture of laryngeal tone. Ordinary *audible speech* consists, it is true, of a mixture of voice and speech, a current of air which has been thrown into sonant vibration by the larynx being employed for at least the greater number of articulate sounds.

The vocal apparatus of the larynx is exceedingly simple, its character being merely that of a membranous reed-instrument, consisting of two elastic plates, stretched so as to leave a narrow fissure between them, so that when the current of air streams through the fissure they are thrown into vibration.

Two circumstances, however, in spite of the simplicity of this principle, tend to give a complex appearance to the larynx. In the first place, we have to distinguish in the larynx, as the term is generally understood, two entirely separate parts, one of which (the lower) is the true vocal organ, and the other (the upper) is a neutral space, which is inserted between the vocal apparatus and the pharynx, and can only be regarded as an integral part of the larynx from being surrounded by the same envelope as the vocal apparatus. The interposition of this neutral space (the *superior cavity of the larynx*) removes the vocal apparatus to such a distance from the alimentary canal as to render any inconvenience or injury from the latter impossible. The second of the above-mentioned circumstances is that the vocal apparatus itself exhibits a certain amount of complication, the disposition of the membranous reeds, and the mechanism by which they are adjusted for musical vibration, and, again, the further adaptation of this adjustment for the creation of tones of various pitch, necessitating a certain multiplication of accessory structures. In spite of this, we must confess that the organization of the larynx is wonderfully simple as compared with all it is able to accomplish.

Our next step will be to examine the vocal apparatus more closely.

The Vocal Apparatus of the Larynx.

The larynx, as already observed, merely constitutes the upper extremity of the windpipe; its entire structure is, therefore, nothing more than a modification of the structure of the windpipe.

The windpipe (trachea) is a tube of the same width throughout, lined with mucous membrane, forming that portion of the air-passage which lies nearest to the lungs, and in its ramifications a component of the lungs themselves. In accordance with the general character of the structure of the air-passages, the walls of this portion are rendered rigid by solid layers interposed between those structures which complete the walls of the windpipe. The rigidity produced by these layers gives a firm character to the whole; it may, therefore, be regarded as the foundation of the windpipe, and as such occupy the first place in our description of the latter.

The layers here referred to consist of a number of cartilaginous rings of about 3 mm. ($\frac{1}{8}$ inch) in depth and 1 mm. ($\frac{1}{25}$ inch) in thickness. They are so curved as to form the anterior and two lateral sides of the windpipe, leaving, however, the posterior wall free. These imperfect rings are so joined together by fibrous membrane (*ligamenta interannularia*), that they present the appearance of a groove, the open side of which faces backwards. The free, rounded ends of these cartilages, as well as the ends of the intervening ligaments, and therefore the free margins of the groove, are connected by fairly strong transverse muscular fibres, which, as a continuous layer, form the posterior level wall of the windpipe. Externally, the tube thus formed is enclosed by a fibrous membrane, which increases in thickness upon the surface of the transverse muscular fibres, the two layers thus completing the posterior wall of the windpipe.

The inner coat of this tube is formed by a mucous membrane, which is provided externally with a layer of small glands, the secretion from which serves to moisten the inner surface of the windpipe. In addition to these smaller glands, there are others of rather larger size, which open by an excretory duct upon the surface of the mucous membrane. The glands attached to these ducts are situated between the cartilaginous rings, or between and behind the muscular fibres of the posterior wall.

This inner lining is completed by bundles of elastic fibres which form a continuous tissue immediately beneath, or even imbedded in, the mucous membrane, and, enclosing the entire periphery of the windpipe, run longitudinally even into its ramifications.

Upon comparing the structure of the windpipe with that of other tubes—for instance, the alimentary canal—we find a remarkable harmony in spite of all differences. Such tubes are, namely, provided with both annular and longitudinal muscular fibres; the former contract the diameter, the latter the length of the tube. In the transverse layer of muscular fibres which form the posterior membranous wall of the windpipe, we recognize at least the rudiments of the annular form of muscular fibre; from their attachment, however, with the cartilages by which the cavity of the windpipe is always kept open, they cannot effect any important contraction, but merely serve to modify this constant condition. As representatives of the longitudinal muscular fibre, we have the elastic fibres mentioned above, the action of which, again, though resembling, is not perfectly analogous to that of longitudinal muscular fibres of other tubes. They lack, namely, that vital contraction which distinguishes muscular fibres, and therefore can never effect a contraction of the windpipe, but only through their elasticity restore it to its previous position of rest after any considerable tension—as, for instance, after it has been filled with inspired air.

We must here again draw attention to the important part played by elastic elements, having already shown how expiration is almost entirely due to the physical action of elasticity. This fact is particularly interesting in connection with the functions of the larynx, which, as will presently be shown, impedes the free exit of the air when the larynx is adjusted for the formation of tone, and consequently when adjusted for audible speech. This obstruction to the exit of the air is, however, constantly counterbalanced by the tension of the elastic elements of the lungs and of the windpipe, and so a continuous current of air is insured for the formation of speech without any special action on our part. Thus the lungs and the windpipe stand in the same relation to the tone-producing apparatus of the larynx as the expanded bellows to the organ, which, by the gradual collapse of the former, is supplied with a continuous stream of air till the air is exhausted, when the bellows must be refilled; or as the indiarubber membrane which, in the child's toy, is attached to a whistle, and which, when blown full of air, by its subsequent elastic contraction gives rise to a sustained note in the whistle.

The elastic condition of the windpipe described above has, however, a further significance, as it supplies the material for the construction of the tone-producing apparatus of the larynx. The elastic fibres, which line the windpipe as a continuous tissue, are in its uppermost portion multiplied and closely packed together, so as to form a strong compact elastic membrane, which, preserving the form of the transverse section of the windpipe, is funnel-shaped. If, now, we suppose the windpipe to terminate with the highest cartilaginous ring, then this funnel-shaped sac will protrude freely beyond the upper end of the windpipe, and it is this protruding portion of the elastic membrane which forms the foundation of the vocal apparatus of the larynx. Before proceeding further, we will, however,

Fig. 7.

The vocal chords as the free edges of an elastic sac. *aa*, Vocal chords; the cricoid cartilage supporting them indicated by a dotted line over the sac; *c*, the thyroid cartilage; the part which produces the tension of the vocal chords given in a continuous line; the outline of the remaining part dotted; *d*, upper part of the windpipe. The arrow shows the direction in which the crico-thyroid muscle pulls.

first describe a simple apparatus, from which we shall easily understand the leading principles of the structure of the larynx.

A tube of moderate length is formed of cardboard or any other material, the diameter of which should be about 2 cm. (⅘ inch). An indiarubber tube about 4 cm. (1⅗ inch) in length is then drawn over one end, so that it shall continue the cavity of the cardboard tube. Care should, of course, be taken that both tubes are securely fastened together, either with glue or by tying them round with strong string. If we blow into this apparatus from the other end of the cardboard tube, the air will pass through without producing any sound. We now, however, take the free end of the indiarubber tube at two diametrically opposite points, and draw these points apart, so that the hitherto round opening assumes the form of a narrow slit. The whole of that part of the indiarubber tube which no longer lies directly upon the cardboard tube resembles the shape of a wedge, the base of which is round. If we now blow again through the apparatus we find that it has become capable of producing tone, the indiarubber plates being to a greater or less extent thrown into vibration. If the tension is slight, more of the plates will vibrate, and the tone will be deeper; when, on the contrary, the tension is greater, only the free margins bounding the fissure vibrate, and the tone is higher.

Upon analyzing this apparatus, we find that the sound is due to the two elastic plates which are inclined towards each other. The current of air, for instance, which has been driven through the spacious "porte-vent" enters the rapidly narrowing wedge-shaped cavity, from which it can only escape by the narrow fissure between the elastic plates, where it produces vibration by its friction. The force with which it is driven out through the fissure and acts upon the margin of the plates, is undoubtedly partly due to the strength of the blast given, partly also, however, to the rapid contraction of the cavity through which it passes, causing an increase in its velocity at the fissure-like outlet. The rigidity of the base of the wedge-shaped cavity, which insures the entrance into the latter of the entire current of air, is not of itself sufficient to produce sound; the tension of the margins bounding the fissure is also necessary. Let A and B stand for the two ends of the fissure, then the tension may be created by drawing these two points (A and B) simultaneously apart; this is the method adopted in the experiment just described. The same result would, however, be equally well attained if one of the two points (e.g. B) were fixed, and the other point (A) drawn away from it. Two conditions must, however, be fulfilled before B can be so fixed; in the first place, it must be so fixed as to offer resistance to the tension exercised upon A, and secondly so as to be held at a constant distance from the base of the wedge.

The apparatus here described illustrates exactly the tone-producing apparatus of the larynx, and we have now only to discover how these fundamental laws of its construction are carried out.

The sac formed of elastic tissue, which projects beyond the upper end of the windpipe, represents the indiarubber tube of the above apparatus; it must, therefore, fulfil all those conditions which rendered the production of tone possible by the indiarubber tube.

The first of these conditions is the fixation of the base of the membranous wedge, and this, together with the second condition of the fixation of one end of the fissure, is accomplished by a single piece of cartilage, namely, by the *cricoid cartilage*. This cartilage presents the appearance of a perfectly closed ring, and is attached to the uppermost ring of the windpipe in the same manner as the rings are united to each other; being, however, in the form of a perfect ring, its posterior portion must rest upon the membranous posterior wall of the windpipe, of which it forms the upper termination, being attached to it by its lower border. In this respect, therefore, it forms a continuation of the windpipe. The lower border of the cricoid cartilage, with the exception of a few unimportant deviations, lies in a horizontal plane, therefore vertical to the axis of the windpipe; the upper border, on the contrary, ascends obliquely backwards and upwards, so that the posterior surface is from three to four times higher than the anterior surface. The posterior portion of the upper border, again, is for a short distance horizontal. It is from this resemblance to a signet-ring, of which this posterior surface forms the "plate," that the cricoid cartilage derives its name. Thus, seen from behind, the middle portion of the upper border of the plate appears horizontally flattened, while the lateral portions descend rapidly forwards. Upon the angle between the middle horizontal and the lateral descending upper borders is, on either side, a small convex articular surface for the attachment of the arytenoid cartilage, which will be described presently. The structure of the cartilage is fairly strong throughout, but is thicker at the sides, and thus the cavity enclosed is not round, but oval, with its longest diameter from before backwards.

Now, the sac of elastic tissue, alluded to above, is firmly attached to the entire inner surface of the cricoid cartilage, except in the immediate neighbourhood of the articular surfaces, thus fixing the lower periphery as the lower periphery of the indiarubber tube was fixed by the cardboard tube. As, however, the elastic sac has precisely the same height as the plate of the cricoid cartilage, support is at the same time given to a triangular portion of the posterior surface of the sac, the apex of which lies in the highest point of the plate. Here, then, we have the necessary fixation of one end (B) of the tone-producing fissure; for the fissure, formed between the free margins of the membrane, and called the *glottis*, commences at this point, from whence it passes diametrically forwards.

For the tension of the margins bordering this fissure, which are called the *vocal chords*, some arrangement is required which shall draw away the anterior end of the fissure from the posterior end, which is attached to the cricoid cartilage. This condition, again, is met in the simplest manner by the organization of the larynx, and at the same time a protective envelope is given to the vocal apparatus. Both objects are again fulfilled by a single

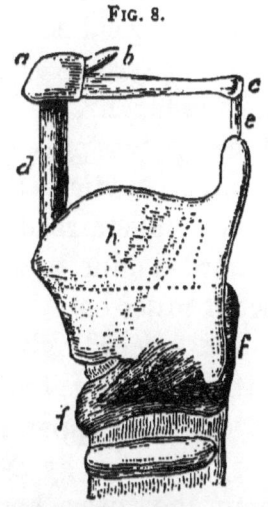

FIG. 8.

Side view of the larynx attached to the hyoid bone; position of the vocal chords and arytenoid cartilages indicated by the dotted lines. *a.* Body of the hyoid bone; *b.* lesser, *c,* greater horn of the latter; *d,* central, *e,* lateral portion of the thyro-hyoid ligament; *f,* cricoid cartilage; *g,* crico-thyroid muscle; *h,* thyroid cartilage.

piece of cartilage, namely, the *thyroid cartilage*. The latter is a plate of cartilage, the surface of which is so curved as to form a sharp angle in the middle line of the body, which gives it almost the appearance of being formed of two lateral plates, firmly blended together in front. Each of these plates is five-sided. The upper, lower, and posterior borders are approximately straight; the anterior border, on the contrary, is marked half-way by such a strong projection as to fall into two halves,

STRUCTURE OF THE ORGANS OF SPEECH. 43

an upper and a lower, meeting at an obtuse angle and constituting the fourth and fifth sides of the plate. By the lower of these two halves the two cartilaginous plates are firmly blended into a whole. As, moreover, the height of the two plates is considerable, the larynx is thus provided with large, rigid walls, and the vocal apparatus which they enclose adequately protected. They also determine the outward form of the larynx, and in thin persons especially are distinctly visible, the projection which they form being called the "Adam's apple." The part played by the thyroid cartilage in connecting the different parts of the larynx, and also as a basis for its movements, will be shown presently; here we have only to consider its direct participation in the structure of the larynx. Now, we have already observed that the tension of the vocal chords is due to the thyroid cartilage. To produce this effect it must be attached to the anterior end of the fissure, and accordingly we find this end firmly attached in the receding angle formed by the union of the two plates. The upper portion only of the elastic sac is affected, however, by this attachment, the rest lying free between the lower border of the thyroid cartilage and the upper border of the cricoid, and presenting the appearance, when viewed from before, of a connecting wall between the two; it is called the *cricothyroid membrane*.

Regular movement cannot be carried out without a pivot and a moving force. The thyroid cartilage acquires the former in the following manner. The posterior border is prolonged above and below into stem-like processes, which are called the *superior* and *inferior horns* of the thyroid cartilage. The superior horn serves for the attachment of the thyroid cartilage to the hyoid bone. The lower horn articulates upon a small elevation on the posterior portion of the lateral surface of the cricoid cartilage. If, now, we cut away any width we please of the lower border of the thyroid cartilage, including the inferior horn of either side and the angle at which the two plates unite in front (see Fig. 7), we obtain a cartilaginous arc, which articulates by its two free ends (the inferior horns) with the cricoid cartilage, and, by the middle of its concave fronts, is fastened to the anterior termination of the glottis. The portion thus artificially

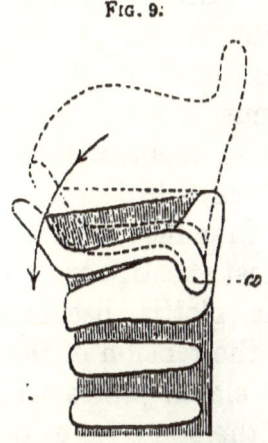

FIG. 9.

To show that the depression, without the advancement, of the thyroid cartilage must cause the tension of the vocal chords. Position of the thyroid cartilage when at rest indicated by dotted lines; also that of the vocal chord. The continuous line shows the arc described by the thyroid cartilage, and also the vocal chord, when depressed. The arrow indicates the path of the point of attachment of the vocal chord with the thyroid cartilage upon the pivot a.

removed from the thyroid cartilage is the sole agent in the adjustment of the vocal apparatus, the other parts merely constituting the protecting envelope.

Two movements are possible to this arc from the manner of its articulation. It can, for instance, be either drawn directly forwards, or it may complete part of a circle upon an axis drawn through the two points of articulation. It is clear that the first movement must cause a tension of the vocal chords; and that the second must have the same effect, will be seen at once from the diagram given in Fig. 9, which shows that the movement in a circle upon the axis of the two articulations must increase the distance between the point of attachment of the vocal chords to the thyroid cartilages, and their point of attachment to the plate of the cricoid cartilage.

A small but powerful muscle (Fig. 8) serves as moving force for these movements of the thyroid cartilage. This muscle (the *crico-thyroid*) springs anteriorly from the outer surface of the cricoid cartilage; it then expands, and is inserted into the lower border of the thyroid cartilage and the anterior border of its inferior horn. The parts of the muscle which are attached to the inferior horn tend rather to advance the thyroid cartilage, those which are attached to the lower border to make it describe an arc. The movements described above as both possible and most effective are thus completed simultaneously, and the glottis becomes depressed in its anterior portion by the tension of the vocal chords which enclose it, while the elastic plates which terminate as the vocal chords are at the same time (their point of attachment with the cricoid cartilage being unmoved) drawn downwards.

Thus we see that the tone-producing (vocal) apparatus of the larynx bears a perfect resemblance to the caoutchouc apparatus described above, the indiarubber tube being represented by the elastic sac, the cardboard tube by the cricoid cartilage and the windpipe. The tension of the margins of the fissure which in that apparatus was performed by the fingers, is one-sided in the larynx, one end of the fissure being fixed in the cricoid cartilage, and the tension being effected from the other end by the aid of the thyroid cartilage.

The Glottis and its Adjusting Cartilages.

There is another point to be considered in connection with the structure of the glottis. It was given above as a general law of the air-passages that their cavities must always be open. If, however, the glottis were a fissure like that in the caoutchouc apparatus, the inspired current of air, by pressing upon the two plates, would press their edges together, and thus itself close the passage into the windpipe. This difficulty is avoided in the simplest manner; the two posterior ends of the vocal chords do not lie close together at the point of their

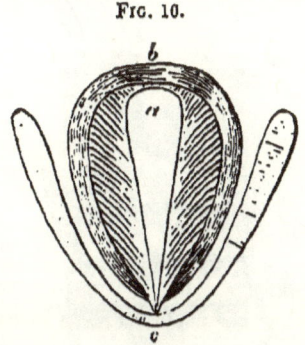

FIG. 10.

Open glottis (when at rest) seen from above. *A*, glottis; *b*, cricoid cartilage; *c*, thyroid cartilage devided horizontally at the level of the glottis.

attachment to the cricoid cartilage, but are removed from each other to a distance of about 5 mm. ($\frac{1}{4}$ inch); in other words, the plate of the cricoid cartilage does not, like the thyroid cartilage, fix one point merely in the periphery of the elastic membrane, but about 5 mm. ($\frac{1}{4}$ inch) of the periphery. Thus the glottis presents the appearance of a triangle, with a narrow base lying posteriorly upon the plate of the cricoid cartilage, its long sides terminating in an apex situated within the hollow of the thyroid cartilage. It is, therefore, always open for both the entering and returning currents of air.

Notwithstanding the necessity and convenience of this arrangement of the glottis, it is undoubtedly a disadvantage when the vocal chords are to be employed for the production of tone. If the vocal chords are to be thrown into vibration by the current of air, the fissure between them must be a very small one. At the utmost the width of the glottis cannot exceed 2 mm. ($\frac{1}{12}$ inch) in the production of tone, while the vocal chords must be brought as closely as possible together for utterance to be easy and without effort. It is clear, therefore, that no

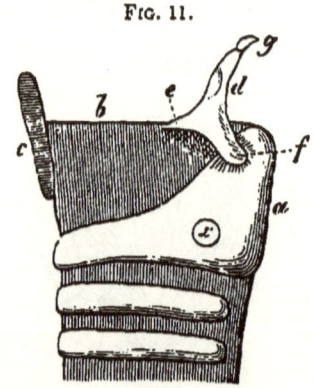

Fig. 11.

Side view of the vocal chords with the arytenoid cartilage. *a*, Cricoid cartilage; *x*, articular surface for inferior horn of thyroid cartilage; *b*, vocal chord; *c*, vertical section of thyroid cartilage; *d*, arytenoid cartilage; *e*, vocal process of *d*; *f*, muscular process of *d*; *g*, cartilage of Santorini.

tone can be created in the wide-open, triangular glottis. We know, moreover, that ordinary respiration, and even the deepest and strongest inspiration or expiration, are effected without tone. Thus we are led to anticipate some arrangement which can be voluntarily employed to place the vocal chords in the necessary relations for the production of tone.

This arrangement is given in the small cartilages (the *arytenoid cartilage*) which are attached to either side of the vocal chords. Each cartilage is triangular and pyramidal in shape, with its base directed downwards and its apex upwards. The internal lateral surface rises almost vertically from the base and bends inwards, while its lower margin is attached to the outer surface of the vocal chords; the two other lateral surfaces face outwards, one to the back, the other to the front: they form with the base a prominent angle, which rests upon that part of the upper border of the cricoid cartilage already described as the articular surface for this cartilage. This angle is directed more backwards, because the posterior of the two external lateral surfaces unites with the vertical

FIG. 12.

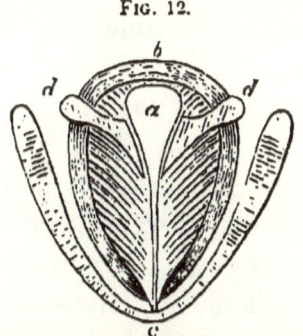

Glottis adjusted for tones. *a*, *Pars respiratoria* of the glottis; *b*, cricoid cartilage; *c*, attachment of the vocal chords to the thyroid cartilage; *d*, horizontal section of the bases of the arytenoid cartilages.

posterior edge of the inner lateral surface at an obtuse angle; the anterior of the two external surfaces must, therefore, meet the two others at a very acute angle.

In considering the adjustment of the vocal chords for the production of tone, we are at present only interested in the relation of the base of the arytenoid cartilage to the vocal chord. If we divide the length of the vocal chord into a larger anterior and a smaller posterior half, and then again divide the posterior half into two almost equal sections, we shall be able to determine

STRUCTURE OF THE ORGANS OF SPEECH.

more accurately the precise position of the base of the arytenoid cartilage upon the vocal chord. We may, for instance, describe this position as the anterior section of the posterior half. If, now, such a horizontal direction is given to the base of the arytenoid cartilage of either side that the anterior angle of their bases come into contact, a very different shape will be given to the glottis. The larger anterior halves of the two vocal chords, which lie between this angle and the thyroid cartilage, will, namely, be so closely approximated, that only a narrow fissure will be left between them; the two posterior halves, on the contrary, form the sides of a short, open triangle, the base of which lies against the plate of the cricoid cartilage. It is evident that tone can only be created by the anterior of these two parts; hence it is called *glottis vocalis*, or better, *pars vocalis glottidis*. The posterior portion, from the manner in which it exemplifies the law that the air-passages must always be open, is called the *glottis respiratoria*, or better, *pars respiratoria glottidis*. The portions of the vocal chords which are thus separated by the arytenoid cartilages are, therefore, regarded as separate ligaments, and are called, from their attachments, the *crico-arytenoid* and the *thyro-arytenoid ligaments*.

Thus the movement of the arytenoid cartilages adjusts, by a voluntary act, the anterior larger portion of the glottis for the production of sound, while, in a quiescent state, the entire glottis stands wide open and allows the current of air to pass through unhindered. If, however, the glottis is to produce a tone after being adjusted in this manner, it is clear that the current of air must be driven through it with a certain amount of force; this, however, is impossible as long as the *glottis respiratoria* remains open, offering an easy escape to the current of air. It follows, therefore, that if the *glottis vocalis* is to be adjusted for sound, the *glottis respiratoria* must be so closed that no air can escape through it. This cannot be effected by the rigid walls formed by the plate of the cricoid cartilage and the bases of the arytenoid cartilages of the *glottis respiratoria* itself; the means of closing it is found elsewhere, and indeed in the form of the arytenoid cartilages themselves, by which the object is attained in the simplest manner.

The arytenoid cartilage rises, as we have already observed, as a triangular pyramid upon the base, the action of which has also been described. The internal lateral surface is free, and situated directly opposite the internal surface of the corresponding cartilage; thus the current of air issuing from the *glottis respiratoria* must pass between these two surfaces. As, however, the two posterior, vertical edges of these surfaces are so connected by a transverse muscle, which will presently be described, that the intermediary space is entirely filled up, the two cartilages form with these walls a kind of channel or groove, into which the air passes upon issuing from the *glottis respiratoria*. This channel is not, however, of the same depth throughout, but from the triangular shape of the cartilaginous walls becomes shallower as it ascends, disappearing entirely at the apex of the arytenoid cartilage. The action of those muscles by which the glottis is adjusted is, however, such that not only the anterior angles of the bases, but the anterior margins of both arytenoid cartilages, are brought into contact with each other. By this means the abovementioned groove is closed; the passage of air through the *glottis respiratoria* is, therefore, entirely stopped, and it is all forced to pass through the *glottis vocalis*.

The contact between the two arytenoid cartilages is rendered more intimate, and the obstruction, therefore, to the current of air more complete, by two small cartilages (the *cartilages of Santorini*), which pass backwards and inwards as prolongations, in the shape of small horns, of the apices of the arytenoid cartilages. By the mutual approximation of the arytenoid cartilages these little cartilages of Santorini are firmly pressed together, and thus are of material assistance in securely closing the upper end of the groove.

The movements of the arytenoid cartilages are, in common with all voluntary movements, produced by muscles which are attached to them, and which, moreover,

FIG. 13.

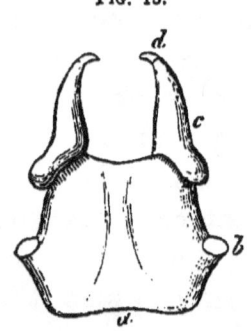

Arytenoid cartilages seen from behind. *a*, Cricoid cartilage; *b*, articular facet for articulation with the inferior horn of the thyroid cartilage; *c*, arytenoid cartilage; *d*, cartilage of Santorini.

offer several points of interest. Two of these muscles contract the glottis, and these adjust it for the production of tone, while two others effect its relaxation.

Before attempting to describe the action of these muscles, we must have a clear conception of those secondary causes which regulate the results of their contraction. There is scarcely a single muscle the stretching action of which works independently, for there are always other forces acting upon the point to be moved, so that the movement arising from any muscular contraction is the double result of the action of the muscle and those other forces. Thus, for instance, the bending of the lower part of the arm towards the upper is not due to the direct action of the flexor muscles, but is the combined result of their action and the resistance of the elbow-joint. It is true, indeed, that those other forces, as in the example just given, consist in the resistance offered by the joint, and we often find, therefore, that the structure of the joint is regarded as regulating the movement caused by the contraction of a muscle. Looking at the question from this point of view, there is a temptation to consider the articulation of the arytenoid cartilage, by which the outer angle of its base rests upon the plate of the cricoid cartilage, as regulating the movements imparted to the arytenoid cartilage by its muscles. We must, however, distinguish two kinds of articulations, differing very essentially from each other. The one kind do undoubtedly, from the clear mathematical contour of their articular surfaces, regulate the direction of the movement made, and thus form a joint in the mechanical sense; the other kind, on the contrary, are characterized by the more indefinite contour of these articular surfaces, and even by the incongruity of the latter, and can less be said to regulate than to allow movements : they do not, therefore, represent joints in the mechanical sense, but merely gliding surfaces ("slot" would be the technical mechanical term). The elbow-joint may be taken as an example of the first kind, while the condyles at the lower extremity of the femur, upon which the knee-cap moves, will illustrate the second.

The more closely we examine the articulation of the arytenoid cartilage with the cricoid cartilage, the more are we convinced that it belongs to the second category, and that its form cannot determine the character of the movements of the arytenoid cartilage. Their character is rather determined by the connection of the inner margin of the base of this cartilage with the vocal chord, and the superposition of its external angle upon the cricoid cartilage can only, by the resistance which that point derives from below, form a component in the result of the muscular action. The interposition of a serous sac between the gliding surfaces of the cartilages is merely an example of the universal presence of serous sacs in all places where there is friction. Serous sacs of this kind are called *bursæ mucosæ*, to distinguish them from the *synovial bursæ* of the joints, with which, however, they are closely connected. The most accurate descriptions of this contact between the arytenoid and the cricoid cartilage would therefore be—that it is a gliding surface provided with a bursa mucosa, and lacking the true character of a joint.

Taking this view, therefore, the resistance by which the result of muscular action upon the arytenoid cartilage is modified arises from the elastic tension of parts or of the whole of the vocal chords, and from the reaction of the cricoid cartilage. The latter, by only acting upon a certain portion of the base of the arytenoid cartilage, gives to this case the character of a two-armed lever, towards which the cricoid cartilage acts as fulcrum.

The muscles by which the arytenoid cartilage is moved have their point of attachment partly without and partly within this fulcrum. It is, therefore, not quite correct to call the angle of the base of the arytenoid cartilage which projects upon the cricoid cartilage the *muscular process*, because it would thus seem that this part were the only point for the attachment of muscles, while the reason for the choice of this name has only been to distinguish this angle of the base from the very acute angle which is connected with the vocal chord, and to which we gave the name of *vocal process*.

The manner in which the different relations and forces described above together effect the resulting muscular action, will be best seen from an analysis of the largest of these muscles, the *thyro-arytenoid*. This muscle arises from the posterior surface of the thyroid cartilage, close to the attachment of the vocal chords, and is inserted into the greater part of the anterior surface of the arytenoid cartilage; a line connecting the central point of origin and of its insertion, which will

Fig. 14.

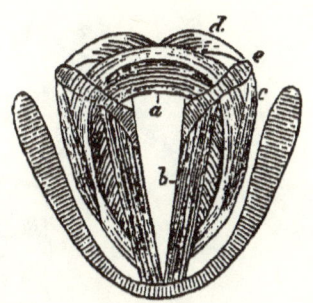

Muscles of the arytenoid cartilages. The muscular processes (*e*) prolonged to show the muscles more distinctly. *a*, Transverse arytenoid; *b*, thyro-arytenoid; *c*, anterior crico-arytenoid; *d*, posterior crico arytenoid.

at the same time give the direction in which the muscle pulls, will therefore ascend outwards. The action of the muscle, if unimpeded, must, therefore, be to bring the central point of its insertion, that is, about the middle of the anterior surface of the arytenoid cartilage, into a straight line with the point of attachment of the vocal chord upon the plate of the cricoid cartilage, and with the central point of the origin of the muscle upon the thyroid cartilage. The cartilage, viewed from above, will then rotate in such a manner that its anterior margin and vocal process will be forced considerably

STRUCTURE OF THE ORGANS OF SPEECH. 55

inwards; a side view would, however, show that the cartilage must be drawn downwards. The central point for both movements must be the point at which the vocal chord is attached to the plate of the cricoid cartilage, round which the above-mentioned point upon the anterior surface of the arytenoid cartilage will rotate till it is brought into that straight line. It never, however, quite attains this position, for its rotation onwards is stopped by contact with the opposite cartilage, and the downward movement impeded by the elastic counter-

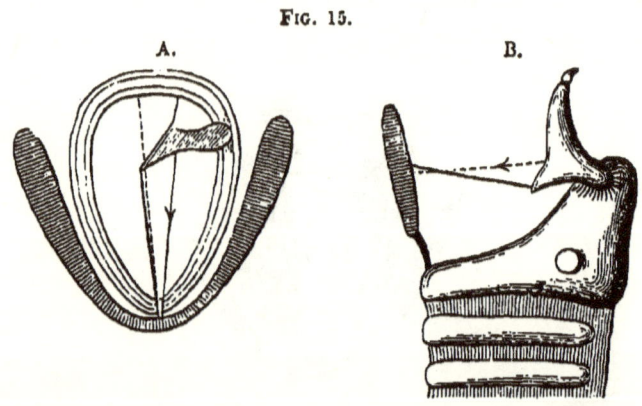

FIG. 15.

Action of the thyro-arytenoid muscle. *A*, Viewed from above; *B*, side view. The arrow indicates the direction in which the muscle pulls. In *A*, the dotted line represents the other vocal chord (of the right side). *A* shows the position which would be given by the muscle to the arytenoid cartilage if there were no impediment in the way of the completion of its action; *B* shows that the muscle must depress the vocal chord.

tension of the vocal chord (in the broader sense), which by this movement is drawn down into an angle, the apex of which lies in the vocal process. The action of the *thyro-arytenoid* muscle is, therefore, to adjust the vocal chord, strictly speaking, for the production of tone, at the same time drawing it downwards. It was often said, formerly, that the *thyro-arytenoid*, being a muscle which runs parallel to the vocal chord from before backwards, must by its pull upon the arytenoid cartilage contract, and therefore relax the true vocal chord; as this, however, did not agree with the necessity for a corresponding tension of the vocal chord, it was thought that this was compensated for by the innermost part of the muscle, which lies close to the vocal chord, becoming thicker in consequence of its contraction, and at the same time forcing the vocal chord inwards. This inner portion of the muscle has on this account even been distinguished as the *thyro-arytenoideus internus*. In addition to the fact that no compensating action is to be found in this

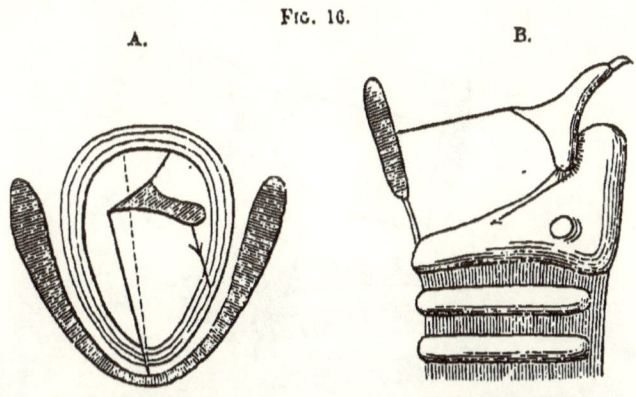

FIG. 16.

Action of the crico-arytenoid muscle. The position, viewed from above, which it would give to the arytenoid cartilage, if no obstruction were placed in the way of the completion of its action. The arrow shows the direction in which the muscle pulls; the dotted line the vocal chord of the other side; *B*, side view, showing that the glottis is raised by the muscle.

manner, it does not appear necessary to seek it when we remember that the chord is always in a state of considerable elastic tension, and becomes still more stretched when depressed.

The action of the *anterior (lateral) crico-arytenoid* muscle is similar to that of the last. It arises upon the upper margin of the lateral portion of the cricoid cartilage, and is inserted into the muscular process of the arytenoid cartilage. Thus it ascends from before backwards, and must, therefore, draw the muscular process downwards.

STRUCTURE OF THE ORGANS OF SPEECH. 57

As, however, the arytenoid cartilage here acts as a two-armed lever, the portion which lies within the cricoid cartilage will move backwards and upwards, and at the same time rotate upon a vertical axis in such a manner that its vocal process will be turned inwards. The central point for all these movements is here, again, the point of attachment of the vocal chord (in the wider sense) to the cricoid cartilage, as the action of the muscle in question, if entirely unobstructed, would be to draw the muscular process of the arytenoid cartilage into a

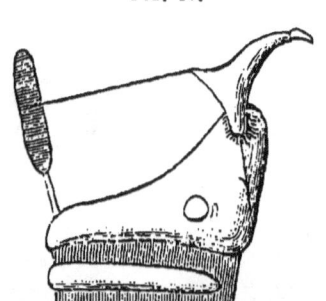

FIG. 17.

Action of the posterior crico-arytenoid muscle. The arrow shows the direction in which it pulls. Side view. (Cf. Fig. 19.)

straight line with the central point of its origin, and with the point of attachment of the vocal chord to the cricoid cartilage. The movement, therefore, which this muscle imparts to the arytenoid cartilage is in all respects similar to that which it derives from the *thyro-arytenoid*, and, like the latter, occasions the closure of the glottis, or its adjustment for the utterance of sound; the one difference being that the glottis is placed higher.

The two other muscles of the arytenoid cartilage have the opposite effect upon the glottis; that is, they widen it. This is most clearly seen in the *posterior crico-*

arytenoid. It arises upon the posterior surface of the plate of the cricoid cartilage, occupying, indeed, each lateral half of the plate; its fibres then converge and are inserted into the muscular process of the arytenoid carti-

FIG. 18.

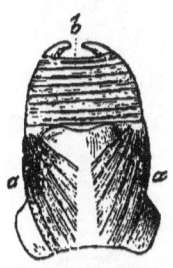

View of the transverse arytenoid muscle (*b*) and the posterior crico-arytenoid muscle (*a*) from behind.

lage. Its action is such that it draws down these points of the arytenoid cartilage backwards and inwards. The greater part of the arytenoid cartilage, which lies within the cricoid cartilage, is consequently drawn outwards, that part which is furthest from the fulcrum upon the

FIG. 19.

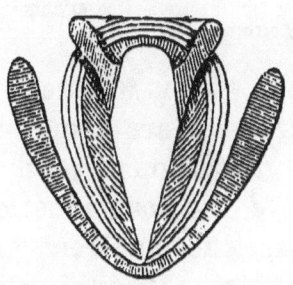

Form given to the glottis by the posterior crico-arytenoid muscle. Direction in which the muscle pulls indicated by arrows.

cricoid cartilage, namely, the vocal process, making the largest excursion in that direction. Thus the action of the *posterior crico-arytenoid* muscle is to widen the entire glottis in such a manner that its greatest width falls between the vocal processes, while at the same time these points are considerably raised.

The *transverse arytenoid* muscle is a broad muscular plate which passes from the outer margin of the posterior surface of one arytenoid cartilage to the corresponding part of the other. The action of this muscle is to approach the two arytenoid cartilages together till that portion of the vocal chord known as the *crico-arytenoid ligament* is rendered tense; the arytenoid cartilage then rotates upon the point where it is attached to the vocal chord in such a manner that the vocal processes are

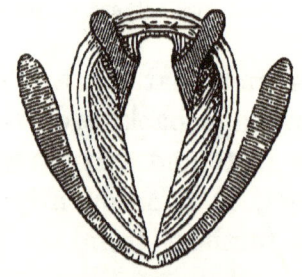

Form given to the glottis by the transverse arytenoid muscle. Direction in which the muscle pulls indicated by arrows.

drawn apart and the glottis widened. But at the same time the vocal processes are somewhat depressed, and the position of the glottis consequently lowered.

By the action of the four muscles attached to the arytenoid cartilages, the quiescent form of the glottis, which was compared to a triangle with a narrow base, can be enlarged to a rhomboidal opening, the shorter diagonal of which passes from one vocal process to the other (*posterior crico-arytenoid m.*, *transverse arytenoid m.*); or its anterior portion (the true vocal chord formed by the *thyro-arytenoid* ligament) can be contracted to a narrow fissure, the posterior portion (*pars respiratoria glottidis*) remaining a triangular opening, but, as already shown, efficiently closed by the meeting of the anterior margins of the two arytenoid cartilages (*thyro-arytenoid m., anterior crico-arytenoid m.*); and both forms of the glottis can be accompanied by its elevation (*anterior crico-arytenoid*) or by its depression (*thyro-arytenoid, transverse arytenoid*).

Naturally those movements only are of importance in the production of tone which are connected with the closure of the *pars vocalis glottidis*. Here, however, it is of importance to mark the results of the depression or elevation of the glottis. From the manner in which the glottis is formed by the free periphery of a sac, it is

Fig. 21.

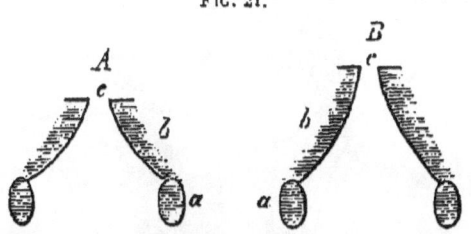

Diagrammatic cross-section of the space between the vocal chords (*A*) when the glottis is depressed, *B* when raised. *a*, Section of the cricoid cartilage; *b*, vocal chord; *c*, glottis.

evident that the entrance to it from below is formed by the converging lateral portions of the membrane, which pass inwards as broad plates (vocal chords) from the upper margin of the cricoid cartilage, to be more or less closely approximated by their edges forming the glottis. Thus the vocal chords together form a kind of roof; and since the base of these plates remains unaltered upon the cricoid cartilage, it follows that they will make a more acute angle with each other when the glottis is raised than when it is depressed. The result must, moreover, be that when the glottis is depressed the vocal chords will be more fully affected by the current of air, and

STRUCTURE OF THE ORGANS OF SPEECH.

therefore a greater part of them can take part in the sonant vibration than when the position of the glottis is higher, as then the current of air flows more gently along the lateral walls which lead to it.

The Superior Cavity of the Larynx.

The neutral space situated between the actual vocal apparatus and the pharynx (the superior cavity of the

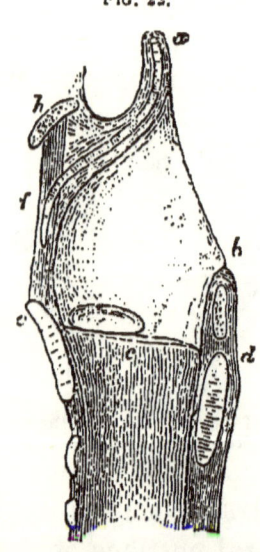

FIG. 22.

Superior cavity of the larynx. *ab*, Opening into the pharynx; *c*, vocal chord; immediately above it the ventricle of Morgagni; *h*, hyoid bone; *c*, thyroid cartilage; *f*, middle portion of thyro-hyoid ligament, in which is seen the long, narrow end of the epiglottis (*a*); *d*, section of the cricoid cartilage, and immediately above that of the transverse arytenoid muscle. The position of the arytenoid cartilage and of the cartilages of Santorini and Wrisberg is also indicated.

larynx) may be described generally as bounded by the hyoid bone and the vocal chords; this, however, would seem to imply that the height of the cavity was the same throughout; it will be better, therefore, to mention at once that, although the lower boundary is formed by the horizontal vocal chords, the upper boundary is characterized as being the entrance from the pharynx into the larynx. This entrance lies in the anterior wall of the pharynx below the cavity of the mouth, and descends, therefore, obliquely backwards. The upper boundary of the superior cavity of the larynx must, therefore, also slant backwards, and the cavity itself be higher before than behind. An examination of the hyoid bone and its relations to the larynx will be the first step towards a clear comprehension of the situation of these parts.

The *lingual* or *hyoid bone* resembles in shape a horse-shoe, and consists of five segments. The central part of the bone (the body), forming the middle of the arch, is a bony plate of about 3 cm. (1·17 inch) in length and 1 cm.

FIG. 23.

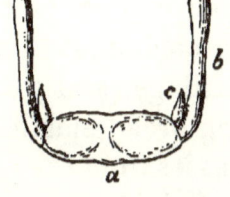

The hyoid bone from above. *a*, Body; *b*, greater horn; *c*, lesser horn.

(·39 inch) in width. This plate lies, with its long axis placed transversely, immediately under the integument of the throat, at the point where the upper horizontal division of the anterior surface of the throat separated by the lower jaw passes into the lower vertical division. Two separate pieces of bone, which are called horns (*cornua*), are attached to the lateral borders of the body; one is termed the greater horn (*cornu majus*), the other the lesser horn (*cornu minus*). The greater horn is a rod-like piece of bone, about 3 cm. in length, which by its broader anterior end is attached to the lower half of the lateral border of the body; it passes, parallel to that of the other side, horizontally backwards, and terminates posteriorly in a small tubercle. The lesser horn is a rod-like piece of bone, only ½ – 1 cm. in length, which rests upon the upper half of the lateral border of the body, and is directed upwards and backwards. It gives attachment to a long, slender ligament (the *stylo-hyoid*), which arises upon the styloid process of the temporal bone. These two muscles (of the right and the left side) thus hold the hyoid bone suspended from the base of the skull; they alone would, however, not be sufficient to effect this object. The position of the hyoid bone is due rather to its connection with a number of muscles, the stylo-hyoid ligaments acting merely as a support, and as a security against undue depression.

The hyoid bone is situated from 2½–3 cm. (·95–1·17 inch) above the upper margin of the thyroid cartilage, with which it is connected in such a manner that it supports the thyroid cartilage, and with it the entire larynx (cf. Fig. 8). A strong broad elastic ligament (the *middle thyro-hyoid muscle*) passes from the posterior surface of the body of the hyoid bone to the anterior depression of the thyroid cartilage; and on either side a rounded ligament (the *lateral thyro-hyoid muscle*) passes from the tubercle at the end of the greater horn of the hyoid bone to the superior horn of the thyroid cartilage. In addition to this, a strong membrane (the *thyro-hyoid membrane*) passes from the entire lower margin of the hyoid bone to the whole of the upper margin of the thyroid cartilage, and is connected with the three ligaments just mentioned. Thus the larynx is firmly suspended from the hyoid bone, and through the latter from the base of the skull, without losing its mobility towards the hyoid bone, or with the hyoid bone towards other parts.

If we now examine the relation of the hyoid bone to the cavities in which we are interested, we find that the floor of the cavity of the mouth passes obliquely backwards and downwards over the upper border of the body of the hyoid bone, till, immediately in front of the cervical vertebræ, it comes in contact with the posterior wall of the pharynx, with which it combines to form the œsophagus. As, however, the body of the hyoid bone is necessarily removed by the entire length of the greater horns from the vertebral column, against which they are directed, it follows that the hyoid bone constitutes the upper periphery of a funnel-shaped space leading into the œsophagus, the posterior wall of which is vertical, the anterior wall descending as an inclined plane from before backwards. Now, the latter contains the entrance into the larynx, or rather into the superior cavity of the larynx, and it is clear, therefore, that the upper limit of this orifice will be so situated that the anterior portion will be considerably higher than the posterior portion.

We are now in a position to consider the form of the superior cavity of the larynx more closely, and, with this object in view, will take the inclined plane just mentioned as our starting-point.

It has already been shown that the arytenoid cartilages are placed upon the posterior division of the vocal chords, from which they rise in a pyramidal form to a height of about 1 cm. (·39 inch), and again that their posterior surfaces are connected by the transverse arytenoid muscle. The two cartilages, with this intervening muscle, thus enclose a cavity situated above the most posterior portion of the glottis (*pars respiratoria*), the important effect of which arrangement we have also pointed out. This space belongs, however, actually to the superior cavity of the larynx; for though it forms, to a certain extent, part of the vocal apparatus, it is clear that it must be immediately connected with the superior cavity of the larynx, and therefore covered by the mucous membrane, which passes from the floor of the cavity of the mouth into the œsophagus. We find, namely, that the inclined plane formed by this mucous membrane commences at the upper border of the body of the hyoid bone, from which it passes to the upper border of the *transverse arytenoid* muscle ; the mucous membrane then descends over the posterior surface of this muscle and the posterior surface of the two *posterior crico-arytenoid* muscles lying upon the plate of the cricoid cartilage, and finally from the lower border of the plate of the cricoid cartilage to the free œsophagus.

Now, in this plate of mucous membrane there is a slit, extending from the hyoid bone to the arytenoid muscle, which marks the entrance from the pharynx into the superior cavity of the larynx, and by means of which the mucous membrane of the pharynx is continued as the inner lining of the air-passages. The surface traversed by the mucous membrane between this slit and the vocal chords is the lateral wall of the superior cavity of the larynx, and as this wall is higher between the hyoid bone and the vocal chord than between the upper border of the transverse arytenoid muscle and the vocal chord, it follows that the superior cavity of the larynx must be higher anteriorly than posteriorly.

If this narrow entrance leading into the superior cavity of the larynx were, however, a simple slit, then its edge would consist of mere folds of mucous membrane placed close together, and which by their mobility would be pressed downwards and against each other by the entering current of air. This, however, would be in direct opposition to the laws of the organization of the walls of the air-passages. We have still, therefore, to discover whether the law which ensures a free course through the

F

air-passages is fulfilled in the form of this slit. This object is attained in a surprisingly simple manner by the structure of the epiglottis. The foundation of the latter is a peculiarly formed plate of elastic cartilage. Its form has often been compared to that of a spoon, a comparison which is in many respects an apt one. The upper part consists of a rounded plate, the lower part of a thin stem, the length of which is, it is true, scarcely more than the diameter of the plate. The great point of interest, and that, moreover, which is particularly well shown in the comparison, is the manner in which the stem is united to the plate. This, namely, is the same as that in which the stem of a spoon is generally joined to the bowl—that is with a double curvature of the surface—so that when the spoon is held vertically the bowl lies in a plane parallel to the stem, and not in the plane of the stem itself. Now, the stem of the epiglottis is inserted in the *middle thyro-hyoid ligament*, so that its axis lies in the direction of the fibres of the ligament (cf. Fig. 22). From this arrangement it follows that, as long as the larynx is suspended by this ligament, when the latter is necessarily stretched, the stem is held in a vertical position. The plate then ascends behind the body of the hyoid bone; its broadest part forces its way through the slit, and so separates its margins, just as the margins of the glottis are separated by its broad attachment to the plate of the cricoid cartilage. Thus the entrance from the pharynx into the larynx is always open, its form being that of a triangular slit, the base of which faces upwards towards the epiglottis. We must remember that this is not the only function of the epiglottis, but, stretching upwards into the free cavity of the pharynx, it acts at the same time as a valve, which according to its position can either close the entrance to the cavity of the mouth or that of the larynx. This point has already been alluded to, but will be discussed more fully as we proceed.

The free passage to the superior cavity of the larynx is not, however, due to the epiglottis alone, for small, solid bodies are found in the folds of mucous membrane (the *aryteno-epiglottidean folds*) which border the slit passing from the side of the epiglottis to the transverse arytenoid muscle. Support is given to each of these folds immediately above the arytenoid cartilage by the *cartilage of Santorini* already mentioned, and between the latter and the epiglottis there lies another small cartilage, the *cartilage of Wrisberg*.

In this manner an open connection is maintained between the superior cavity of the larynx and the pharynx, whilst the œsophagus is, on the contrary, always closed by the larynx pressing against the posterior wall of the œsophagus which lies upon the vertebral column, and by the free walls of the œsophagus below the larynx contracting upon themselves. This relation is only altered during the passage of food, when the entrance to the larynx is closed and the œsophagus opened. Thus, of the two continuations of the pharynx, that which, as the superior cavity of the larynx, leads to the vocal apparatus, is always open, and we must, therefore, in considering the relation of the organs in question to respiration and the formation of voice, regard the superior cavity of the larynx as the lowest portion of the pharynx, when the latter acts as an air-passage.

The entrance to the superior cavity of the larynx, like the similarly organized passages of the nostrils and the glottis, can be directly contracted by means of a muscular layer which surrounds it. This layer varies greatly with the individual; but as a rule we find a number of bundles of muscles, which, arising upon the base of the arytenoid cartilage of one side, ascend obliquely over the posterior surface of the transverse arytenoid muscle to the apex of the arytenoid cartilage of the other side, and then, passing upwards in the aryteno-epiglottidean fold, are inserted into the side of the epiglottis. That part of this muscle which lies behind the transverse arytenoid is called the *arytenoideus obliquus,* and that within the aryteno-epiglottidean fold the *arytcno-epiglottideus.* The action of this muscle is twofold : it must, for instance, by lateral pressure draw the arytenoid cartilage inwards towards the cavity of the larynx, and, on the other hand, it must depress the epiglottis. The action of this muscle is in both cases reinforced by two bundles of muscles which are generally found in the larynx. Thus its action upon the arytenoid cartilage is reinforced by a muscular bundle in the form of a loop, the *depressor cartilaginis arytenoidis,* which, with the *anterior crico-arytenoid,* arises upon the lateral portion of the cricoid cartilage, and, spreading backwards over the lowest portion of the arytenoid cartilage, is inserted into the upper border of the plate of the cricoid cartilage; this presses the arytenoid cartilage inwards towards the cavity of the larynx. In connection with the epiglottis its action is reinforced by a muscular bundle, the *thyro-epiglottideus,* which, arising upon the inner surface of the lateral plate of the thyroid cartilage, is inserted into the side of the epiglottis; it draws the epiglottis downwards.

The upper cavity of the larynx is, generally speaking, a broad space between the glottis and the entrance from the pharynx, which has just been described. The walls are formed entirely of mucous membrane, and present a certain degree of rigidity in front only, where the mucous membrane is firmly connected with the *middle thyro-epiglottic ligament,* and behind, where again it acquires a firm support from the arytenoid cartilage and the transverse arytenoid muscle. Its lower border is horizontal, corresponding to the position of the glottis; its upper opening into the pharynx is, on the contrary, inclined backwards and downwards. This inclination, moreover, does not exactly correspond with that of the inclined plane which we took as a foundation for our description, but is considerably more abrupt, its upper end being driven more backwards and upwards by the epiglottis, which ascends in a backward and upward direction. The current of air, which ascends vertically as far as the glottis, will then gradually assume a more backward direction as it passes into the pharynx, against the posterior wall of which it will strike, and then, gliding upwards upon this posterior wall, enter the posterior nares (cf. Fig. 6). In the same manner, the current of air entering through the nose will first strike the posterior wall of the pharynx and glide downwards upon it into the larynx. Thus the entrance to the cavity of the mouth, situated between the posterior nares and the upper entrance into the larynx, never comes directly in contact with the current of air during quiet respiration, the air being further prevented from entering by the two valves, the soft palate and the epiglottis, which, with the dorsum of the tongue, form a fairly perfect partition between the cavity of the mouth and the pharynx.

Yet another structure demands our special attention, the so-called *ventricles of Morgagni,* situated in its lateral walls, and most intimately connected with the production of tone in the larynx. If the edges described as the vocal chords are to vibrate so as to produce a tone, they must be free chords or edges. The vocal chords cannot, however, be free in this manner from below, as they are not independent structures, but merely the terminations of the vocal plates which converge upwards towards them. They acquire this freedom, however, sufficiently from above, as immediately above the actual vocal chords (thyro-arytenoid ligaments) a deep depression occurs in the lateral wall of the superior cavity of the larynx, which, at first passing outwards along the entire length of the ligaments, afterwards ascends upon the outer side of the mucous membrane with which the superior cavity of the larynx is lined. It is this pouch

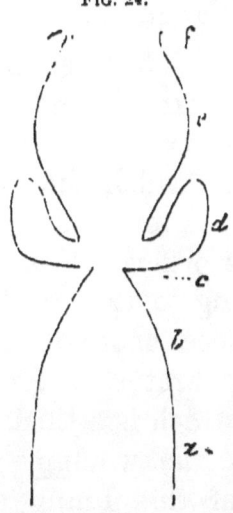

FIG. 24.

Vertical cross-section of the cavity of the larynx. *a*, Cavity of the windpipe; *b*, cavity between the vocal plates; *c*, glottis; *d*, ventricles of Morgagni; *e*, superior cavity of the larynx; *f*, lateral folds marking the outlet of the larynx into the pharynx.

which is called the *ventricle of Morgagni*. Its anterior rises somewhat higher than its posterior portion. These ventricles give to the vocal chords the form of sharp edges, which are well adapted to perform musical vibrations. Without them the glottis would merely present the appearance of an isthmus, bounded by blunt prominences in which the current of air could only have created a whistling sound. The ventricles of the larynx may also possibly reinforce the tone by resonance.

Summary.

We have now completed our examination of the larynx, and may briefly sum up the conclusions we have arrived at as follows:—

(1) The external form of that organ which is called the larynx is determined by the thyroid cartilage.

(2) Two parts must be distinguished in this organ; namely, the vocal apparatus, and the superior cavity of the larynx.

(3) The superior cavity of the larynx is merely a neutral space interposed between the pharynx and the vocal apparatus. It exhibits no special organization beyond the rigidity given to its walls by the cartilages embedded in them, of which the epiglottis is the most important, and the weak muscular layer which serves for the contraction of its orifice. The ventricles situated in its walls rather belong to the vocal apparatus, as they give freedom to the vocal chords.

(4) The vocal apparatus is formed by the elastic lining of the larynx, which is a thickened continuation of the elastic lining of the windpipe; the approximated edges of two sides of this lining constitute the tone-producing " vocal chords."

(5) The cricoid cartilage is the foundation upon which the apparatus is constructed.

(6) The thyroid cartilage and the crico-thyroid muscle effect the tension of the vocal chords.

(7) The glottis when quiescent is in the form of a triangular fissure; when adjusted for tone its anterior larger half becomes a narrow fissure, its posterior portion a rounded opening.

(8) The glottis is adjusted for the production of tone

by the arytenoid cartilages, and by two of the four muscles to which the movement of the latter is due.

(9) That portion only of the vocal chord which lies between the thyroid cartilage and the arytenoid cartilage can act as a vocal chord in the true sense of the word —that is to say, can produce tone. The activity of the apparatus mentioned in (6) and (8) is therefore entirely or chiefly directed to this point.

The Pharynx.

Having thus fully described in the preceding section the interesting apparatus which determines whether the current of air in passing from the windpipe to the succeeding cavities shall be accompanied by tone or shall be toneless, we must now proceed to examine that cavity which it must traverse before finally escaping either through the nasal cavity or the cavity of the mouth.

The pharynx is the immediate upward continuation of the œsophagus, and is therefore, like the latter, nothing more than a tube of mucous membrane enclosed externally by a muscular layer. Posteriorly and on either side its walls are closed; it has no such anterior wall, and stands, therefore, in open connection with the three spaces which are situated one immediately above the other, namely, the larynx, the cavity of the mouth, and the nasal cavity. Above it presents a blind termination against the base of the skull, to which it is firmly attached; passing downwards behind the larynx, it contracts, immediately below the entrance into the latter, into a narrow slit, from the antero-posterior pressure to which it is there subjected, and this slit leads into the cavity of the œsophagus, which is closed by the contraction of all its walls, and which passes downwards

STRUCTURE OF THE ORGANS OF SPEECH. 73

below the larynx. We may thus regard the pharynx as closed, from our point of view, by this slit situated between the larynx and the posterior wall of the pharynx; for here the latter ceases to be an open cavity, in which condition alone it can act as an air-passage, and therefore be of interest in our present investigation.

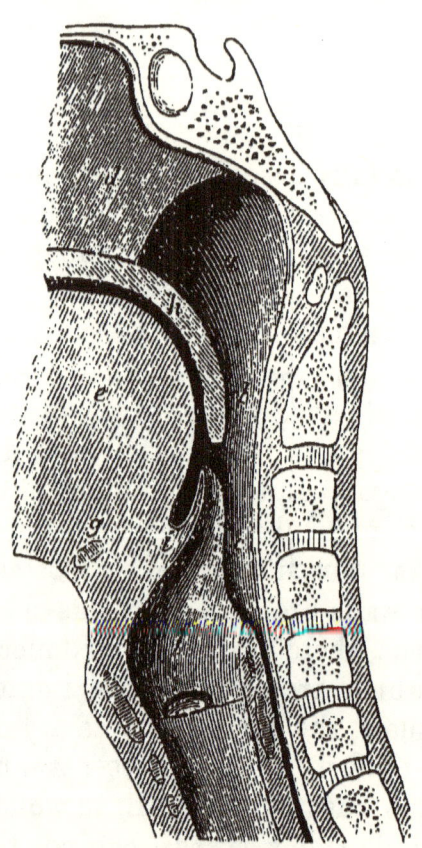

FIG. 25.

The pharynx. *a*, Nasal portion; *b*, oral portion; *c*, laryngeal portion; *d*, posterior portion of the nasal septum; *e*, posterior portion of the tongue; *f*, superior cavity of the larynx; *g*, hyoid bone; *h*, soft palate; *i*, epiglottis.

In the formation of voice the importance of the pharynx is not only due to the free passage which it presents to the current of air, and to its connection with the cavity of the mouth and the nasal cavity, but also especially to the fact that it is attached as a direct resonance tube to the superior cavity of the larynx, and, moreover, a resonance tube of variable length, thus exercising an influence upon the pitch of the tones produced. We must defer for the present the discussion as to how this alteration in the length of the pharynx is effected, and proceed now to examine its form when at rest.

In the first place, we must not imagine the pharynx to be an upright tube of equal diameter. Its form is in a great measure determined by the parts which surround it, in connection with which it must, therefore, be considered.

Now, in order that it may always present a free passage, it is of the greatest importance that it should possess the same breadth throughout its length. Its uppermost part (the nasal portion) is firmly attached to the base of the skull by a surface which measures a little more than the posterior entrance to the nasal cavity— about 3 cm. (1·17 inch)—in breadth, while its depth from before backwards is about 2 cm. (·78 inch). Its lower termination is firmly connected with the inner circumference of the hyoid bone, the greater horns of which lie about 3 cm. (1·17 inch) apart. Thus its breadth is fixed by these two attachments, and is, as the measurements show, the same at the base of the skull and at the hyoid bone. Below the hyoid bone it falls off rapidly, disappearing below the larynx in the contracted walls of the cavity of the œsophagus. Between the two points of attachment just mentioned, the lateral walls receive no support from any imbedded structures; they are, however, kept apart by several causes. This object is attained by their being, in the first place, continuous with the rigid lateral walls of the nasal cavity and with the lateral walls of the cavity of the mouth, which, if not rigid, are at least widely separated; they are, moreover, still further separated by the *stylo-pharyngeus* muscles, which descend from the styloid process of the temporal bone situated even further apart; while the effect is increased by the weight of the larynx, which, with the parts below, is attached to the hyoid bone, drawing it downwards, and thus necessarily stretching the walls of the pharynx between the two points of attachment.

The depth (antero-posterior diameter) of the pharynx is less regular, and presents several peculiarities. The depth depends upon the distance of the posterior from the anterior wall, and may, therefore, be varied by an alteration in the position of either wall, or both walls may be concerned in the alteration at once. This is the case in the pharynx.

The conformation of the posterior wall is, on the whole, simple, as it lies upon the anterior surface of the cervical portion of the vertebral column, by which its form is determined. This surface is, it is true, covered by muscles, but they are of small size, and have no perceptible effect upon the surface they occupy. Now, a curve occurs in this portion of the vertebral column, which is convex in front, and therefore the posterior wall of the pharynx will also be curved forwards. The highest part of this curve lies almost opposite the gap between the soft palate and the epiglottis, from which point it gradually recedes upwards to the base of the skull, and downwards to the commencement of the œsophagus. The height of this curve of course varies greatly according to the individual, but may be roughly estimated at 2 cm. (·78 inch).

The conformation of the anterior wall of the pharynx is less simple, for although its upper and lower divisions are so fixed as to be equally distant from the posterior wall—those parts, therefore, always constituting an open cavity—the conformation of the middle division is both different and variable. In the upper (nasal) portion we cannot, strictly speaking, distinguish an anterior pharyngeal wall, as the lateral walls of the pharynx here pass directly into the lateral walls of the nasal cavity, so that instead of an anterior wall we have merely the direct transition of the cavity of the pharynx into the nasal cavity. We may, however, still obtain an antero-posterior diameter of the pharynx at this point. As the nasal cavity is divided into two parts by a vertical septum, the posterior end of this septum forms the end of the nasal cavity, and at the same time the anterior limit of the pharynx. If, now, we examine the posterior margin of the nasal septum, we shall find that it does not descend in a vertical line from the base of the skull, but that it runs distinctly forwards, so that its lower end is further from the anterior surface of the vertebral column than its upper end, although this part of the vertebral column itself advances. This line, therefore, remains at almost the same distance from the posterior wall of the pharynx upon the vertebral column (the distance being a little greater at its lower extremity), and gives to this part of the pharynx a constant depth of about 2 cm. (·78 inch).

The same is the case with the lowest (laryngeal) portion of the pharynx. As the ends of the greater horns of the hyoid bone lie against the vertebral column, the hyoid bone forms with the latter a framework, the antero-posterior diameter of which is from 2-3 cm. (·78-1·17), and from which, as we have already shown, the larynx is suspended. The space below this frame is so entirely occupied by the larynx that its posterior wall lies upon the vertebral column, the entrance from the pharynx to the œsophagus being only marked by a narrow slit between the two. The space above the horizontal vocal chords is thus necessarily open, and this we found to be the necessary characteristic of that space, which we have already described as the superior cavity of the larynx. As, however, it is directly connected by its orifice with the cavity of the pharynx—with which, in fact, it is continuous—it may be regarded as the lowest portion of the pharynx in its capacity as an air-passage. This view is, indeed, contrary to that generally taken of the superior cavity of the larynx as part of the larynx, but the foundation for it will at once be seen if we allow that the pharynx in its two capacities terminates in a slit, and that the *transverse arytenoid muscle* constitutes a kind of valve, separating the anterior portion (leading to the larynx and windpipe) from the posterior portion (leading to the œsophagus).

The middle (oral) part of the pharynx does not offer the same securities for a constant width as those observed in the parts just described. It appears, indeed, considerably contracted in the direction from before backwards, at that part which lies directly behind the cavity of the mouth. Two causes contribute to effect this contraction. In the first place, it is at this point that the curvature of the cervical portion of the vertebral column reaches its height; and, secondly, the hindermost portion of the tongue projects, when at rest, backwards, so that the two curves lie opposite to each other, merely separated by a narrow slit-like passage. The tongue does not, however, advance freely into the pharynx, but is covered above by the soft palate, which hangs down from the hard palate, and below by the epiglottis, which rises upwards from the anterior wall of the pharynx.

THE ORGANS OF SPEECH.

Thus the cavity of the pharynx possesses an anterior wall sufficient for the purposes of closure, which is formed by the posterior surface of the epiglottis, the posterior surface of the soft palate, and a portion of the dorsum of the tongue situated between their free edges. The part marked by the free surface of the dorsum of the tongue between the two valves, is the narrowest portion of the pharynx.

Thus the pharynx, in its capacity as air-passage, has the same breadth throughout ; its depth (antero-posterior diameter) is greater above (behind the nasal cavity) and below (above the larynx) than in the middle (behind the cavity of the mouth). It would appear that this conformation of its cavity must be detrimental, and in opposition to the law which demands that all air-passages should be open. We find, however, that there is on the one hand no disadvantage in this arrangement, while on the other it is of great value in the formation of articulate sounds. It is of no disadvantage because the narrowest space is sufficient to allow the current of air to pass in and out during quiet respiration; in cases of great want of breath it is undoubtedly too small, and under such circumstances the cavity of the mouth must also be employed as an air-passage. Its advantage is due to the fact that by this arrangement a very slight backward movement of the soft palate is sufficient to completely shut off the nasal cavity from the returning current of air, the full volume of which is thus led aside into the cavity of the mouth, where it can be employed in the formation of sounds. The mechanism by which this is effected will be explained hereafter.

The Nasal Cavity.

The nasal cavity may be described generally as a long narrow passage through the bones of the face, beginning with the nostrils and terminating at the upper part of the pharynx. The construction of this passage is, however, not so simple as to render further description unnecessary. The mere circumstance that it also contains the organ of smell shows that the construction must to some extent be intricate, while, considered simply as an air-passage, it exhibits many interesting and important complications.

The Relation of the Organ of Smell to the Air-Passages.

Our attention is at once drawn to the fact that the nasal cavity contains the organ of smell, because it is by means of the latter that we become cognizant of the fact that the nasal cavity constitutes the commencement of the air-passage, not by any peculiarities of the cavity itself. We shall see the reason of this if we consider the important part played by the organs of sense in the maintenance of the organism. Thus, while they inform us of the presence and properties of external objects, they at the same time caution us against those objects which will be injurious to the organism, and thereby afford us the opportunity of avoiding them. The eye and the ear act in this manner for more distant objects; the other organs perform the same duty for objects which are near to us—the skin in the case of immediate contact or temperature, while the tongue tests the properties of the substances placed in the mouth for mastication, and the nose the properties of the inspired air. The organs of sense may, therefore, to a certain extent be said to play the part of sentinels to the organism. This peculiarity is particularly remarkable in the skin, all those parts which are brought most necessarily and frequently into contact with external objects, the palms of the hands and feet and the natural orifices, being especially sensitive. This attribute is also unmistakably the property of the tongue, which not only possesses a delicate perceptive faculty for testing immediate contact or temperature, but also for ascertaining the chemical properties of the objects with which it is brought into contact. It is scarcely necessary to remark that the tongue thus becomes a most important critic upon all the substances which are brought into the mouth. This is also the case with the nasal cavity as a whole, which is, indeed, only sensitive to actual contact, here of rare occurrence, and to temperatures; a certain part, however, the *organ of smell*, properly so-called, has a peculiar perceptive faculty for testing the properties of gaseous substances. Now, since the part specially organized as the organ of smell is only accessible to gaseous substances, it is evident that it must act as a sentinel towards the latter, and that, therefore, the gaseous substances which enter come as naturally and necessarily into contact with the organ of smell, as the solid and liquid substances introduced into the food-passages come into contact with the tongue. The nasal cavity seems, therefore, to possess every characteristic of the natural air-passage, a view entirely borne out by its construction, which will be most easily and clearly understood if regarded in its relation to the entering and the issuing currents of air.

From what has been said, it would appear that one portion of the mucous membrane must be specially adapted for the organ of smell, and this would lead us to

STRUCTURE OF THE ORGANS OF SPEECH. 81

infer that there must be some peculiarity attached to that part. It will, therefore, be well to discover the relation which it bears to the rest of the nasal cavity, at the same time obtaining some general information as to the construction of that cavity itself.

Division of the Nasal Cavity into an Air-Passage and an Olfactory Chamber.

Although the nasal cavity has been compared to a canal traversing the bones of the face, its width is not the same throughout, but less at both ends than in the middle. The base in no way contributes to this increase

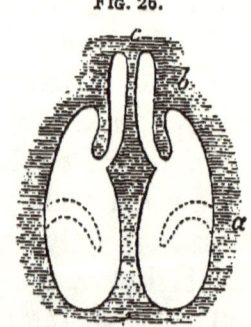

FIG. 26.

Relation of the organ of smell to the air-passage of the nasal cavity (diagrammatic transverse section). *a*, Air-passage, in which the inferior turbinated bone is indicated by the dotted line; *b*, chamber of the organ of smell; *c*, septum.

of dimension, as it proceeds backwards in a straight line. We shall see presently the effect produced in this respect by the side walls. The point which is of greatest interest to us now is to find that the middle portion is characterized by its greater height, being only separated from the skull by a thin lamina of bone, which, from the numerous holes with which it is perforated, is called the *cribriform plate*. In the middle line of the chamber we find a plate composed of bone and cartilage,

G

which acts as a partition or *septum*, dividing the nasal cavity into two parts, so that we have a cavity of the right side and a cavity of the left side; the anterior portion of the septum divides the entrance to the nasal cavity into the two "nostrils," while the posterior portion divides the orifice of the nasal cavity which is directed towards the pharynx into the two hinder openings, which are known as the *posterior nares* (*choanae narium*).

If we take a vertical section of the nasal cavity at the point of its greatest height, we see very clearly the relation between the cavity of the nose (strictly speaking) and the organ of smell. Thus we find that the upper portion of the side wall approaches so closely to the septum that there is only a narrow crevice left between the two. The organ of smell lies in the mucous membrane which lines this crevice, and which is provided with an immense number of nerve filaments. These filaments belong to the lobes of the *olfactory nerve* which rest upon the upper side of the cribriform plate, passing through the holes of the latter to the olfactory mucous membrane. Below the crevice containing the olfactory organ the nasal cavity suddenly expands, forming the air-passage, properly so-called. We see from the section that the form of the latter is oval, the long axis being vertical, and the air-passage, consequently, is higher than it is broad. As the upper part of this oval is necessarily further from the septum than the middle, the entrance to the organ of smell is not at the extreme summit of the air-passage, but in the upper portion of the inner circumference. The upper part of the air-passage and the lower portion of the organ of smell are, therefore, in close proximity, only separated by a thin plate, which, when examining the side wall of the nasal cavity, we shall find to be the middle turbinated bone. In the section it has the appearance of a tongue, which acts as a partition between the two cavities. It is remarkable that the approach to the organ of smell is still further contracted by the margin of the inferior turbinated bone being enlarged, a similar thickening also appearing upon the septum, a little below the latter, so that between the two swellings a comparatively narrow crevice leads from the air-passage to the organ of smell. Now, as this insignificant entrance is the only means of direct communication with the inspired air, it follows that the cavity must to a great extent be filled by diffusion. At the same time we see why a cold in the head is always prejudicial to the sense of smell, the entrance to the crevice in which the organ is situated being more or less completely closed, and consequently excluded from the air, by the swelling of the mucous membrane with which a cold is accompanied.

A closer investigation of the construction of the side wall of the nasal cavity will give us still more information as to the shape of the air-passage and its relation to the organ of smell. With this end in view we must first become acquainted with the roof of the nasal cavity, reserving, however, our special attention for those parts which constitute the side walls.

The Bony Framework of the Nasal Cavity.

The cranial and facial bones of the skull both take part in the construction of the nasal cavity, which may be roughly described as that portion of the skull which lies between the base of the cranium and the arch of the upper jaw. The latter is composed entirely of bone, commencing in front of the ears with the zygomatic arch and united in the median line of the face to the corresponding bone of the other side. The central portion of this arch receives the upper row of teeth, and is therefore called the *superior maxillary bone.* The entire arch of the upper jaw is composed of a number of separate bones, and is strongly attached on each side and in the centre of the face to the base of the skull. The lateral connection is formed by that part of the upper jaw known as the *malar bone,* which at once constitutes the anterior border of the temporal fossæ and the external border of the orbits; below the outer angle of the eye this portion of the upper jaw thickens considerably, forming the prominence known generally as the "cheekbone."

The central point of attachment, forming at once the inner walls of both orbits, is of the greatest interest from our point of view, forming as it does the framework of the nasal cavity. Looking more closely, we find that this attachment is double, and only appears single because, in the immediate neighbourhood of the frontal bone of the cranium, the two nasal bones form an arched connection between the highest portions of the two attachments. In the skull of the adult it is difficult to realize that the bony eminence between the eyes, which we readily recognize as the bony framework of the upper portion of the external nose, is only a double continuation of the arch of the upper jaw. This difficulty is merely caused by the elevation of the superior maxillary bone, which forms with the teeth the central portion of the arch of the upper jaw. In the skull of the infant, where the superior maxillary bone is not developed to so great a height, the difficulty disappears, the continuity of the arch of the upper teeth with the malar bone is at once evident, and the arch of the upper jaw can be seen passing beneath the orbits.

In that portion of the superior maxillary bone which

lies close to the median line of the face, we find a process passing obliquely upwards and inwards, and forming the inner wall of the anterior opening of the orbit. The processes of the two sides are attached close together to the central part of the frontal bone, being only separated by the narrow nasal bone. The gap left between these two processes, which above is partially covered by the nasal bone, constitutes the pear-shaped opening of the *anterior nares;* in the living subject it is so covered by cartilage and integument as to form the external nose.

This description gives a general idea of the nasal cavity, and especially of the relation of its anterior opening to the surface of the face; we have still to investigate the interior of the cavity. We shall do this most easily if we consider the arch of the upper jaw from below. We then see at once that the portion of this arch formed by the superior maxillary bone widens out considerably backwards, and that the margin of the surface thus formed constitutes the alveolar arch, into which the upper teeth are inserted. The posterior margin of either superior maxillary bone is attached to a downward process of the base of the skull (or, more strictly speaking, of the sphenoid bone) by which they are supported. A small bone (the *palate bone*) is partly the medium for this attachment; it is, however, unnecessary to describe its form and position here. The space contained within the arch of the teeth is filled by a thin, horizontal, bony plate (the *hard or bony palate*), and this forms, while separating the cavity of the mouth from the cavity of the nose, the roof of one and the floor of the other. The side walls of the nasal cavity are about as far removed from each other above the hard palate as the posterior extremities of the arch of the teeth are below it; they extend, however, further backward than the hard palate, for they are so closely connected with the whole internal surface of those processes of the base of the skull (the *pterygoid processes* of the sphenoid) as to only terminate with their posterior margin. On either side, therefore, these margins constitute the posterior extremity of the nasal cavity, the floor of which, however, terminates earlier with the posterior margin of the hard palate, and the roof is

Fig. 27.

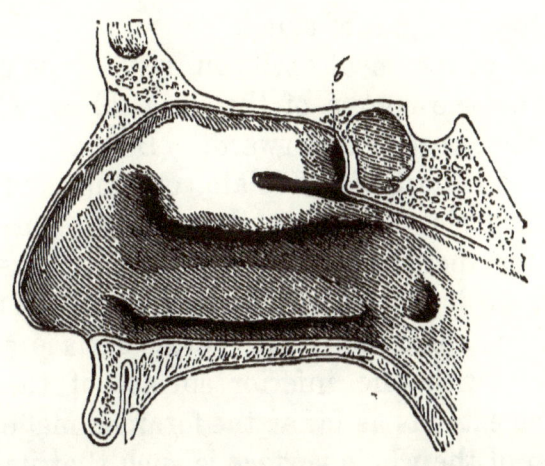

Lateral wall of the nose. *a*, Partition separating the narrow entrance to the organ of smell from the passage under the middle turbinated bone; *b*, *recessus spheno-ethmoidalis*.

formed by the whole of that portion of the skull which lies between the articulation of the nasal bone with the frontal and the posterior border of the pterygoid processes.

We have already remarked that the middle portion of the nasal cavity rises to a considerable height. The roof of this part is formed by the *cribriform plate*. This thin lamina of bone lies almost horizontally between the internal margins of the orbital vaults formed by the horizontal portion of the frontal bone. Its upper surface may be seen in the position described, at the base of the cavity of the skull, and is characterized by a number of sieve-like perforations. Upon its median line, which passes from before backwards, may be seen a small prominence somewhat resembling a cock's comb, and therefore called the *crista-galli*. This prominence divides the surface of the cribriform plate into two lateral halves, upon each of which lies the broad extremity of the *olfactory nerve* (the *olfactory bulb*), which sends an immense number of small filaments through the holes of the plate to the organ of smell.

The roof of the nasal cavity in front of the cribriform plate follows the course of the *nasal bones*, which pass obliquely downwards and forwards. Beyond the posterior margin of the cribriform plate, on the contrary, the anterior surface of the body of the sphenoid bone descends as an almost perpendicular wall, which, however, soon turns backwards almost at right angles to form the under surface of the sphenoid. This latter surface articulates immediately with the inferior surface of the occipital bone, which extends as far as the foramen magnum. The inclination of the whole surface is such that its posterior extremity (the anterior margin of the foramen magnum) is about on a level with the floor of the nasal cavity. The anterior portion of this surface, so far as it is laterally bordered by the pterygoid processes, belongs to the roof of the nasal cavity, and within the same limits is also attached to the upper margin of the nasal septum.

If we were to continue this surface forwards we should find that it would strike the lower extremity of the nasal bone, thus connecting the upper margin of the *anterior nares* with the upper margin of the *posterior nares*. The nasal cavity is, therefore, divided into two parts, which may be generally described as the air-passage and the organ of smell. The space between the continuous surface just described and the floor of the nasal cavity, being the direct connection between the anterior and posterior nares, is plainly marked as the air-passage. The upper space, situated between that surface and the cribriform plate, contains the organ of smell; it has the appearance of an upward extension of the air-passage, from which alone it can be approached; its anterior wall is formed by the nasal bone, its posterior by the sphenoid bone. Further, with regard to the air-passage, we find that it is lower behind than before, expanding like a trumpet as it proceeds forwards; the extent of this expansion is indicated by the fact mentioned above, that the posterior prolongation of the floor of the nasal cavity upon reaching the anterior margin of the foramen magnum comes in contact with the under surface of the sphenoid and the occipital. The angle at which this connection takes place gives the degree of divergence, or rather convergence, between the upper and lower extremities of the air-passage. We shall speak presently of the peculiar construction presented by a horizontal section of the air-passage; we need here only remark that it is considerably wider in the middle than at either end.

These two divisions of the nasal cavity are bounded laterally by several distinct pieces of bone, a fact which, upon closer investigation, furnishes us with an important feature in our description of the bony framework of the nasal cavity. We have thus far only regarded the nasal cavity as a space enclosed by the two superior maxillary bones, stretching upwards between the orbits as far as the base of the skull. If, however, we examine the inner wall of the orbit, we find that only the foremost portion (the nasal process) of the superior maxillary bone extends to the base of the skull; the greater part of the superior maxillary bone, which with its upper surface forms the floor of the orbits, being considerably removed from the vaults of the orbits which are formed by the frontal bone. Thus a gap is left, bounded below by the superior maxillary, above by the portion of the frontal forming the orbital vaults, anteriorly by the nasal pro-

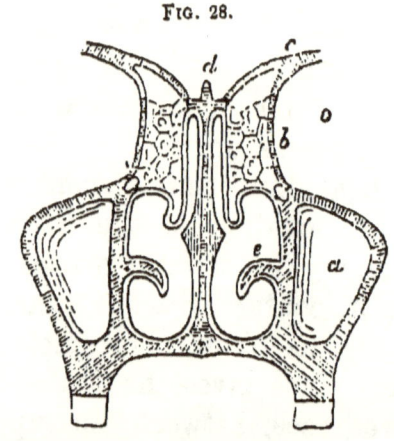

Fig. 28.

Vertical transverse section of the nasal cavity; the boundaries between the different bones marked by dots. *a*, Superior maxillary bone with the antrum; *b*, ethmoidal cells separated from the orbit *o* by the os planum; *c*, part of the orbital vault formed by the frontal bone with the frontal sinus; *d*, the upward continuation of the septum of the nose, the crista-galli, under which lies the horizontal cribriform plate; *e*, the inferior turbinated bone.

cess of the superior maxillary, and posteriorly by the sphenoid. This gap is filled by a thin plate of bone, the *os planum* of the ethmoid, which thus forms the inner wall of the orbit. With regard to the lateral border of the nasal cavity, we find, therefore, that the superior maxillary forms the lateral wall of the air-passage; the os planum of the ethmoid, on the contrary, closes externally the portion of the nasal cavity containing the organ of smell.

The inner surfaces of the superior maxillary and the

os planum of the ethmoid lie almost in a vertical plane, and yet it has been shown that the organ of smell must be sought in a crevice forming the upper space of the nasal cavity. If the os planum of the ethmoid is the true external boundary of the portion of the nasal cavity containing the organ of smell, these two facts offer a contradiction which must be cleared up. The difficulty at once disappears when we find that the os planum is not a separate free plate of bone, but only the outer coating of a large cellular mass of bone which projects into the nasal cavity, where it terminates in a similar bony plate (the *turbinated bone*). The space between these two plates is filled by the ethmoidal cells.

We shall have another opportunity of speaking of the cellular cavities of these lateral masses of the ethmoid and similar appearances in the surrounding bones, and considering their general importance; we must, however, now devote a few words to the relation between the ethmoidal cells and the adjoining bones. The lateral mass of the ethmoid is a plane right-angled parallelogram, the larger surfaces of which, the os planum and the superior and middle turbinated bones, have already been mentioned. With regard to the latter we must, however, further observe that the os planum is composed of two parts, a posterior (the *os planum*, strictly speaking) and an anterior (the *lachrymal bone*). The lachrymal bone differs from the actual os planum in not forming, like the latter, an unbroken continuation of the walls of the cells, but may, on the contrary, be compared to a loose lid placed upon their outer surface; in all other respects it has so entirely the appearance of being part of the os planum, that we shall generally use the latter term for the two bones, which, however, it is usual to separate.

The lateral mass of the ethmoid has the same borders as those which have already been described as belonging to the os planum. They are, however, of some thickness, corresponding to the distance of the turbinated bones from the os planum; thus they assume the character of narrow surfaces, and as such may be regarded as the lateral surfaces of the plane parallelogram, with which the lateral mass of the ethmoid has been compared. The lower of these surfaces rests with its outer edge, where it joins the os planum, upon the upper margin of the superior maxillary bone, and thus forms the roof of the air-passage. The further characteristics which this gives rise to will be described more minutely as we proceed. On either side of the upper of these narrow surfaces are half-broken spaces, a closer acquaintance with which is important for our thorough investigation of the cavity of the nose. In order to understand this characteristic we must examine a little more closely that part of the frontal bone which forms the orbital vaults, and remark particularly the thickness of the inner wall. This fact is quite apparent in any skull without dissection. The surface of the orbital vaults, namely, which is directed towards the cavity of the cranium is only separated from that of the other side by the intermediate cribriform plate; the surface, however, which turns towards the orbits is divided from that of the other side by the whole of the space lying between the orbits. If the frontal bone is removed, we find that the inner part of the orbital vault consists of two plates, the one of which joins the os planum of the ethmoid, while the other is attached to the lateral wall of the cribriform plate. As, however, the two turbinated bones of the lateral mass of the ethmoid are connected with the same wall of the cribriform plate, it appears that each half of the cribriform plate forms the roof of the organ of smell in the corresponding division of the nasal cavity, determining by its breadth the width of the crevice in which the organ is situated.

The construction which we have thus described as that of the bony framework of the nasal cavity, will be found to harmonize perfectly with the relation between the air-passage and the organ of smell, to which we have already alluded. We have, namely, only to prolong the lower edge of the inner surface of the lateral mass of the ethmoid (the middle turbinated bone), and we shall obtain the thin tongue-like wall of division between the upper portion of the air-passage and the lower part of the organ of smell, which has already been mentioned.

The External Nose.

We see from this sketch of the bony framework of the nasal cavity, which we shall presently make more complete, the importance of the bony case to the cavity, giving as it does the characteristic conformation to the air-passage, and setting aside a special chamber for the organ of smell; nevertheless, the walls of the nasal cavity do not entirely consist of this bony foundation, but are provided with an external prolongation of such a form that the whole of the pear-shaped orifice is closed, and the entrance to the nasal cavity confined to the comparatively small openings of the two nostrils. This prolongation affects the side walls as well as the septum, and is partly produced by plates of cartilage, partly by the external skin. The result of the combination is the *external nose*.

The cartilages of the external nose are of two different kinds, which differ materially from each other. The

STRUCTURE OF THE ORGANS OF SPEECH. 93

one, namely, has more the characteristics of bone, the other those of the accessory parts of the external skin.

The cartilages of the first kind are remains of the rudimentary skull, by which is meant the earliest form of the skull—the exact miniature, indeed, of the fully developed skull, but consisting merely of a continuous capsule of cartilage, instead of the separate bones of the latter. These separate pieces of bone, which are united when the skull is fully developed, are produced from cer-

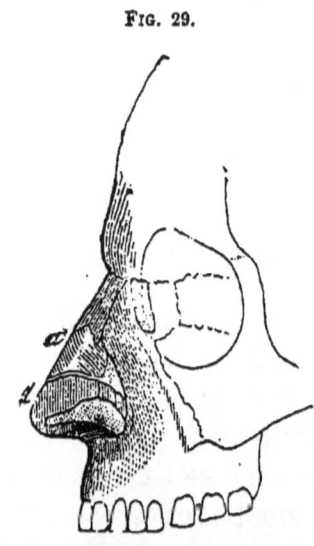

FIG. 29.

Cartilage of the external nose. *a*, Triangular cartilage; *b* (shaded with vertical lines), the lower lateral cartilage of the nostril.

tain points or centres of ossification, which are found partly in the cartilage of the rudimentary skull, and partly in the perichondrium. A portion of this rudimentary cartilaginous skull remains unossified at the anterior extremity of the nasal cavity, standing in the same relation to the bones with which it is united as the costal cartilages to the ribs, of which these cartilages are also merely extensions of undeveloped bone. This cartilaginous prolongation of the walls of the nose consists of a middle plate, which forms the anterior lower portion of the septum, and two lateral plates, which form a continuation of the nasal bone. Although these three plates are composed of a single piece of cartilage, the central plate is generally distinguished as the *cartilaginous septum*, and the two smaller lateral plates, which unite with the latter upon the dorsum of the nose, the *triangular lateral cartilages*.

The cartilaginous septum protrudes to such a distance beyond the pear-shaped opening of the anterior nares, that, with the exception of the tip, it supports the dorsum of the whole external nose; it does not, however, extend either to the extreme tip of the nose, or to the edge of the septum, which may be seen dividing the outer margin of the nostrils. Thus it forms, if not a perfect, yet a very efficient extension of the bony septum. The lateral cartilages are, on the contrary, unimportant, and represent the side walls of the cavity in a much less decided manner. The well-known form of the external nose is completed by the integument of the face, which is continuous with the mucous membrane lining the interior of the nasal cavity.

The lowest marginal portion of the septum, formed entirely by the skin, is short, but possesses, as we know, considerable mobility; it is called the *septum mobile*. The lateral portions of the external nose, which are formed in the same manner, are considerably expanded, and hang like a loose curtain between the skin of the cheek and the dorsum of the nose; they are therefore called the *alae* of the nose.

The mobility and softness of the alæ of the nose, to which we have just alluded, are, however, in direct opposition to that fixity which we pronounced as an indis-

STRUCTURE OF THE ORGANS OF SPEECH.   95

pensable characteristic of the walls of an air-passage; and the alæ of the nose afford, therefore, an excellent means of demonstrating the importance and the necessity of such a peculiarity in an air-passage. If, namely, the entrance of the air is impeded by lightly laying the finger upon the nostril, and a strong inspiration taken, the ala of the nose falls in, and if a great inspiratory effort is made, remains in such close contact with the septum that the passage is more or less entirely closed to the air. This experiment shows, however, at the same time that there is no danger of the air being excluded in this manner in ordinary quiet breathing. On the other hand, the mobility of the nose offers the great advantage, that by this means the entrance of air to the nasal cavity can be regulated, as we shall presently show. There is, moreover, another peculiarity in the formation of the nostril, which, without affecting the mobility of the nose, secures the entrance of air into the nostrils. A cartilaginous ring is, namely, inserted in the periphera of the nostril, where it does not come in contact with the lower margin of the anterior nares, which stiffens the skin forming the nostril and thus keeps the latter open. The principal portion of this ring is formed by the *lower lateral cartilage,* a moderately broad, thin plate which is situated in the lower central portion of the ala, and, curving round the lobe of the nose, runs into a narrow process which is enclosed in the fold of integument forming the septum mobile. Posteriorly the plate of integument situated in the ala is produced into several united cartilaginous plates—the *sesamoid cartilages*—which extend as far as the anterior nares. The lobe of the nose, therefore, is formed of the curved portion of the lower lateral cartilages of the right and the left side, the inward processes of which are situated in the septum mobile. This construction of the lobe of the nose can often be distinctly recognized by a shallow vertical groove, but still more plainly if, as it sometimes happens, one cartilage projects beyond the other.

The Muscles of the Nose.

The great advantage of the mobility of those parts of the nose which are in close proximity to the nostrils, especially the alæ of the nose, is that by this means the entrance of air into the nasal cavity can be regulated. It is true that this arrangement chiefly affects the organ of smell, but this fact is in itself a reason why a certain amount of importance should attach to the quantity of air admitted. The development of this mobility into actual motion is, of course, due to certain muscles, the disposition of which we find to be such that some produce an alteration in the width of the nostril, while others affect its position. Here, again, much is attained by the smallest means, for it is through the action of four muscles only that all this is accomplished. There are, indeed, other smaller muscles distributed over the surface of the nose, but these are much too unimportant to exercise any perceptible influence, even where they are fully developed, which, however, is very rarely the case. Their whole value lies in the fact that they are indications of similarly arranged, but much more powerful and therefore more active, muscles in the lower animals.

Of the four muscles mentioned above, the largest is the one which distends the nostril by raising the ala of the nose. It arises upon the side of the bony external nose, close to the inner angle of the eye, and descends in a straight line to the angle between the ala of the nose and the cheek, where its fibres terminate partly in the ala of the nose, and partly a little lower down in the upper lip. When in action it draws the last-mentioned angle upwards, thus raising the ala of the nose and the adjoining portion of the upper lip, and at the same time dilating the nostril. It is therefore called the *levator labii superioris alaeque nasi*. Its action may be seen when a very strong inspiration is taken, especially in shortness of breath, when it affords entrance to a greater amount of air.

The antagonist of this muscle is one which it partly covers, and which arises upon the incisive fossa immediately above the outer incisors, passing upwards to angle between the ala of the nose and the cheek. A number of its terminal fibres are here inserted in the ala of the nose; the rest, however, extend further, spreading out in a fibrous aponeurosis over the entire dorsum, especially that part which has no bony foundation. The first division of this muscle is called the *depressor alae nasi;* from a false conception of its position and consequent action it is, however, sometimes called the *levator alae nasi*. The second division, from its fibrous expansion over the moveable portion of the dorsum, draws that part of the nose downwards, and is therefore called the *compressor narium*. The two muscles act unanimously in one respect, for they both cause a diminution in the quantity of air admitted into the nasal cavity—a fact which has no effect upon the process of breathing, but, as we shall presently see, is of some importance to the organ of smell.

The two muscles which we have just described are the most important, and most frequently brought into action, from their position upon the exceedingly mobile alæ of the nose. Closely related to them we find, however, two smaller muscles, the action of which is restricted to the lobe of the nose; the one again being an elevator and the other a depressor.

The elevator of the lobe of the nose—the *m. pyramidalis nasi*—is a double bundle of fibres, which does not arise upon any particular surface of bone, but is a prolongation of some of the fibres of the *frontal muscle*, running down the dorsum of the nose towards the lobe. Its size varies in different individuals; as a rule, it does not extend beyond the lower margin of the nasal bone. As it finally blends with the integument, its action is to draw the integument of the dorsum of the nose slightly upwards, and therefore slightly to raise the lobe.

In opposition to this muscle is the *depressor septi mobilis*. This, again, does not arise from any special bone surface, but consists merely of a few bundles of the *orbicularis oris*, which, passing upwards, terminate in the septum mobile. Their action is to draw the latter downwards, and with it the lobe of the nose.

Summary.

If, now, before proceeding to a closer examination of the walls of the nasal cavity, we briefly review the facts obtained from the foregoing description of the construction of the nasal cavity in general, we have the following results:—

(1) The nasal cavity, with the exception of a portion of the external nose, is a space entirely enclosed by walls of bone, which opens anteriorly by a narrow orifice in the face to the outer air, and posteriorly by an equally narrow orifice in the uppermost part of the pharynx.

(2) A septum, also for the most part composed of bone, occupying a vertical position in the median line

of the cavity, divides the latter from the anterior to the posterior orifice into a right and a left portion.

(3) An almost horizontal cross-piece, which, however, ascends forwards, again divides each half into two spaces distinguished by their difference in width, but immediately connected with each other.

(4) The lower, wider space is the air-passage, strictly speaking; it is bounded laterally by the superior maxillary bone, and the pterygoid processes of the sphenoid with the accompanying palate bones; the floor is formed by the hard palate, with which posteriorly the soft palate is directly continuous; posteriorly the roof is formed by the under surface of the body of the sphenoid, and anteriorly by the under surface of the lateral mass of the ethmoid.

(5) The upper, narrow space is the organ of smell. It has the appearance of a small crevice-like upward extension of the air-passage, which is bounded laterally by the inner plate (middle turbinated bone) of the lateral mass of the ethmoid. It ascends to the cribriform plate, and is bounded posteriorly by the anterior surface of the body of the sphenoid, anteriorly by the nasal bone; its lower boundary is given by the plane (sec. 3), which, from the under surface of the sphenoid, extends as far as the nasal bone; below it is slightly enlarged by the middle turbinated bone, without, however, being in any way detrimental to the air-passage. (This point will be treated more fully presently, and is only alluded to here, that the division between the two spaces should not seem too pronounced.)

(6) The external nose, where the nasal bone does not form its foundation, is principally to be regarded as the most anterior portion of the air-passage; it consists partly of plates of cartilage, which are direct con-

tinuations of the nasal bones, partly of folds of integument, which round the two nostrils are stiffened by rings of cartilage.

(7) That part of the septum also which is situated in the external nose, is formed of cartilage retaining this character also for some distance into the nasal cavity.

(8) The cartilaginous portion of the external nose can be moved by muscles in such a manner, that by one pair of muscles the ala, and by another the lobe, of the nose can be elevated and depressed.

(9) The whole of the nasal cavity is lined with a mucous membrane which is continuous with the outer integument at the nostril, and at the posterior nares with the mucous membrane of the pharynx. The mucous membrane of the crevice, in the upper part of the nasal cavity, has a peculiar organization which enables it to act as the organ of smell.

The Inner Wall of the Nasal Cavity.

We have already observed that the space which is commonly called the nasal cavity is really divided into two spaces, so that, to be perfectly accurate, we should distinguish a right and a left nasal cavity; as, however, both cavities stand in precisely the same relation to the current of air passing through them, and therefore act as a whole, the term "nasal cavity" is still generally applied to the two spaces. Still, in a closer examination, this division must not be forgotten. We must remember, namely, that each cavity has two walls, the inner one of which is formed by the septum, and the outer one by the superior maxillary bone and the ethmoid.

The inner lateral wall formed by the septum offers

little of importance, it being simply a smooth and even surface, bearing the single characteristic of that fold of mucous membrane which serves to narrow the entrance to the organ of smell. It consists fundamentally of two thin plates of bone and a plate of cartilage, which are so united at their margins as to represent a single plate.

In fact, the septum in the rudimentary skull consists of a single plate of cartilage, of which the two bony plates

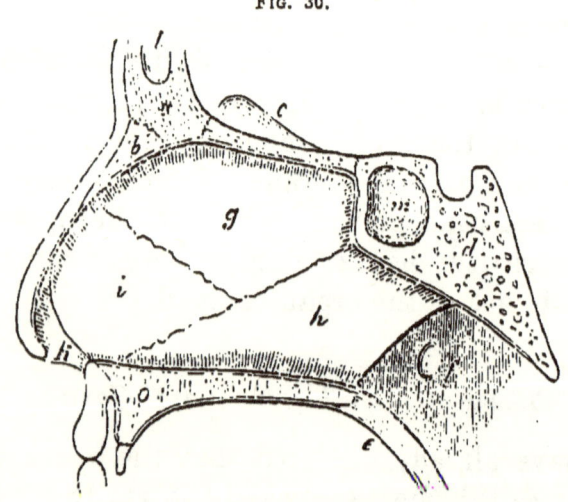

FIG. 30.

Septum of the nose. *a*, Frontal bone with the frontal sinus (*l*); *b*, nasal bone; *c*, the crista galli and the cribriform plate; *d*, sphenoid and sphenoidal sinus (*m*); *o*, hard palate; *e*, soft palate; *f*, entrance to the Eustachian tube; *g*, perpendicular plate of the ethmoid; *h*, vomer; *i*, cartilaginous septum; *k*, septum mobile.

described are only ossified portions. These bony plates are the *perpendicular plate of the ethmoid* and the *vomer*. The latter is situated between the under surface of the body of the sphenoid and the upper surface of the hard palate, its upper border (guttural edge) forming a line extending from the anterior lower angle of the body of the sphenoid to the forward termination of the hard palate. The perpendicular plate of the ethmoid is attached before to the nasal bone, above to the cribriform plate, behind to the anterior surface of the body of the sphenoid, and below to the posterior half of the guttural edge of the vomer; a fifth free border passes from the middle of the vomer to the lower extremity of the nasal bone. Between this border and the anterior half of the guttural edge of the vomer lies the *cartilaginous septum*, the curved margin of which projects in front of the anterior nares, between the lower extremity of the nasal bone and the anterior extremity of the hard palate. The portion of the septum still remaining between the latter and the nostrils is composed of the fold of integument which we already know as the septum mobile.

It not unfrequently happens with this construction that the septum is unsymmetrical, that its central portion is bent in on one side, bulging out at the corresponding point on the other side into the opposite cavity.

Far more complicated are the lateral walls of the two nasal cavities, for they present all the peculiarities connected with the passage of the air through the nose.

The first thing which strikes us in this wall is the difference between the chamber of the organ of smell and the air-passage. We see on the latter, namely, two convoluted mussel-shaped plates of bone, so situated that their concavity faces downwards, and covered with the mucous membrane which lines the nasal cavity. The lower of these two plates (the *inferior turbinated bone*) may for the present remain unnoticed; the upper one, however, is more important. It is called the *middle turbinated bone*, although this title is most unsuitable, as it implies the existence of an upper turbinated bone. There is, it is true, another similar small plate of bone to be seen above the middle turbinated bone, which is

STRUCTURE OF THE ORGANS OF SPEECH. 103

called the superior turbinated bone; but its formation and its relations are so different, that it cannot be considered as equal in importance to the middle turbinated bone. Strictly speaking, the relations of the inferior turbinated are quite different to those of the middle, and the common designation bestowed upon these two bones is equally misapplied; nevertheless there is more excuse in the latter case, as the two bones bear an outward resemblance to each other.

The middle turbinated bone divides the air-passage from the organ of smell. It is, in fact, a downward prolongation of the inner surface of the lateral mass of the ethmoid, leaving between the latter and the septum a narrow crevice-like space, which is an immediate downward extension of the chamber of the organ of smell. There is, however, an intermediate space between this middle turbinated bone and the superior maxillary, which is the highest part of the air-passage. Thus the upper part of the air-passage and the lower part of the organ of smell lie on the same plane, only separated by the middle turbinated bone, and the crevice of the organ of smell opens into the upper and inner portion of the air-passage. The entrance to the former is, as we have already observed, greatly contracted by the thickening of the mucous membrane upon the lower margin of the middle turbinated bone, and by a similar swelling upon that part of the septum which is opposite to it. The chamber of the organ of smell commences in the narrow opening thus left, expanding slightly as it passes upwards.

In shape the middle turbinated bone may be compared to a right-angled triangle. Its lower margin begins a little below and before the lower angle of the body of the sphenoid, and proceeds parallel with the horizontal floor of the nasal cavity forwards, terminating under the upper end of the nasal bone; the anterior margin then starts upwards at a right angle, passing nearly to the roof of the nasal cavity. The hypotenuse which connects these two lines is formed by the attachment of the turbinated bone to the lateral mass of the ethmoid. It is the same line which has already been mentioned as continuing the under surface of the body of the sphenoid, and forming the upper boundary of the air-passage. It is clear that this line must ascend as it

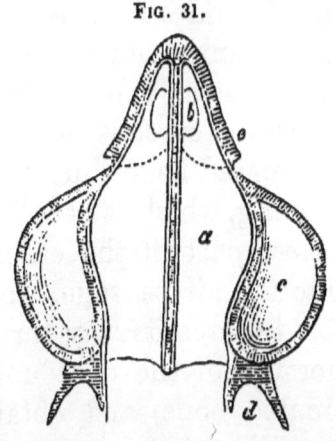

Fig. 31.

Horizontal section of the nasal cavity below the attachment of the inferior turbinated bone, viewed from above. *a*, Floor of the nasal cavity, terminating behind with the posterior margin of the hard palate, the anterior margin of the bony floor indicated by the dotted line; *b*, view through the nostril; *c*, antrum; *d*, pterygoid process of the sphenoid; *e*, integument of the external nose.

passes forwards, and consequently that the air-passage, the roof of which is marked by the under surface of the middle turbinated bone, must be higher before than behind. The importance of this construction probably consists less in forcing the air through the ensuing posterior contraction, as in the fact that space is given for all the air which enters the nasal cavity in the air-passage, and that it is thus kept back from the chamber of the organ of smell.

This view is borne out by the peculiarity of the anterior margin of the turbinated bone and the manner of its union with the side wall of the nasal cavity. The anterior portion of the nasal cavity, so far as it is formed by the external nose and the anterior nares, is very narrow; the inner wall of the superior maxillary bone then recedes considerably, the nasal cavity becoming proportionately wider, to contract again at the posterior nares. It is precisely this wider portion which is roofed by the turbinated bone, the anterior margin of which curves forwards and outwards into the narrower portion, where it is continued for some distance parallel to the dorsum of the nose as a low fold, losing itself in the even surface, which extends to the nostril. The space below the turbinated bone thus commences with a trumpet-shaped opening, which is peculiarly well adapted to take up the greatest part of the entering air and to direct its course into the air-passage, while only a small quantity will be able to force its way through the narrow slit between the dorsum of the nose and the thickened edge of the turbinated bone, and obtain direct access to the organ of smell, this chamber being generally filled by diffusion from the air passing through the air-passage.

These characteristics also throw some light upon the relation between the external muscles and the act of smelling. The *m. compressor narium*, acting in unison with the depressor of the septum, impedes the entrance of air through the narrow opening leading to the organ of smell, and therefore we make use of these muscles when wishing to avoid unpleasant smells. On the other hand, an elevation of the alæ of the nose, accompanied by a slight depression of the septum mobile, will draw the current of air inwards against the septum, and thus facilitate its entrance under the lower edge of the turbinated bone into the chamber of the organ of smell, which will take place still more easily if the air is inhaled slowly, so as not to be forced at once into the air-passage when it has passed through the nostril. Thus, when we wish to perceive any odour very distinctly—as, for instance, in smelling a rose—we elevate the alæ of the nose and then slowly draw up the air.

In the middle of the air-passage, and therefore in its widest part, we meet with another mussel-shaped plate lying parallel with the floor of the nasal cavity. It is formed of a separate piece of bone (the *inferior turbinated bone*), which is united with the inner wall of the superior maxillary. It divides the above-mentioned lateral dilation of the air-passage into two parts, an upper and a lower, and is situated at about the same distance from the septum as the middle turbinated bone. The two divisions thus caused by these bones in the air-passage are known as the *middle* and *inferior meatus*. We shall also find mention of a "superior meatus" below the "superior turbinated bone," but it can as little be compared with the two other meatuses as the superior turbinated can with the middle and inferior bones. Moreover, we cannot attribute a common significance to the two lower meatuses, as they possess none whatever when considered apart, and must only be regarded as accidental appearances in the air-passage produced by the interposition of the inferior turbinated bone. It is, indeed, difficult to discover the significance of the inferior turbinated bone in this passage. It seems most probable that it is designed to warm the air which enters before it passes further inwards. In support of this view, it appears that the mucous membrane of the inferior turbinated bone is so vascular as to form almost a spongy tissue, which is filled with blood; and as, in accordance with a well-known law, the current of air must flow more slowly in the expanded portion of the air-passage, there would be sufficient time for it to be warmed by the constantly renewed blood of the vascular membrane. As the process just described must in any case be always going on, we may venture to regard it as the office of the inferior turbinated bone—a view which we shall find confirmed by the relation of the inferior turbinated bone in many mammals. In the latter, for instance, it is often not merely a simple convoluted plate, but a complicated construction filling the whole of the air-passage. The two principal forms which we meet with are (1) a plate, which near its point of attachment splits into two plates, each of which is convoluted upon itself, one in an upward, the other in a downward direction; (2) a plate, split in the same way, but these secondary portions split again, so that a cross section of these series of plates has a delicately branched appearance. In either case there can be no mention of the division of the air-passage into two channels, but the air streaming through the passage is thus forced to find its way through the numerous windings between these plates, and consequently must be warmed by its long-continued contact with the mucous membrane, which is so rich in blood, just as the inhaled air is warmed by passing through the threads of a respirator.

The Side Chambers of the Nose.

The side chambers of the nasal cavity are a very characteristic part of its construction. We may describe them generally as excavations in the bones enclosing the nasal cavity, into which they open by means of comparatively narrow orifices. In each of the two nasal cavities there are three distinct side chambers—the *sphenoidal sinus*, the *antrum* or *maxillary sinus*, and the *ethmoidal sinus*.

The *sphenoidal sinus* (Fig. 27) is a spherical cavity which is found in the body of the sphenoid, and is separated from that of the other side by a thin lamella of bone. It opens by a small round aperture upon the anterior surface of the body of the sphenoid into the posterior part of the nasal cavity, or, more correctly, into the *spheno-ethmoidal recess*. The manner of opening peculiar to this sinus is of some interest, as affording a possibility of discovering the function of the side chambers; we shall, therefore, refer to it again.

The *antrum* is a cavity which runs through the entire maxillary bone. It is a large cavity, and opens by a small round aperture into the upper part of the air-passage, below the centre of the middle turbinated bone.

The *ethmoidal sinus* is an extensive and very irregular cavity, which owes its origin to the hollow character of the lateral mass of the ethmoid, and to the fact that this character extends beyond the limits of the lateral mass, and is more or less continued in the contiguous bones. It is not so noticeable in the sphenoid, the palate, or the maxillary bone, but very striking in the inner walls of the orbital vaults, and particularly so in the frontal part of the frontal bone; so much so that this extension is commonly regarded as a separate cavity (the frontal sinus). The system of ethmoidal cells possess two entrances into the nasal cavity. By one of these—the *superior ethmoidal fissure*, generally called the "superior meatus"—the posterior ethmoidal cells open into the back part of the chamber of the organ of smell; by the other—the *inferior ethmoidal fissure* (known as the "middle meatus")—the anterior cells and the frontal sinuses open into the nasal cavity under the middle turbinated bone, at almost the same place as the antrum. Both entrances are long and narrow.

We may also regard as one of the side chambers of the nose, the tympanic cavity of the organ of hearing, which opens into the hindermost part of the air-passage, close to the posterior nares, by the Eustachian tube. As, however, this cavity and the passage by which it is connected with the nasal cavity have a very decided and important influence upon the organ of hearing, it is not generally included with the side chambers, though from its hollow nature it so strongly resembles them.

We must further, to leave nothing unnoticed, remember that the *lachrymal canal*, which conveys the tears, opens under the foremost end of the inferior turbinated bone, so that the tears, after having moistened the eye, are conveyed into the nasal cavity, where they evaporate in the passing current of air. It is only in cases where the fluid flows very freely, and when, indeed, the lachrymal canal cannot carry it all off, so that some of the tears flow over the lower eyelid, that the quantity of fluid forced into the nasal cavity cannot evaporate, and therefore either flows down through the nostril, or by repeated short inspirations is drawn back into the pharynx. These short inspirations are either voluntary, or they belong to the phenomenon of "sobbing," which is caused by spasmodic contraction of the diaphragm.

But now what significance are we to attribute to these side chambers? That they have no connection with the organ of smell, is sufficiently proved by the fact that in cases where, perhaps from injuries sustained, the more easily approached side chambers—as, for instance, the frontal sinus or the antrum—have been exposed, it has been evident that the mucous membrane with which they are lined is not adapted for the sensation of smell. They must, therefore, be more especially connected with the air-passage, particularly as they all open into the air-passage and not into the chamber of the organ of smell. Their exact significance from this point of view has not, indeed, been yet discovered, still we may venture to form some opinion from the manner in which they open into the nasal cavity.

We find that there are only two entrances into the nasal cavity, one leading from the sphenoidal sinuses and the posterior ethmoidal cells, and the other from the antrum, the anterior ethmoidal cells, and the frontal sinuses. The construction of both entrances is such that the entering current of air must flow past them; but the returning current will be caught by them, and will be able to penetrate the cavities to which they lead.

This peculiarity can be most clearly seen in the entrance below the middle turbinated bone which leads to the antrum, the anterior ethmoidal cells, and the frontal sinuses. It is, namely, a groove, shallow where it commences posteriorly, but becoming deeper as it proceeds forwards, till at last it leads into a canal which ascends to the ethmoid bone and the frontal sinuses. A round opening in the groove leads to the antrum. Such is the first entrance, and there is no difficulty in following the course of the second.

The posterior extremity of the middle turbinated bone lies at a slight distance—about 3 mm. ($\frac{1}{8}$ inch) —below and before the lower angle of the body of the sphenoid. The passage formed by this separation at once divides into two branches. One of these ascends in front of the anterior wall of the body of the sphenoid, and terminates abruptly at the cribriform plate; it forms

STRUCTURE OF THE ORGANS OF SPEECH. 111

a groove of some depth (the *spheno-ethmoidal recess*), upon the posterior wall of which the sphenoidal sinus opens. The other branch, rising obliquely upwards, cuts deep into the ethmoid bone, and passes into a canal which penetrates into the posterior ethmoidal cells. It does not, however, penetrate the lateral mass of the ethmoid in a direction vertical to the surface of the plate of the turbinated bone, but passes obliquely upwards and outwards; thus its lower edge falls sharply towards the septum, and its upper edge appears as a sharp border directed downwards. This indentation (the superior ethmoidal fissure) is what is commonly called the *superior meatus*, and its upper edge the *superior turbinated bone*. In some cases it is double, the lateral mass of the ethmoid being indented by two fissures of this kind running parallel to each other. The upper of the two passages is then called the "uppermost meatus," and its upper edge the uppermost turbinated bone.

The remarks just made will sufficiently show how entirely unsuitable the comparison is which is commonly drawn between the crevice here called the *superior ethmoidal fissure*, with the divisions of the air-passage made by the inferior turbinated bone (whence the terms "superior turbinated bone," "superior meatus"), and that it can only properly be coupled with the *inferior ethmoidal fissure*.

The construction of both fissures plainly shows that they can only admit the expired current of air to the cavities to which they lead, and that the inspired air must flow past them. The necessary repletion of the side chambers with air must, therefore, be the work of the retreating current of air. That the air really is renewed in the side chambers is shown by the example of the tympanic cavity, where the air undoubtedly changes periodically, producing an effect upon the organ of hearing with which we are fairly well acquainted. We know, however, very little about the influence of the side chambers, and must, therefore, endeavour to form some opinion out of the foregoing facts.

The expired air, like all liquid currents, has a certain lateral pressure; it flows out through the narrow nostrils, entering the nasal cavity, however, through the comparatively wide posterior nares; an accumulation of the air in the nasal cavity necessarily ensues, accompanied by increased lateral pressure, which will affect even the side chambers, compressing the air which they contain considerably. Expiration, therefore, fills the side chambers with compressed warm air. When the act of expiration is over, part of this air, from its subsequent expansion, will return to the nasal cavity. When inspiration commences, the expansion of the air in the side chambers still continues, the result of inspiration being a rarity of air in these chambers. Thus the side chambers are constantly ventilated by the currents of air passing through the nose. This cannot be of much value to the side chambers themselves; and the recognition of this fact, if we consider the side chambers separately, can throw no light upon their significance in connection with the nasal cavity. We must, therefore, see if we can discover any benefit resulting from this arrangement to the nasal cavity, or still more to the breathing process. If, now, we have already been led to form the opinion that the inferior turbinated bone exercises a warming influence upon the inhaled air, and when we find that the ventilation just described not only supplies the nasal cavity before inspiration with a supply of warmed air, but that also during inspiration a stream of warmed air flows out of the side chambers and is mixed with the inspired air, we shall seem to be justified in holding that the side chambers, like the inferior turbinated bone, may be regarded as a warming apparatus for the inspired air.

They have, moreover, a further significance in connection with the formation of articulate sounds, when they take part in the resonance of the nasal cavity.

In conclusion, we must draw attention to the relation of the *superior ethmoidal fissure* to the chamber of the organ of smell. The upward course of this fissure in front of the body of the sphenoid, and the way in which it cuts through the turbinated plate of the ethmoid covered by the olfactory mucous membrane, would seem to stand in contradiction to the description we have already given of the chamber of the organ of smell, as being entirely isolated from the direct current of air through the nose. If, however, we look at the relation more closely, we shall find in the arrangement of this fissure another cause for the isolation just mentioned. The fissure, namely, takes up that smaller portion of the exhaled air which forces its way over the posterior root of the middle turbinated bone in the direction of the chamber of the organ of smell. This side stream can, however, never reach the chamber of the organ of smell, for it is conducted by the fissure into the sphenoidal sinus and the posterior ethmoidal cells, and that portion of it which cannot force its way into these cavities is thrown back by the wall in which the fissure terminates into the great current of air below. In complete accordance with this, we find that odorous substances entering through the posterior nares are not so easily perceived as those which come in through the nostrils with the inspired air.

The results obtained in this section may be briefly stated as follows :—

(1) Of the two walls which enclose each nasal cavity, that which constitutes the septum is unimportant in its construction, as, with the exception of the fold which serves to narrow the entrance to the chamber of the organ of smell, its surface is plane.

(2) The lateral wall, on the contrary, composed of the superior maxillary and the ethmoid bones, possesses every characteristic form which gives to the nasal cavity its varied significance. We find, namely, (*a*) in the upper part an even surface situated close to the septum, which forms the outer wall of the chamber of the organ of smell, and to which, from the nostril, there is only access by a shallow groove running parallel to the dorsum of the nose ; in the lower, larger part, we find (*b*) the air-passage, which is partly roofed by the middle turbinated bone, and which commences anteriorly with a height almost corresponding to that of the whole external nose, and terminates with about half the height at the posterior nares.

(3) The air-passage, in a transverse section, is narrower anteriorly and posteriorly, and wider in the middle; the wider portion is divided by the inferior turbinated bone into an upper and a lower half.

(4) The side chambers of the nose open into the air-passage by two narrow fissures, into which fissures only the expired air can enter, the inspired air flowing past them.

(5) The probable significance of the inferior turbinated bone and the side chambers is that they act as a warming apparatus for the inspired air.

(6) There is no doubt that the side chambers exercise some influence upon the resonance of the nasal cavity.

Individual Variations in the Nasal Cavity.

As in all parts of the body, so also in the nasal cavity, we find many individual variations, which, it is true, have no significance when considered in connection with the function of the nasal cavity in breathing and smelling, but become of importance for the part which they play in speech, as they must considerably influence its resonance.

Some of the peculiarities which we have now to consider are due to difference in age, while others are variations in the nasal cavities of adults.

If we compare the face of a young child with that of an adult, we find a very considerable difference in the relation of the several parts to each other. In the child's face, for instance, the middle of its elevation falls between the eyelids; the elevation from the root of the nose to the chin is therefore equal to the elevation of the forehead, and the lower half of the face consists of two, roughly speaking, equal parts, the first being the elevation of the nose and the second the elevation of the region of the mouth. In the face of the adult, on the contrary, we find that the horizontal line formed by the space between the eyelids divides off the elevation of the forehead as a third of the face, and that the second third consists of the elevation of the nose, and the third of the elevation of the region of the mouth as far as the chin.

This difference of relation arises from the changes which the bones of the face undergo during their development into the perfect form. With regard to the region of the mouth, it is clear that the development of the alveolar processes of the jaws and the appearance of the teeth must cause a considerable elevation, till at last it reaches the same height as the region of the forehead.

The region of the nose, on the contrary, acquires its increase of elevation entirely from the enlargement and development of the nasal cavity.

We find in the side wall of the nasal cavity of the infant all those peculiarities of construction which characterize it in the adult; but they are remarkably compressed from above downwards. The turbinated bones stand out distinctly, but the spaces between them are mere narrow crevices, although the anterior trumpet-shaped opening in the inferior turbinated bone already distinctly betrays its characteristic shape. The whole cavity appears as a very low, and in comparison to its height, as a very long canal. But, again, the side wall approaches so closely to the septum that, in a transverse section, it also looks very narrow. There is as yet no trace of the side chambers. These facts are quite sufficient to explain why a cold in the head with small children is accompanied by such difficulty in breathing. The narrow space must be nearly entirely closed by the inflammation of the mucous membrane which accompanies this complaint, and what does remain open will be filled by the discharge of mucous fluid, which, from want of a strong current of air, cannot be carried away in the usual manner. Gradually, and with the advancing growth only, do these relations change; the nasal cavity begins to develop in height and breadth, and the side chambers appear.

The antrums of the superior maxillary bone, which are not present in the infant, begin during this gradual development to increase considerably in height; the floor of the nasal cavity is thus further removed from the roof, so that the space within gains much in height, and the side walls are able gradually to develop those forms with which we are familiar in the adult. The development of the teeth also expands the superior maxillary bone from before backwards, so that by this means, again, the nasal cavity gains in depth; this advantage is also increased anteriorly by the rapid development of the external nose, which, through the enlargement and elevation of the nasal bone, acquires that commanding form which distinguishes it from the short, round nose of the child.

Simultaneously with these changes there is a development of the sphenoidal sinuses, which are not present in the infant, of the ethmoidal cells, of which also there is little trace in the infant, and of the frontal sinuses with which they are connected.

This process of development can only be considered complete at about the twentieth year.

That the development just described is not carried out in all persons to the same extent, is evident from the fact that the external nose assumes every variety of form, from the small round nose to the noble aquiline. The striking resemblance of the short pug-nose to that of a child shows at once that in such cases the development of the nasal cavity has been less perfect than in that of the larger external nose.

It is remarkable that the general characteristic of this variation in development—that is, greater or less development—is not so much an accident of individuality as a characteristic of a typical form of head. In the classification of skulls, namely, two principal forms are distinguished—the *brachycephalous*, or short-headed, and the *dolichocephalous*, or long-headed; the former being characterized by a spherical horizontal periphery of the skulls, while in the second this periphery is an oval, the long diameter of which passes from before backwards. This difference is not, however, produced by individual development, but, as we learn from accurate comparative measurement, is most distinctly perceptible in the infant; it is, therefore, unmistakably a characteristic of race. We may, therefore, consider it to be a general law that in brachycephalous skulls the development of the nasal cavity and its side chambers is not so complete as in the dolichocephalous, and that, therefore, an equal characteristic difference may be observed in the form of the face.

The dolichocephalous head, besides the long cranium, has a long face, in which the lower part of the forehead, from the great development of the orbits, projects considerably and overhangs the eyes, which appear, therefore, more deeply set, while between the eyes rises a long high nose, which is generally arched; in the region of the chin the profile again retreats.

In the brachycephalous head, on the contrary, from the development of the frontal sinuses being defective or entirely wanting, the forehead is upright; the nose is short and low, with a straight or even depressed dorsum; the eyes are more advanced, and the chin does not fall away so much from the nose.

An apparently retreating forehead is, therefore, characteristic of the dolichocephalous skull, but bears no resemblance to the retreating forehead peculiar to idiots, which arises from an absence of brain in the upper region of the forehead, while the retreat in the dolichocephalous skull is caused by the presence of the frontal sinuses in the lower part of the forehead, and is, therefore, rather a projection of the lower part of the forehead.

The Cavity of the Mouth.

The mouth, as we have already observed, in a natural classification of the organs of the body, would not be considered to belong to the air-passages, but rather to the alimentary canal of the organs of digestion. It contains the necessary mechanical apparatus for the mastication of the food; the salivary glands open into it, and during the process of mastication moisten the food with their secretions, thus preparing it for solution; and here, also, we find the apparatus which carries down the mass thus formed through the pharynx into the œsophagus. At the same time, from being immediately connected with the pharynx, it is adapted to act occasionally as an air-passage both in inspiration and expiration. This use is made of it in cases of distress for breath—when a person is out of breath, for instance, or suffering from asthma, which occasions a constant difficulty in breathing; and also in those cases where, from general weakness, the stronger respiratory action which is necessary to inhale the air through the nose cannot be performed. Consumptive people generally have the mouth slightly open, so as to breathe with less exertion.

The complicated mechanism which is connected with the natural function of the cavity of the mouth, gives it the power of assuming a great number of different forms, which partly affect the orifice, partly its internal cavity. The air, moreover, passing through the cavity of the mouth, derives a characteristic noise from each form assumed by the latter; and again, if the current of air is vibrating with a musical sound, the momentary conformation of the cavity of the mouth will give to the air thus passing through it a different resonance. These relations explain the use of the cavity of the mouth in speaking, for noises and resonances just alluded to represent the elements of articulate speech. As, however, the cavity of the mouth is not adapted by any special apparatus for the part it plays in speech, but is only provided with that which fits it for its natural position as part of the alimentary canal, and is merely occasionally otherwise employed, it will be well first to study the cavity of the mouth from this point of view.

The mouth is a moderately wide cavity, bounded laterally by the cheeks, having a roof formed by the hard palate of the upper jaw, and a floor by a plate of mucous membrane, which, commencing with the lower lip, extends to the upper margin of the hyoid bone. This plate finds attachment and support from resting upon the upper border of the lower jaw, with which, moreover, it is strongly connected. Thus there are bony foundations to both the roof and the floor of the cavity, giving to part of it at least relations incapable of modification. The anterior orifice of the mouth is formed by the space between the lips, while posteriorly it is immediately connected, by means of a narrow opening (the *isthmus* of the *fauces*), with the pharynx. Imbedded in the mucous membrane which covers the alveolar processes of the upper and lower jaws, we find the upper and lower rows of teeth projecting into the cavity of the mouth. The mucous membrane which surrounds the teeth, and is closely attached to the alveolar processes, is generally known as "the gums." The cavity of the mouth is imperfectly divided by the teeth into two chambers; into that, namely, which is enclosed by the teeth (the cavity of the mouth, strictly speaking, or the *oral cavity*), and that which lies between the teeth and the cheeks (the cavity of the cheeks, *cavum buccarum*). This peculiarity will be alluded to again as we proceed.

STRUCTURE OF THE ORGANS OF SPEECH.

The Teeth.

Each jaw is provided with sixteen teeth, arranged in a wide arch, so that four incisors are situated in the crown of the arch, followed on either side by one canine; upon the sides of the arch, which are prolonged backwards to some distance, we find in succession behind the canine two bicuspids and four molars. The two arches, following the well-known form of the crowns of the teeth, are thin in front, gradually thickening towards the molars, with which the broad ends of the arch terminate symmetrically.

There is a striking difference between the two rows of teeth, the crown of the arch of the lower teeth being flatter than that of the upper. The result of this peculiarity is that, when the teeth are closed, the incisors of the upper jaw project beyond those of the lower. It, therefore, generally happens that the upper incisors overlap the lower, and that when the two rows of incisors are made to meet, a gap is left between the molars of the two jaws; and further, that the incisors of the upper jaw thus prolong the roof of the cavity of the mouth (the *oral cavity*) anteriorly. This latter peculiarity is carried out still further by the upper incisors, and especially the two middle ones, being much broader and longer than the corresponding teeth of the lower jaw.

The Mechanical Movements of the Cavity of the Mouth.

To obtain a proper acquaintance with the changes in form of which the cavity of the mouth is capable, it will first be necessary to consider the various mechanical movements which, from this point of view, exercise an influence upon the mouth.

Now, that which naturally strikes us first is the

movement of the lower jaw. In the process of digestion it plays the important part of chewing, or mechanically dividing the food; in speech it is also of importance, its action being first to remove the floor of the cavity of the mouth from the roof, and then to bring them together again, or, in other words, to regulate the size of the *orifice of the cavity of the mouth.*

A second mechanical movement is that of the lips, which regulates *the form* of the orifice of the mouth. It assists in the digestive process by receiving the food into the mouth; in speech it gives a different form to the orifice of the mouth, thus exercising an important influence upon the production of articulate sounds.

A third mechanical movement is that of the soft palate. The soft palate comes into play in that part of the process of digestion which consists in the act of swallowing; in speech it regulates the degree to which the nasal cavity is shut off from the cavity of the mouth, and, therefore, the strength of the current which is diverted into the cavity of the mouth. With the action of the soft palate is connected the mechanism of the constrictor of the pharynx.

The fourth mechanical movement is that of that complex bundle of muscles lying upon the floor of the cavity of the mouth, which is called the *tongue*. In the process of digestion it is called into play in the reception of the food, in mastication and in the act of swallowing; in speech it has the power of altering the shape of the inner cavity of the mouth in such a variety of ways that it has the greatest influence upon the creation of certain articulate sounds.

STRUCTURE OF THE ORGANS OF SPEECH.

THE MOVEMENT OF THE JAWS.

Of the two jaws the upper is rigid, being immoveably connected with the rest of the skull; the lower jaw, on the contrary, articulates by a moveable joint with the skull. When, therefore, we speak of moving the jaws, the lower jaw alone must be understood, the movement of which causes it to assume different positions in relation to the skull, and especially to that part which articulates immoveably with it, namely, the upper jaw.

The movements of the lower jaw are, in common with the movements of all portions of the bony framework of the body, produced by muscular action. The kind of movement resulting from this muscular action is, however, due to the character of the joint in which it arises; and it is precisely in this respect that the lower jaw displays peculiarities which distinguish it greatly from other joints, and to a great extent decide the share which the movements of the lower jaw are to take in speech.

It is to the hinder portion, the *ramus*, of the lower jaw that these movements are due. The body, or horizontal portion bearing the teeth, bends upwards at its posterior extremity in an angle which is little short of being a right angle. It is this ascending posterior portion which is called the *ramus*. The upper border of the ramus presents two processes, separated from each other by a deep concavity (the *sigmoid notch*). The anterior process (the *coronoid process*) is pointed, and serves for muscular attachment; the posterior process (the *condyloid process*) is, on the contrary, broad and round at its upper end, and serves for articulation with the temporal bone of the skull.

The round end (*condyle*) just mentioned may be

compared to a cylinder placed transversely upon the process, and lies, when quiescent, in a hollow (*glenoid cavity*) of the temporal bone immediately in front of the outer ear. When the lower jaw is depressed, a rotatory movement of the two (right and left) condyles upon an horizontal axis immediately takes place in the corresponding hollow articulating surfaces of the temporal bones; it is, however, only in the ruminants that this movement is sufficiently great to constitute the whole of the movement by which the mouth is opened; in the human lower jaw we find a distinct mechanism which provides for its perfect removal from the upper jaw. In front of the *glenoid cavity* of the temporal bone, namely, may be observed a transverse rounded eminence (the *eminentia articularis*) upon which the condyle of the lower jaw is carried forward when the mouth is opened; when this happens two rounded bodies come into contact, thus allowing the movement to be continued still further. As a necessary precaution in this movement, a biconcave fibrous plate (the *inter-articular fibro-cartilage*) is placed between the two articulating surfaces, and being more closely attached to the condyle of the lower jaw, is carried forward with this bone, returning with it to a state of rest in the *glenoid cavity*. This forward movement of the condyle is very perceptible in thin persons, a hollow appearing in front of the ear which is caused by the external air depressing the skin into the empty cavity of the joint; when the mouth is shut, the condyle returns to the glenoid cavity which it fills, and the hollow disappears.

The question now follows as to the forces by which the lower jaw is set in motion—a question which, though at first sight a simple one, offers many difficulties in its solution. With regard to the forces which bring the lower jaw into contact with the upper, thereby closing the mouth, the answer is easy, for we find several powerful muscles exercising this function. When, however, we turn to consider those forces which depress the lower jaw, and therefore open the mouth, we are placed in the not inconsiderable predicament of being unable to discover a single muscle which we can with equal justice designate a depressor of the lower jaw in opposition to the former, which may be considered as the elevators of the lower jaw. We can, indeed, refer to muscles as taking some parts in the depression of the lower jaw, but at the same time must confess that they perform other functions which are more important. It would seem, therefore, that the removal of the lower jaw from the upper must be effected by some other force than that of direct muscular action, and this force we shall find to lie in the weight of the lower jaw. Remarkable as this fact may at first sight appear, it is soon explained when we consider what force it is which brings the lower jaw to a state of rest against the upper jaw. If we compare the laws to which the natural positions of different parts of the body, particularly in the living subject, are due, we find that, besides different statical momenta, there are muscles which act by their "contractility." By this term is meant a chronic state of contraction which is natural to every muscle when at rest, and corresponds to the degree of expansion of which the muscle in question is capable. We can, therefore, have no hesitation in referring the raised position of the lower jaw to the contractility of its constrictor muscles. At the same time it should be remembered that this contractility, in order to maintain the raised position of the lower jaw, must overcome the weight of the latter, so that this position depends upon the equilibrium existing between the contractility of the elevating muscles and the weight of the lower jaw. If this equilibrium is destroyed by the action of the muscles being too strong, the raised position will still be maintained, and the teeth merely pressed more tightly against each other. If, however, the muscular action is too weak, and equilibrium consequently destroyed by the weight, the lower jaw drops. Thus a depressed lower jaw, and therefore open mouth, may be regarded as a sure sign of general weakness, or of temporal paralysis caused by fright, astonishment, etc. It is upon this fact that the common expression "gaping with astonishment" is founded. It appears, therefore, that the weight of the lower jaw is quite sufficient to account for the opening of the mouth, and it only remains to be proved whether we have it in our power to call this weight into action. We can, of course, only do so by putting an end to the state of muscular contraction. There is, indeed, no doubt that we are able by an effort of the will to relax those muscles which are in a state of active contraction, but how this process is accomplished it is difficult to say. It is not improbable that the cause of this contraction arises from some unconscious psychical action upon the motor nerves, and therefore the state of the mind finds expression in the bearing of the whole person which is due to general muscular contractility; the character of this bearing, especially in the face, gives, therefore, some idea of the mental life of a person. This being so, it seems as natural that we should be able to exercise an influence upon this contractility as that we should be able to arrest any voluntary muscular contraction. We cannot continue this discussion here, but must be satisfied with knowing that we have it in our power, when we wish to open the mouth, to destroy the equilibrium between the weight of the lower jaw and the contractility of the elevating muscles, and so to drop the lower jaw.

The freely suspended lower jaw of a dead body is held in position by two lateral bands, the *external lateral ligaments*. The point of attachment of each band lies a little below the corresponding condyle, upon the outer surface of the *condyloid process*. The centre of gravity of the lower jaw falls below this point of attachment, which causes the whole body of the bone to fall backwards, while the condyle, which lies above the point of attachment, is carried forward as far as the *eminentia articularis*. This forward movement of the condyle upon the eminentia articularis, therefore, necessarily takes place when the lower jaw is moved from the upper in the manner just described. If now, for a moment, we imagine the point of attachment to be fixed, it is clear that, if the condyle were drawn forward, the same movement would be imparted to the lower jaw as that which it experiences when allowed to fall. The condyle, in fact, is drawn forward in this manner by a short powerful muscle (the *external pterygoid*), which arises upon the pterygoid process of the sphenoid, or, more accurately, upon the outer surface of the external plate of the latter, and is attached to the anterior surface of the condyle. There is no question that this muscle must have an influence upon the depression of the lower jaw; indeed, its action is distinctly perceptible when the mouth is very widely opened, as, for instance, in yawning, the unpleasant sensation then experienced in front of the ear, especially when a yawn is suppressed, merely arising from a spasmodic contraction of this muscle.

Although there is no doubt that the *external pterygoid* muscle is of use in the opening of the mouth, yet it is chiefly important from another point of view. When, namely, this muscle acts in harmony with the elevating (or closing) muscles, its forward action alone comes into play, and it then causes the molar teeth to grind upon each other. If the muscle of only one side is in action, the movement is oblique; but if both muscles act simultaneously, the lower jaw is propelled directly forwards, and can, indeed, be carried so far that the incisor teeth of the lower jaw can be placed at some little distance in front of those of the upper jaw. Although the importance of these movements is chiefly connected with the process of mastication, the position thus given to the lower jaw is scarcely less influential in the formation of individual or national peculiarities of pronunciation.

NOTE.—With regard to the muscles which take part in the depression of the lower jaw, we must further remark that there is a group of small muscles upon the anterior surface of the neck, to be described presently, the action of which is connected with the movements of the hyoid bone and larynx; they are, however, also called into play when the mouth is very widely opened. The powerful contraction can be felt during a yawn upon the anterior surface of the neck.

When the lower jaw has been depressed in the manner described, and is to be replaced in its former position, those muscles come into action which have already been mentioned, and which are generally called the *masseters*, because they effect the division of the food. The *external pterygoid*, moreover, is generally included amongst the masseters, and rightly so, because of the grinding action to which it gives rise.

The muscles which act as elevators of the lower jaw may be regarded as a single muscular mass, which finds its attachment upon the external and internal surfaces of the ramus of the lower jaw. If we continue the line of the anterior margin of the *coronoid process* downwards upon the internal and external surfaces of the ramus, we shall obtain upon each surface a triangle, the apex of which lies in the point of the coronoid process and the base given by the angle, in which the lower border of the body of the lower jaw bends upwards to form the posterior border of the ramus. These two surfaces are occupied by the attachments of the muscles in question, only a small space being left upon the inner surface for the opening through which the inferior dental nerve and its accompanying artery pass. This muscular mass arises upon the outer side of the skull, partly outside and partly within the *coronoid process* of the lower jaw. The *temporal muscle* may be regarded as the centre of the group, which arises upon the entire surface of the temple, and is attached to the external and internal surfaces of the *coronoid process*. Upon the zygomatic arch, which forms the external boundary of the temple, arises the *masseter muscle*, another of this group of masticatory muscles; it is attached to that part of the triangle upon the external surface of the ramus which is not occupied by the *temporal muscle*. The more isolated inner part of the group, the *internal pterygoid*, arises in the fossa between the two plates of the *pterygoid process* of the sphenoid bone, and is attached in the lower division of the triangle to the inner surface of the ramus, below the opening for the dental nerve mentioned above.

At the same time that these muscles raise the lower jaw, they also produce a backward movement of the condyle of the lower jaw, so that it falls back again into the *glenoid cavity*. A change is, moreover, also produced in the mutual position of the incisor teeth of the upper and lower jaws, the latter being again placed behind the former, which is very striking, if, as described above, the lower jaw, from a position of slight contact, is not actually depressed, but only carried forward.

THE LIPS.

The lips are two transverse fleshy folds which mark the external orifice of the cavity of the mouth. They surround the narrow transverse entrance to the mouth. The latter is, however, generally speaking, merely an opening made from without into the cavity of the mouth, and consequently pierces through both the outer integument of the face and the mucous membrane of the cavity of the mouth. The outer surface of the lips is, therefore, formed by the integument of the face; the inner, on the contrary, by the mucous membrane of the cavity of the mouth. The construction of the two integuments is very similar, the only difference being the extreme thinness and delicacy of the mucous membrane. The transition from one integument to the other at the margin of the orifice is, therefore, almost imperceptible. The point of transition, however, which is marked by the red margin of the lips, has somewhat the character of thickened mucous membrane, but beyond this line it rapidly assumes the character of the integument of the face.

We are all familiar with the fact that the lips, when quiescent, are closed against each other, and that they have also the power of performing a great number of voluntary movements, by means of which the orifice of the mouth can be made to assume almost any shape. This purpose is answered by a number of muscles, which are either situated in the lips, or approach them from different sides; all, however, are so strongly attached to the integument of the lips, that their action has an immediate effect upon them. The fibres within each lip are, however, so numerous, that it is scarcely possible to distinguish the separate fasciculi and to arrange them as distinct muscles. This has given rise to much discussion upon the question as to how many and what muscles are to be considered as typical muscles of the mouth.

It would occupy too much time if we were here to enter into a minute discussion upon the best analysis of the system of the muscles of the lips. We must, therefore, be satisfied with a rapid glance at the arrangement which is generally accepted at the present time.

Following, therefore, this arrangement, we must distinguish two layers of muscles, an upper and a lower.

The lower layer is not confined to the mouth, but is merely part of a broad, thin muscular layer, the larger part of which constitutes the *buccinator muscle*. The entire cavity of the mouth, and the adjoining portion of the pharynx, is surrounded by a broad layer of muscles, the fibres of which run horizontally (cf. Fig. 38). This layer attains its greatest width upon the cheeks, and it is here that it bears the name of *buccinator* (also called the trumpeter-muscle, since by its contraction the air collected in the cheeks is driven out in the act of blowing a trumpet). It is of an annular form, passing without interruption from one side of the lips to the other, thus forming the foundation of the system of the muscles of the lips. The orifice of the mouth, considered in connection with this layer of muscles, is merely a long narrow opening situated between its fasciculi; and yet these fasciculi cannot be regarded as passing simply upon either side of the opening, for we find that the bundles of fibres interlace each other at the corners of the mouth, and that some, which, if they proceeded directly forwards, would run along the upper margin of the lower lip, alter their course to the lower margin of the upper lip, and in the same manner others, which would run along the lower margin of the upper lip, cross over to the upper margin of the lower lip. The two sets of fasciculi, by intersecting each other in this manner, give a more definite form to the lateral ends of the orifice of the mouth.

Above this first layer of muscles lies another, in which it is usual to distinguish two antagonistic systems, one of which closes the orifice of the mouth and the other opens it. The system of expanding muscles radiates from all sides towards the orifice of the mouth, and can draw back its margins in every direction. In opposition to this system we have that which closes the mouth, an annular layer of muscle surrounding the orifice of the mouth, which is known as the *orbicularis oris;* the layer is, however, by no means a simple one, but is unquestionably composed of different elements. For the present, however, we will still regard this circular layer as a simple annular muscle, and proceed to investigate the radiating system of the expanding muscles of the orifice of the mouth; the modifications which must be made in our conception of the closing muscle will then be self-evident.

The muscles which act as expanders of the orifice

of the mouth are arranged upon a very simple plan, and are partly attached to the lips themselves and partly to the angles of the mouth. Each lip has its abductor—the *levator labii superioris* and the *depressor labii inferioris;* and at the angle of the mouth we find an elevator and a depressor—the *levator* and the *depressor anguli oris.* As all these muscles are in pairs, we have already eight

FIGS. 32, 33.

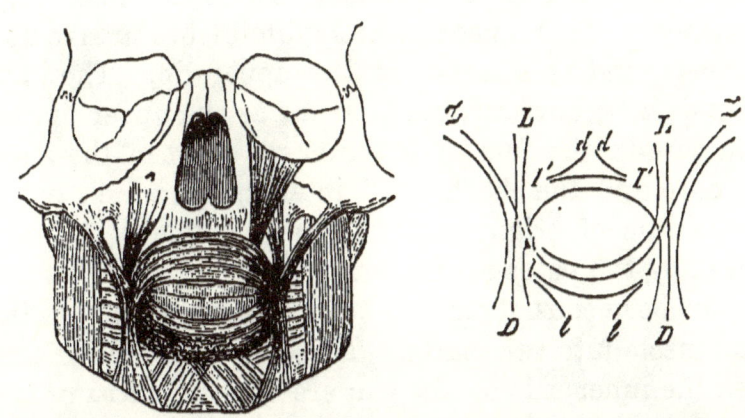

The muscles of the mouth. The diagram, Fig. 33, shows how, by the partial interlacing of their fibres, they form a constrictor muscle for closing the mouth. L, Elevator of the angle of the mouth (*levator anguli oris*); D, depressor of the angle of the mouth (*depressor anguli oris*); Z, *zygomaticus*; I, lower muscles of the incisors (*incisivi inferiores*), partly blending with the *orbicularis oris*, and partly descending as the muscles raising the chin (*levatores menti*)—l, to the integument of the chin; I', *incisivi superiores*, partly blending with the *orbicularis oris*, partly passing to the nasal septum as the depressor of the nasal septum (*depressor septi narium*)—d. In the complete figure we see the *levator anguli oris* on the left side partially covered by the *levator labii superioris;* between the *depressor anguli oris* of the right and left sides lie two quadrilateral muscles which partially intersect each other—the *depressor labii inferioris*. Running vertically upon either side: the masticatory muscle (*masseter*), and behind horizontally, the *buccinator*.

muscles which act upon the orifice of the mouth in the manner described. Acting in concert with these, moreover, we find a muscle (the *zygomaticus*) which descends obliquely to the angle of the mouth, and in many cases another (the *risorius*) which ascends obliquely to the angle of the mouth, so that we have altogether ten or twelve muscles, the action of which is to distend the

STRUCTURE OF THE ORGANS OF SPEECH. 133

orifice of the mouth. We must now consider these muscles singly, both as regards their action and their relation to the annular layer of muscle.

Two muscles are generally distinguished upon each side as *elevators of the upper lip*, though the distinction rests upon a very slight foundation. A very broad plate of muscle arises from the inner half of the lower margin of the orbit, the line of origin extending as far as the lateral surface of the nasal bone, close to the inner angle of the eye. This muscular plate diminishes in size as it descends, and is inserted in the upper lip. The inner fibres do not, however, reach as far as the upper lip, but terminate in the fold of integument between the ala of the nose and the cheek. An interruption which occurs in the line of origin near the inner angle of the eye, caused by the passage of a small nerve to the lower eyelid, has been considered as a sufficient reason for dividing this muscle into two parts. Those fasciculi which arise upon the inner side of this gap are called the *levator labii superioris alaeque nasi*, because they contain those fibres which terminate near, and consequently raise, the ala of the nose ; the rest of the muscle, however, which arises from the outer side of the above-mentioned gap, is called the *levator labii superioris proprius*. It is evident that this division is entirely artificial, and that the two muscles should more properly be regarded as one (the *levator labii superioris*), although a few of its fasciculi cannot directly elevate the upper lip, but do so only through the ala of the nose. If any artificial division is to be made, it would be better to call the latter fasciculi the *levator alae nasi*.

Corresponding to this muscle, we have a depressor of the lower lip, the *depressor labii inferioris* (*quadratus menti*). This arises upon the lower jaw in the hollow which lies near the triangular eminence, called the *mental process;* it strikes upwards and inwards, and is lost in the under lip, after having intersected the corresponding muscle of the other side. Its action is to draw down one side of the lower lip, but also, from its fibres extending beyond the middle line, to draw down the other side obliquely; both muscles (of the right and left sides) therefore draw the lip downwards in such a manner as to form a groove beneath it.

The *levator anguli oris,* which raises the angle of the mouth, arises upon the surface of the superior maxillary bone below the margin of the orbit, and descends obliquely, diminishing at the same time in size, to the angle of the mouth.

In antagonism to this muscle we find the *depressor anguli oris (triangularis menti),* which depresses the angle of the mouth; it arises in a long line upon the anterior portion of the lower margin of the lower jaw, diminishing in size as it approaches the angle of the mouth.

From the angle of the mouth also the *zygomatic* muscle passes upwards and outwards to the zygomatic arch.

By the *risorius (Santorini)* muscle we understand an irregular and uncertain fasciculus which passes towards the angle of the mouth from behind and below, arising upon the margin of the lower jaw, but which is generally nothing more than a few fasciculi of the great muscle of the neck, the *platysma myoides.*

The last-named muscles stand in a peculiar relation to the annular muscular layer (constrictor) of the orifice of the mouth. The *depressor anguli oris* does not, for instance, terminate at the angle of the mouth, or at least does so only partially; the greater part curves round this angle to blend with the muscle of the other side, and thus not only acts as a depressor of the angle of the mouth, but also as a depressor of the upper lip. The *levator anguli oris* and the *zygomaticus* behave in the same manner towards the lower lip, curving round it to blend with the corresponding muscles of the other side, and therefore acting as elevators of the lower lip. A few fasciculi of the two last-named muscles even pass by the angle of the mouth, and, blending with the *depressor anguli oris*, run with it to its point of origin. They form, therefore, a convex loop towards the angle of the mouth, which consequently they draw outwards.

NOTE.—It is usual to distinguish a second *zygomatic muscle*, which, the first being the *major*, is described as the *zygomaticus minor*. This muscle is, however, only a variety of part of the *zygomaticus major*, or indeed of the *levator anguli oris*, which displays no regularity either in its appearance or in its arrangement when present. As, moreover, this muscle has no independent effect upon the mobility of the mouth, we can have no hesitation in omitting it from the group of the typical muscles of the mouth, and in regarding it merely as a variety.

We may now return to the constrictor muscular layer which surrounds the mouth, and proceed to examine its component parts.

We have already seen that it is partly composed of the interlacing portions of the *buccinator*, and of the portions detached for that purpose from the three muscles of the angle of the mouth, and we must now inquire whether other elements enter into the annular system, or whether these alone are sufficient to form the constrictor muscle. When we consider that these elements are undoubtedly able to press the lips together, but not to draw the angles of the mouth inwards, so as to give a round appearance to the orifice of the mouth, it is clear that other elements must be found in the lips to which this latter function belongs, and this we shall find to be the case upon closer investigation.

We are at once confronted with an annular layer of muscle, fully corresponding to the definition of a constrictor (sphincter) muscle, namely, the *orbicularis oris*. The greater part of this layer is, moreover, so strongly connected with the integument at the angle of the mouth, as to make it appear that the continuity of the fibres must be broken. Although the constrictor may thus be considered as divided into two half-circles, one of which lies in the upper lip and the other in the lower, its character as a whole is not destroyed, its function of drawing in the angles of the mouth merely becoming in this manner more pronounced, and the possibility given for the independent action of one or other of the half-circles.

The function of the closure of the orifice of the mouth is further shared by two muscles, the *incisivi*, the construction of which is somewhat complicated. One of these muscles (the *incisivus superior*) is situated upon the upper jaw, the other (the *incisivus inferior*) upon the lower jaw.

The *incisivus superior* arises above the external incisor tooth and the canine tooth of the upper jaw. The fibres proceeding from this point of origin pass (1) upwards towards the nose as the *depressor alae*, (2) downwards to the upper lip, which they draw upwards, and (3) obliquely to the angle of the mouth, where they are lost in the integument. The last division draws the angle of the mouth inwards, and thus completes the action of the *orbicularis oris*.

The *incisivus inferior* behaves in a similar manner. It arises beneath the external incisor and the canine of the lower jaw, and also separates into three portions, which are the exact analogues of those of the *incisivus superior*. One portion (distinguished as the *levator menti*) descends to the integument of the chin, and therefore draws the chin upwards; a second portion is dispersed along the lower lip, which it draws downwards; and the third portion passes obliquely to the angle of the mouth, in the integument of which it is lost. The action of the latter portion is, therefore, exactly similar to that of the corresponding portion of the *incisivus superior*, except that it draws the angle of the mouth more downwards and inwards, while the corresponding portion of the *incisivus superior* draws it upwards and inwards.

The sphincter system of muscles which effects the closure of the orifice of the mouth is, therefore, composed of the following elements:—

(1) Part of the *buccinator* muscle.
(2) A true annular (sphincter) muscle.
(3) Loop-muscle of the corner of the mouth.
(4) Parts of the *incisivi* muscles.

The great variety of the muscular forces acting upon the orifice of the mouth at once explain its great mobility and power of assuming such a variety of shapes, all of which are of greater or less importance in the formation of articulate sounds. The close connection between the shape given to the orifice of the mouth and those articulate sounds which are influenced by it will be discussed more at length in another section.

THE TONGUE.

A definition of the tongue offers considerable difficulties, for it is impossible to isolate it as an independent structure from its surroundings, as we are accustomed to isolate and to describe independently a given bone or muscle. All that we can say about it is, that it is a moveable fold, which occupies nearly the whole of the floor of the cavity of the mouth; this mobility depends partly upon its power of assuming different shapes, and partly from the relatively great power it possesses of altering its position.

If we proceed to examine the structure of this fold, we find that the entire substance of the tongue apparently consists of a confused mass of muscular fibres and a little intermediary fat. Upon following the course of these fibres, we are able to distinguish three separate muscles on each side, arising upon certain bone surfaces, and thus we find that six muscles, three upon each side, passing from different directions, are intimately bound together at their free ends so as to form a complicated muscular mass, which penetrates into the cavity of the mouth and rests upon its floor in the form of that fold which is known to us as the *tongue*. In addition to the elements contributed by these three muscles, we find, though in a less degree, muscular fibres which are peculiar to the tongue, their origin, course, and termination being all within its limits.

The external appearance presented by the tongue in the cavity of the mouth is that of a long flattened rounded body, the greater part of the under surface of which is implanted in the floor of the cavity of the mouth, while the upper surface, the *dorsum*, faces freely upwards, and the *apex*, or tip, free both above and below, is directed forwards. The broad posterior end, the *base*, or root, lies near the epiglottis, with which it is connected by a small fold of mucous membrane passing from before backwards (the *glosso-epiglottic ligament*), which, being attached to the upper surface of the epiglottis, helps to keep it in a raised position. A similar fold of mucous membrane, the *frenum linguae*, passes from the under

STRUCTURE OF THE ORGANS OF SPEECH. 139

surface of the apex of the tongue, at the point where it rises from the floor of the cavity of the mouth, downwards to the latter.

The groundwork of the formation of the tongue is, as we have already remarked, laid by three pairs of muscles, which, arising from fixed points of origin, after a free course of greater or less length, terminate in the body of the tongue. The most important of the three, and that at the same time which contributes most to the form of the tongue, is the *genio-hyo-glossus*. It arises upon the upper genial tubercle on the inner surface of

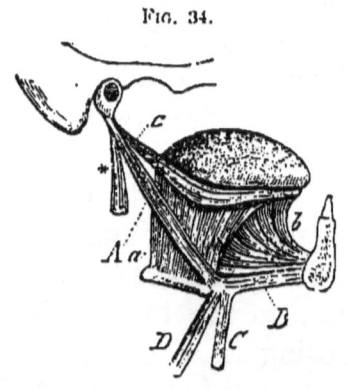

Fig. 34.

The muscles of the tongue and the hyoid bone. *A, stylo-hyoid; B, genio-hyoid; C, sterno-hyoid; D, omo-hyoid; a, hyo-glossus; b, genio-hyo glossus; c, stylo-glossus; *, stylo-pharyngeus; C, D,* and * divided.

the symphysis of the chin. It passes first backwards for a short distance and then spreads out upwards and backwards throughout the entire length of the tongue, so that its uppermost fibres terminate in the apex of the tongue, and its lowest upon the upper margin of the body of the hyoid bone at the hindermost end of the dorsum of the tongue. The two (right and left) *genio-hyo-glossi* muscles, lying close together in the middle line of the body, form to some extent the foundation of the tongue, constituting both a considerable part of its substance, and a central point of support to which the other muscles are attached.

Next to it we find the *hyo-glossus* muscle. This muscle arises upon the upper part of the greater horn of the hyoid bone, and then passes, close to the lateral wall of the pharynx above the hyoid bone, forwards upon the external surface of the *genio-hyo-glossus* to the tongue, in which its fibres spread out and terminate.

The third muscle is the *stylo-glossus*. This is a long, thin, round muscular band which arises upon the styloid process of the temporal bone, and passes freely downwards near the upper part of the pharynx. It bends forward above the hyoid bone, and then runs to the apex of the tongue upon the external surface of the *hyo-glossus*.

The muscles which are entirely situated in the tongue are the following:—

(1) The *lingualis longitudinalis inferior*, a round muscular band, running between the *genio-hyo-glossus* and the *hyo-glossus* through the whole length of the tongue.

(2) The *lingualis longitudinalis superior*, a flat layer of muscular fibres which spreads over the entire dorsum of the tongue under the mucous membrane.

(3) The *lingualis transversus*, an aggregation of separate fasciculi, which traverse the whole of the tongue from side to side.

As regards the action of these muscles, it is clear that the second group, comprising the three muscles just mentioned, can only have an influence upon the form of the body of the tongue, while the muscles of the first group effect a change of position in the body of the tongue in addition to a change of form.

Let us first consider the second group, and we find

that the two *longitudinal muscles* produce by their contraction a *shortening* of the body of the tongue, which of course makes it *wider* and *thicker*. A similar effect is also produced in a single muscle, *i.e.* the flexor of the elbow-joint situated in the anterior region of the upper arm, in which this simultaneous shortening and thickening is plainly perceptible. A difference will, however, be observable, according as the *longitudinalis superior* or the *longitudinalis inferior* is in action, or both at once. The first, namely, can only effect a contraction of the *upper* portion of the tongue; and as the lower portion remains quiescent, this contraction must produce a *concavity* upon the dorsum of the tongue or cause an *elevation* of its apex. Similarly, the *longitudinalis inferior* only acts upon the *lower* part of the tongue, the dorsum being quiescent, and therefore the dorsum of the tongue becomes *convex* and the apex is bent downwards. If the two longitudinal muscles act simultaneously, the whole tongue is contracted; if, however, the muscles of one side only are called into action, half of the tongue only is contracted, and directed upwards or downwards according as the upper or lower muscle is most powerful.

The transverse layer of muscle (the *musculus transversus*) draws the sides of the tongue together, thus lessening the body, but at the same time lengthening it, and thickening it in a vertical direction.

Of the muscles of the first group the action of the *genio-hyo-glossus* is the most important, and at the same time the most striking, for it draws the whole body of the tongue *forwards*, so that the apex of the tongue protrudes beyond the incisor teeth and the lower lip. The *hyo-glossus*, on the contrary, draws it *backwards* and *downwards*, rendering the back part of the tongue convex, and forcing it into the pharynx. The stylo-glossus also draws the tongue *backwards*, but in an *upward* direction, thus bringing it into contact with the palate; the muscle of either side raises the corresponding edge of the tongue, thus forming a sort of fold throughout its length; if both muscles act at once they create, by thus raising the edges, a groove along the dorsum of the tongue.

Enough has been said to explain the cause of the extraordinary mobility of the tongue. Great variety is shown even by the simple action of the separate muscles, which must, however, be infinitely increased when a number of muscles act simultaneously, or when there is a succession of simple or compound actions.

Three movements of the tongue predominate in the process of mastication: (1) it is alternately stretched out and drawn back for the purpose of receiving the food; (2) it is moved in different ways, but especially raised laterally for the purpose of replacing the food, which has fallen during mastication into the cavity of the mouth, under the molar teeth—the *buccinator* performs the same service to the food which has fallen into the cavity of the cheeks; (3) it is raised backwards to perform the act of swallowing.

The influence of the movements of the tongue upon the formation of articulate sounds will be particularly noticed in another section.

THE HYOID BONE.

The movements of the tongue which we have just described are all derived from muscles which either enter into or are situated in the tongue; they may, therefore, be termed independent movements, or, if we prefer it, active movements of the tongue. In addition

STRUCTURE OF THE ORGANS OF SPEECH. 143

to these there are, however, a great number of movements which we may describe as passive, as through them an alteration is effected in the position of the tongue as a whole. These movements are imparted to the tongue as part of the floor of the cavity of the mouth, and are therefore, strictly speaking, movements of the latter. They are, moreover, of considerable importance in the formation of articulate sounds, because they at the same time act upon the pharynx in such a manner that the position of the latter, especially in a vertical direction, is altered, and the resonance tube of the vocal apparatus contracted or lengthened.

The diaphragmatic floor of the cavity of the mouth may be regarded as the foundation for these movements.

What is meant by a diaphragmatic floor, and how it is produced, will best be seen from a consideration of the *diaphragm* itself. The latter is a thin plate of muscle which throughout its periphery is united with the thorax, the fibres passing from this attachment as from their origin towards a central point in such a manner that if we follow the course of any two fibres which meet here, we find that they arise from opposite points upon the periphery. As, therefore, all the fibres have a fixed attachment at both ends, they cannot possibly, like other muscles, bring these ends together by contraction. This contraction must, therefore, have a different effect, which we find to be as follows. The muscular plate, which constitutes the diaphragm, is situated between the abdominal viscera and the contents of the thorax. The pressure exerted by the latter in transmitting the pressure of the abdominal walls, is greater than that of the contents of the thorax, and the diaphragm, therefore, is forced upwards. When it contracts it becomes flatter, and thus exerts a pressure upon the abdominal viscera. In generalizing this construction, we must represent a diaphragmatic muscle as a muscular plate stretched between two fixed points of attachment, forming the boundary of a cavity upon one side, concave when quiescent from unequal pressure, but becoming flatter when in action, and thus exerting a pressure upon that side, from which at other times the pressure proceeds.

This diaphragmatic construction may be observed in the *levator ani* muscle of the pelvis as well as in the diaphragm; and again in the lower boundary of the cavity of the mouth. The floor, for instance, of the mouth is formed in this manner; we will therefore proceed to examine it somewhat closely.

The principal part of the *diaphragmatic floor* of the cavity of the mouth consists of a flat muscle which, in current terminology, bears the inappropriate name of *mylo-hyoid*, but which would be much better described as the *diaphragma oris*, because the relation in which it stands to the cavity of the mouth is purely diaphragmatic, while its relation towards the hyoid bone is only of secondary importance. Upon the inner surface of the lower jaw may be seen a small ridge, the *internal oblique line*, which passes backwards upon the body of the lower jaw from the *genial tubercle*, to which we have already alluded. The muscle we are describing crosses from one of these lines to the other, thus closing the lower part of the cavity of the mouth, strictly speaking (the *oral cavity*); it is covered above by the mucous membrane which lines the cavity of the mouth and the tongue. The weight of the latter presses down the middle of this muscular plate, so that it presents a concave appearance from below. From this it is clear that a contraction of this muscle will only produce an *elevation of the floor of the cavity of the mouth*, and consequently of the whole body of the tongue.

In the muscle just described, the fibres run only in one, namely, a transverse direction. The diaphragmatic character of the floor of the cavity of the mouth requires, however, that another series of fibres should cross the former; and as we find this to be the case with the fibres of the *digastric* muscle, we need not hesitate to include this muscle as participating in the diaphragmatic closure of the cavity of the mouth. Before describing it, we must first show the relation of the hyoid bone to the *mylo-hyoid* muscle.

The form and construction of the hyoid bone has already been described, so that here we need only remark that the body of the hyoid bone is connected with the free posterior border of the *mylo-hyoid* muscle in such a manner that it projects into the posterior fasciculi of the latter, and interrupts their continuity. This gives rise to two important relations. One result of this connection will be that the hyoid bone, and with it the parts dependent upon it, especially the larynx, must be raised by the posterior fasciculi of the *mylo-hyoid*; another, that all movements which the hyoid bone has the power of performing must have an influence upon the floor of the cavity of the mouth, thus, for instance, creating the possibility of its depression.

The *digastric muscle* is composed of two short muscular bellies, and an intermediate long tendon. The posterior belly arises from the mastoid process of the temporal bone behind the ear, and presently blends with the tendon, which descends to the hyoid bone, and is here attached to the side of the body by an aponeurotic loop. From this point the anterior belly passes to the lower jaw, and is attached below the *mylo-hyoid* muscle to the

L

lower margin of this bone close to the genial tubercles. It not unfrequently happens that this anterior belly has an independent origin upon the hyoid bone; but the construction is not materially effected by this variation. Thus the *digrastic muscle* is in the form of a curve, the lowest point of which is the hyoid bone, from the base of the skull to the lower jaw. When in action, it will become tense, and therefore raise the hyoid bone; but as this elevation of the hyoid bone necessitates that of the floor of the cavity of the mouth, the activity of this muscle reinforces and completes that diaphragmatic action of the *mylo-hyoid* muscle.

From these relations it appears that the hyoid bone acts as a fixed central point of the floor of the cavity of the mouth; it follows that the position of the latter may be indirectly affected by movements or alterations of position in which the hyoid bone is primarily concerned. As, moreover, the situation of the hyoid bone also decides that of the larynx, which is suspended from it, the movements and changes in the position of the hyoid bone must be further imparted to the larynx.

The *movement of the hyoid bone* is due to a number of muscles which radiate towards it from several fixed points of origin, and are attached to the body of the bone. The mechanism presented by these muscles as a whole is the most wonderful of the whole body, the small number of four muscles upon each side being sufficient to ensure the movement of the hyoid bone in any direction. The number of these muscles is, therefore, really eight, but may be reduced to six, two of the four muscles in the middle line of the body being immediately connected with those of the other side, and thus acting singly from a mechanical point of view.

The fixed points from which the muscles of the hyoid bone arise are—

The *genial tubercles* of the lower jaw.

The posterior surface of the upper part of the breast-bone.

The *styloid process* of the temporal bone.

The upper border of the internal surface of the shoulder-blade from the *supra-scapular notch* behind the *coracoid process* which rises from the upper part of the neck of the shoulder-blade.

The names of the four muscles are derived from the points where they terminate, and following the same order as above, will be therefore—

The *genio-hyoid*.
The *sterno-hyoid*.
The *stylo-hyoid*.
The *omo-hyoid*.

As regards the position of the latter, we need only observe that the *genio-hyoid* passes directly along the lower border of the *genio-hyo-glossus*, which has already been described, and above the *mylo-hyoid*, so that it is covered inferiorly by the latter. The other three muscles are free. (Cf. Fig. 34.)

If we regard the group of the muscles of the hyoid bone from before, we find that the *genio-hyoid* descends directly towards it, and that the *sterno-hyoid* and the *omo-hyoid* ascend vertically to the side of the bone. Thus all transverse movements of the hyoid bone are provided for, though at the same time the action of these muscles is most powerful in a vertical direction.

If we take a side view of the group, we find that the direction of the *genio-hyoid* is distinctly from before backwards, its rise being much less pronounced. On the other hand, the *sterno-hyoid*, the direction of which is undoubtedly also from before backwards, is much more remarkable for its upward tendency—so much so that our attention is almost entirely claimed by the latter peculiarity. The direction of the *stylo-hyoid* and of the *omo-hyoid*, again, is distinctly forward, the former from above and the latter from below. Movement in every direction is thus provided for in the middle line of the body of the hyoid bone.

The glance we have taken from these two points of view shows that the upward direction is the one least provided for, the *genio-hyoid* having a more forward direction, and thus that the upward movement through muscles of the hyoid bone is chiefly due to the *stylo-hyoid*; it seems probable, therefore, that the whole of the diaphragmatic apparatus of the cavity of the mouth, described above, must take part in the production of the movement. The demonstration of the muscles which are either directly or indirectly concerned in the movements of the floor of the cavity of the mouth would gain greatly in simplicity if we could regard the *genio-hyo-glossus* and the *stylo-glossus* as part of the diaphragmatic apparatus which raises the floor of the cavity of the mouth, and therefore unite them into one group with the *mylo-hyoid* and the *digastric* as " elevators of the floor of the cavity of the mouth and the tongue," which group would then be opposed by another consisting of the *sterno-hyoid* and the *omo-hyoid*, or "depressors of the floor of the cavity of the mouth and the tongue." The first of these groups would also, from reasons already explained, act as elevators of the larynx, and the latter as depressors of the larynx.

The larynx is not, however, entirely dependent upon the movements of the hyoid bone for its elevation and depression, but possesses for this purpose special forces, which are most closely connected with the group of the muscles of the hyoid bone, and especially with the *sterno-hyoid*.

Covered by the *sterno-hyoid*, a long muscle passes upwards from the sternum to the hyoid bone, being apparently nothing more than a deeper layer of the sterno-hyoid, but distinguished from the latter by having another point of attachment upon the thyroid cartilage of the larynx, thus separating into two parts, which from their attachments are called respectively the *hyo-thyroid* and the *sterno-thyroid*. This band of muscle, which might be called the *sterno-hyo-thyroid*, has, as a whole, the same action as the *sterno-hyoid*. The action of its separate parts differs, however, with regard to the larynx, the *hyo-thyroid* raising it towards the hyoid bone, and the *sterno-thyroid* depressing it in the direction of the sternum.

The *hyo-thyroid*, again, has a special influence upon the act of swallowing. When, for instance, it is then called into action, it relaxes the *median hyo-thyroid ligament*, the tension of which keeps the epiglottis upright, and thus facilitates the fall of the epiglottis by which the entrance to the larynx is protected from the passing food.

THE PHARYNX.

The hinder portion of the cavity of the mouth is closed towards the pharynx by the apparatus which is known to us as the soft palate, or the *velum palati*. The latter may be generally described as a soft pendulous fold, which according to its position either shuts off the cavity of the mouth from the pharynx, or the nasal division of the pharynx from that belonging to the cavity of the mouth. The apparatus is not, however, quite so simple as it appears at first sight, for we find that the walls of the pharynx are included in the mechanism. We must, therefore, first consider the walls of the pharynx with regard to the movements of which they are capable.

The pharynx is distinguished from the rest of the alimentary canal, especially the œsophagus, of which it is the upper termination, in not being, like the latter, an enclosed circular tube, for it is entirely without an anterior wall, the cavities of the nose, mouth, and larynx all opening into this side; unless, indeed, we regard as an anterior wall the posterior margins of the septa between these cavities, or, since these septa are prolonged into the soft palate and the epiglottis, the free margins of these two folds. The pharynx, therefore, has only a posterior wall and two lateral walls, the latter being continuous with the lateral walls of the cavities of the nose, mouth, and larynx.

The muscles in the walls of a perfect tube are so arranged that some surround the tube as an annular plane of fibres, while the rest run downwards as a longitudinal plane. The first contract, the latter, on the contrary, shorten the tube.

The absence of an anterior wall in the pharynx makes it impossible that there should be a perfect constrictor muscle, and yet the same movements take place in the pharynx as in a free tube—shortening, namely, and contraction. This becomes possible from a modification in the typical muscles of a tube in accordance with the relations of the pharynx. The constrictor muscles being chiefly concerned, we will first examine them; the modification of the longitudinal muscles is closely connected with the adjustment of the soft palate, and will, therefore, be discussed with the latter.

STRUCTURE OF THE ORGANS OF SPEECH. 151

The contraction effected by the constrictor muscle of a tube is due to the fasciculi of fibres of which it is composed, which, in shortening, form the circumference of a smaller circle, and thus all the points of the circumference are equally approached to the axis of the tube. The same contraction may, however, take place if one point of the circumference is fixed. The only

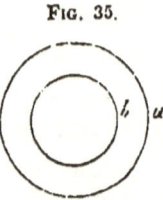

Fig. 35.

Diagram of a free constrictor muscle: *a*, when relaxed; *b*, when contracted.

difference will be that here the separate points of the circumference are approximated to this point, when the contraction takes place.

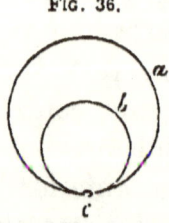

Fig. 36.

Diagram of a constrictor muscle, in which a point (*c*) of the periphery is fixed: *a* and *b* as in Fig. 35.

The relation of the circle at rest to the contracted circle is in the first case that of two concentric circles, in the second that of a smaller circle, which touches the inner surface of a larger circle at one point; in the first case the two circles have a common centre, in the second a common tangent.

A similar relation to that just described will, however, result when two points of a circumference are separated by, for instance, one-fourth of the circumference, when, of course, the remaining portion between the points may be absent. The remaining arc will, therefore, be drawn towards a line connecting the two fixed points. Here we can no longer speak of a constrictor muscle, but must regard the entire construction as a "loop" with two fixed points, or points of attachment.

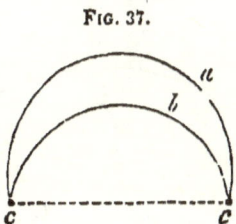

FIG. 37.

Diagram of a loop-muscle; *c c*, fixed points of the loop: *a* and *b* as in Fig. 35.

It is a metamorphosis of this kind which takes place between the constrictor muscles of the œsophagus and the muscular planes which we find in the pharynx, from the lower border of the cricoid cartilage of the larynx to the base of the skull.

Before passing to the examination of this arrangement in the pharynx itself, let us first consider the mechanism of such a loop. Let us still imagine a loop as constituting three-fourths of the circumference of a circle, and instead of the remaining fourth a line connecting the two fixed points as the base of the loop, we shall then be able to divide the loop into three parts, namely, into the part opposite to the base line and the two lateral parts. Now, the contractile action of a loop will be most readily understood if we imagine the highest portion of the loop to be brought nearer to the base line, and the lateral portions to each other. Referred to the pharynx, this implies that by the contraction of the loop-muscles of the

STRUCTURE OF THE ORGANS OF SPEECH. 153

pharynx the posterior wall of the pharynx is drawn forwards and the lateral walls inwards.

The fixed points of the loop-muscles surrounding the constrictors of the pharynx are three in number: (1) the larynx, (2) the hyoid bone, and (3) the maxillary portion of the skull. A loop-muscle enclosing the pharynx arises from each of these points, and the three loops are called either, from their position, the *inferior*,

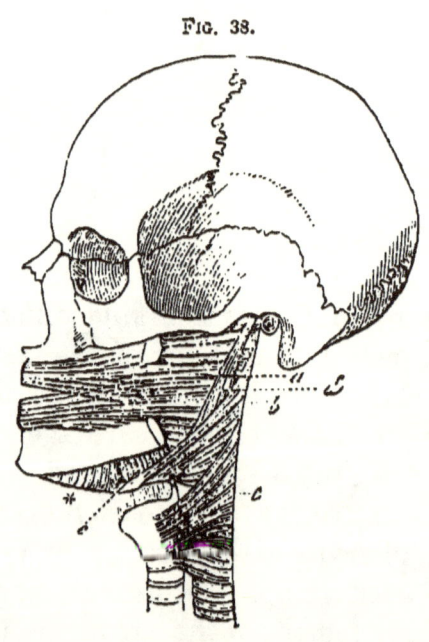

FIG. 38.

The muscles of the pharynx. *a*, Superior constrictor, passing anteriorly into the buccinator; *b*, middle constrictor; *c*, inferior constrictor; *d*, stylo-pharyngeus; *e*, hyo-glossus; *, diaphragma oris (mylo-hyoid).

middle, and *superior constrictors*, or, from their points of attachment, the *laryngo-pharyngeus*, *hyo-pharyngeus*, and the *gnatho-pharyngeus*.

The arrangement of the three constrictors presents this peculiarity, that their fibres, closely packed together at the two points of attachment, diverge as they pass backwards—so much so that the two halves of each muscle meet in a comparatively long line in the middle of the posterior wall of the pharynx. As each of the constrictors spreads out backwards in this manner, they must partially cover each other, which in fact we find to be the case, the upper margin of the lower loop in each case overlapping the lower margin of the one above it. We must further remember that the oblique direction which their divergence gives to the greater number of the fibres, introduces a longitudinal component into their action, thus making up for the absence of longitudinal fibres.

The inferior constrictor consists of a lower portion (the *crico-pharyngeus*), which arises from the outer surface of the cricoid cartilage, and of an upper portion (the *thyro-pharyngeus*), arising from the raised oblique line on the lateral surface of the thyroid cartilage. The lower margin of the entire muscle is horizontal, and rests immediately upon the circular plane of fibres of the œsophagus; the upper margin ascends rapidly from the divergence of the fibres, and overlaps the greater part of the adjacent muscle.

The greater part of the middle constrictor (the *kerato-pharyngeus*) arises upon the upper border and the posterior rounded end of the greater horns of the hyoid bone; a small portion (the *chondro-pharyngeus*) arises upon the lesser horns of the hyoid bone. In this muscle the descent of the lower margin is slight; the upper margin, on the contrary, ascends very abruptly, and overlaps the greater part of the succeeding muscle.

The superior constrictor is an exceedingly broad layer of muscle; one portion (the *mylo-pharyngeus*) arises upon the inner surface of the lower jaw, immediately in front of the attachment of the *greater* or *internal pterygoid muscle;* another portion (the *pterygo-pharyngeus*) from the lower part of the posterior free margin of the internal pterygoid plate. Between these two a larger middle portion, lying against the inner surface of the *pterygoid muscle*, passes directly into the *buccinator;* it forms with the latter, therefore, one muscle, which might be called the *stomato-pharyngeus*. This muscle is, however, generally understood to be interrupted by a narrow tendinous band, which is observed in that part which is in relation with the *greater pterygoid muscle*, and the portion in front of this ligament is called the *buccinator muscle;* the portion situated behind it, which is directly continuous with the two first-mentioned parts of the superior constrictor, is known as the *bucco-pharyngeus*. The divergence of the fibres is not so striking in this muscle, though its lower margin is seen distinctly to descend, and its upper margin ascends to the base of the skull, to which it is attached by a narrow prolongation.

In spite of a certain similarity in their arrangement, the three constrictors have each a significance of their own. The two lower ones, namely, are only brought into service in the act of swallowing; for, always being in the contracted state, they press the larynx and the ends of the greater horns of the hyoid bone against the posterior wall of the pharynx, and can only be called into action during the passage of food. The upper constrictor has, however, a free space in front of it which it can diminish by its own contraction. We shall presently show the part which such a movement plays in the formation of articulate sounds, and how the superior constrictor thus assumes the character of a muscle belonging to the action of speech just as much as the two lower ones assume that of loop-muscles.

THE SOFT PALATE.

In considering the apparatus of the soft palate, the idea of a pendulous fold is of the greatest assistance towards a true comprehension. This idea moreover is, within certain limits, as convenient as it is correct, being specially well adapted for a sectional illustration; at the same time, it by no means fully represents the mechanism of the soft palate. We obtain an idea which in many respects is more accurate, if we regard the soft palate as an apparatus consisting of a double constrictor muscle,

FIG. 39.

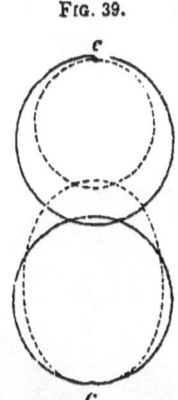

Diagram of two constrictor muscles united to each other in a part of their circumference, each with a fixed point (*c*). The dotted line represents the change of form which takes place when one of them (here the upper) is contracted.

which on the one hand cuts off the cavity of the mouth from the adjacent portion of the pharynx, on the other, the portion of the pharynx which adjoins the nasal cavity from that which belongs to the cavity of the mouth.

If, now, in our examination of the construction of the soft palate, we take as our starting-point the simplest diagram of a constrictor muscle, we shall find that our first diagram of this apparatus will consist of two circles, which meet in one point of their circumference. One of

STRUCTURE OF THE ORGANS OF SPEECH. 157

these circles would embrace the circumference of the posterior nares, the second the posterior aperture of the cavity of the mouth. If, further, we imagine each circle to represent a constrictor muscle, the result inferred in both cases will be correct: (1) that this double apparatus on the one hand will effect a closure of the nasal cavity, on the other a closure of the cavity of the mouth; and (2) that if the points opposite to the points of contact of the two circles are fixed, the two constrictor muscles must act antagonistically in such a manner that the contraction of the one must cause an expansion of the other, so that, there-

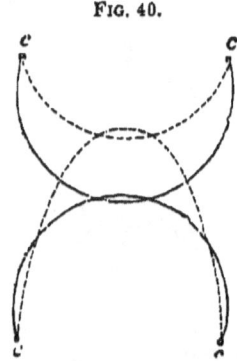

FIG. 40.

Diagram representing the change of the two constrictor muscles into loop-muscles with two points of fixation (c c). Dotted line as in Fig. 39.

fore, the closure of the nasal cavity must be accompanied by the opening of the cavity of the mouth, and that of the cavity of the mouth by the opening of the nasal cavity.

The above result is, however, in reality obtained by the two muscles not being constrictors but loop-muscles, and the apices of the two loops being connected. The upper loop effects the closure of the nasal cavity, the lower that of the cavity of the mouth. The apices of the two loops come into contact upon the boundary between the cavity of the mouth and that of the nose; that is to say,

158   THE ORGANS OF SPEECH.

at the posterior end of the hard palate, or, more definitely still, in that prolongation of the hard palate which is known to us as the *velum palati*, or soft palate.

The distinctive features of the soft palate are derived from that part which lies in the cavity of the mouth. The foundation is laid by a loop-muscle (the *palato-pharyngeus*), which is situated immediately upon the mucous membrane of the pharynx and is covered exter-

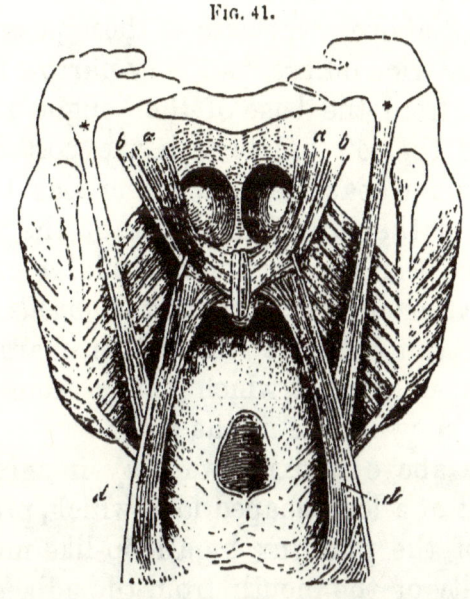

FIG. 41.

Muscles of the soft palate. *a, Levator veli*; *b, tensor palati*; *c, azygos uvulae* (*levator uvulae*); *d, palato-pharyngeus*; *, *stylo-pharyngeus* (elevator of the pharynx).

nally by the constrictors. The fixed points of the loop rest upon the posterior border of the thyroid cartilage; it then ascends the sides of the pharynx, curving inwards to form its apex in the soft palate. External evidence of this muscle is given by a fold of mucous membrane which projects into the interior of the pharynx. This fold is very indistinct at first, but becomes more pronounced above the hyoid bone, finding its greatest breadth in the soft palate. If we trace its course from the latter, we find that the two together form a crescent-shaped fold, the broad middle portion of which passes into two lateral processes which descend backwards. This broad middle portion, which appears as a soft continuation of the hard (bony) palate, is called the *soft palate;* the two processes which are direct continuations of it are, however, known as the *posterior pillars of the soft palate,* and are nothing more than the fold which was mentioned above. Opposite to these posterior pillars we find the anterior pillars, two very narrow folds, which run upwards from the base of the tongue and unite in the margin of the soft palate with the posterior pillars. In the triangular space left on either side between the two pillars and the lateral margins of the base of the tongue may be seen two rounded glandular bodies, about the size of a hazel-nut, namely, the *tonsils.* The free margin of the soft palate is still further characterized by a conical-shaped process which hangs from its centre, and which is known to us as the *uvula.*

From the above remarks we may imagine the soft palate as part of a loop-shaped fold, which, projected into the interior of the pharynx by a loop-like muscle, separates the cavity of the mouth from the adjacent portion of the pharynx; this will also explain the pendent position of the soft palate when at rest.

Turning now to examine the influence and action of this closing apparatus, we will for the moment regard the thyroid cartilage as a fixed starting-point for this action. The apex of the loop will in the first place be drawn downwards towards this point, and the soft palate consequently depressed; as, however, this depression will soon be opposed by the connection of the latter with the hard palate, the sides will be drawn out into a straight line; the posterior pillars will, therefore, be driven inwards so far that they almost come into contact with each other. The closure of the cavity of the mouth from the pharynx is, therefore, chiefly effected by the simultaneous advance of the posterior pillars of the soft palate towards each other, the soft palate itself doing little more to effect this result than when at rest.

It must, however, be remembered that the position of the larynx is not absolutely fixed, so that when a further descent of the soft palate meets with opposition, it is the larynx which forms the basis of any further action. Thus, if the action is continued, the larynx, together with the lowest part of the pharynx, is drawn upwards. The *palato-pharyngeus* muscle acts, therefore, in a twofold manner during swallowing; in the first place, closing the aperture of the cavity of the mouth, thus preventing the return of the food which is to pass into the pharynx; and, secondly, facilitating the descent of the food into the œsophagus by drawing the latter up towards it.

The action of this muscle has, therefore, a secondary effect upon the pharynx and œsophagus, which gives it the character of a longitudinal muscular layer; it may, therefore, be regarded as a modification of the longitudinal muscular layer of the alimentary canal, and the more so as the effect produced is partly due to a layer of muscle situated beneath the mucous membrane of the posterior wall of the pharynx, and not attached to the thyroid cartilage; the soft palate here acts as the fixed point for the ensuing elevation.

The longitudinal character of the action of this muscle becomes still more striking when we find that two portions of it have their attachment in the base of the skull, from which point they act only as elevators of the pharynx.

The first of the attachments here alluded to is that of the free fasciculi of the *palato-pharyngeus*, which, instead of passing into the soft palate, ascend still further, and are attached to the Eustachian tube (*salpingo-pharyngeus m.*).

The second attachment belongs to a comparatively strong, round fasciculus, which breaks off at the boundary between the middle and superior constrictors, passing outwards between these two muscles, and then rising freely upwards, to find attachment upon the styloid process of the temporal bone (*stylo-pharyngeus m.*).

The upper loop-like constrictor muscle which belongs to the nasal cavity has a similar oblique position, having, like the lower, its fixed point of origin near the vertebral column, from whence it descends obliquely forwards as far as the soft palate. The *levator palati* muscle must be regarded as the leading feature in this part of the apparatus of the soft palate. It arises from the apex of the petrous portion of the temporal bone, and from the adjoining margin of the Eustachian tube. In this origin it is closely contiguous with the mucous membrane of the pharynx, which here forms the concave roof of the latter below the base of the skull; but instead of following this surface, it descends to the soft palate, and, like the *palato-pharyngeus*, is covered externally by the superior constrictor. In the soft palate it expands with the same muscle of the other side into a loop which lies behind the corresponding loop of the *palato-pharyngeus*. The position of this muscle upon the nasal side of the soft palate gives it the character of a muscle for closing the nose, as the position of the *palato-pharyngeus* upon the oral side of the soft palate gives to the latter the character of a muscle for closing the mouth. This course enables the muscle in question, or rather the loop formed by the muscles of both sides, to raise the soft palate backwards, so that the lower margin of the latter is approximated to the posterior wall of the pharynx; by this means the nasal portion of the pharynx is shut off from the oral portion.

The action of this loop is, moreover, strengthened by that of the *azygos uvulae* (*levator uvulae*). This muscle consists of a pair of fasciculi, which arise from the posterior border of the hard palate, and pass immediately below the mucous membrane of the posterior surface of the soft palate to the apex of the uvula. When in action it helps to raise the posterior margin of the soft palate, and especially the uvula, in a backward direction.

In addition to these two elevators, a third muscle enters the soft palate from above, in which the character of an elevating loop is curiously modified. This muscle, the *tensor palati*, arises on the outer side of the *levator palati* from the *scaphoid fossa* of the internal pterygoid plate, and from the contiguous margin of the Eustachian tube. It descends upon the external surface of the superior constrictor, and winding round the hooked (annular) process of the internal pterygoid plate with its tendinous end, enters the soft palate from the side; its fibres here spread out, and form with those of the other side a tendinous plate (aponeurosis), the anterior margin of which is attached to the posterior margin of the hard palate. When this muscle acts the aponeurosis is made tense horizontally, giving the same direction to the upper half of the soft palate. Thus the two *levatores palati* form a loop, modified, it is true, which acts as an elevator of the soft palate, and takes part in the closure of the nasal portion of the pharynx.

If we now look back upon the different mechanisms

and apparatus in the cavity of the mouth with which, from the foregoing remarks, we have become acquainted, we find that its adjustment rests upon a most simple foundation, and yet that it is adapted for the greatest variety of purposes. We may make a brief summary of these characteristics as follows:—

(1) The cavity of the mouth is a large, spacious cavity, the roof being formed by the rigid hard palate, which is a part of the upper jaw.

(2) The parts composing the floor of the cavity are soft, and only partially fixed through their connection with the lower jaw.

(3) The anterior border of the cavity of the mouth is formed by the orifice which is bounded by the lips. A number of muscles, some entirely situated in, others entering the lips, give to this orifice the power of assuming different shapes, and especially of opening and shutting in a variety of ways and degrees.

(4) The posterior border of the cavity of the mouth is indicated by the apparatus of the soft palate and its pillars. In this apparatus a constrictor muscle for closing the nasal cavity, and another for closing the cavity of the mouth, are connected in such a manner that the soft palate, strictly speaking, is entirely under their control, so that it can be employed in shutting off the cavity of the mouth from the pharynx, or, again, in shutting off the nasal from the oral portion of the pharynx.

(5) The interior of the cavity of the mouth is divided by the teeth into two imperfectly separated spaces, the cavity of the mouth and the cavity of the cheeks.

(6) The interior of the entire cavity of the mouth can be enlarged by the depression of the lower jaw, and modified in its form by the advancement of the latter,

(7) The interior of the cavity of the cheeks is dependent upon the tension or contraction of the *buccinator* muscle.

(8) The interior of the cavity of the mouth, strictly speaking, can be modified in a great variety of ways in form and width by the activity of the tongue.

(9) The tongue produces these changes through alterations in its own form and position.

(10) The tongue, however, is more passive in the movements of the floor of the mouth, which are partly diaphragmatic elevations of the latter, and partly depressions caused by lowering the hyoid bone.

(11) Among the group of muscles which draw down the hyoid bone are two, one of which draws the larynx to the hyoid bone, while the other draws it away.

(12) Further, the elevation or depression of the larynx is dependent upon that of the hyoid bone, to which it is attached.

The Nerves of the Air-Passages.

The air-passages which we have described are, like all parts of the organism, provided with nerves, which are partly sensory nerves for the skin with which they are covered, and partly motor nerves for the muscular parts. So far as the air-passages are in connection with the animal part of the body, these nerves give the possibility of conscious perceptions and voluntary movements. Their nerves, therefore, proceed from the centres of the animal nervous system—the brain, namely, and the spinal cord.

Now, since the creation of articulate sounds depends partly upon the presence of a suitable current of air, and partly upon the modifications to which the latter

STRUCTURE OF THE ORGANS OF SPEECH.

can be subjected, the nerves belonging to the organs of speech may be regarded from these two points of view.

As regards the nerves which regulate the current of air, it would appear at first sight as if nerves took no part in the production of this current; for, as we have already shown, the current of expired air, which from the present point of view is of the greater importance, is due to the purely physical action of the elasticity of the tissue of the lungs and the costal cartilages. On the other hand, it must be remembered that the force of a current of air produced in this manner must to a great extent depend upon the degree of elasticity called into action, and this, again, depends upon the degree of the preceding tension. The latter, however, is created by the force to which the inspiratory act is due. The stronger and deeper the inspiration, the stronger and fuller will be the current of the expired air. Those nerves which give activity to the inspiratory muscles will, therefore, undoubtedly have a great, if indirect, influence upon the general characteristics of the expired current of air. Ordinary quiet inspiration is effected by the activity of the diaphragm alone; when deeper and more powerful, several groups of muscles already described are called into play, the action of which is principally directed towards raising the walls of the thorax. All these movements take place automatically without any effort of the will, but they may be so modified by the will, that they may either be carried on with greater force, or the separate acts may be more rapidly performed, or, again, the number of these acts within a certain space of time varied. Thus we have to a great extent the power of regulating the current of air according to requirements; and so we see in ordinary quiet speech that the quiet course of inspiration is scarcely interrupted, but in loud speech, which requires a stronger current of air, we observe a deeper and stronger inspiration, and in rapid speech, when a great quantity of air has to pass through the vocal organs in a short space of time, we find a quick repetition of the separate acts of inspiration.

The degree to which the will may regulate the current of air expelled by the force of elasticity alone is not, however, confined within the above limits. A more direct influence is derived from the voluntary muscular activity by which the current of air may be prevented from escaping too quickly, and thus become better adapted for use. This is achieved by the attention being directed to the inspiratory muscles, and after the completion of the inspiratory act not allowing them to relax suddenly, but forcing them to do so by degrees. The necessity of asserting this effort of the will for ordinary speech will most clearly be seen if we consider the peculiarities in the speech of delicate persons. They speak, for instance, in jerks, because from the too rapid escape of the current of air they are obliged to take breath more frequently, and, what makes this necessity more striking, cannot at any time take a deep breath on account of the weakness of their muscles.

Healthy persons when awake always hold back the respiratory current in this manner in ordinary quiet breathing, so that the time employed in inspiration and expiration is almost the same. When asleep, however, on account of the absence of this modifying element, another rhythm is followed, namely, a prolonged quiet inspiration followed by a quicker expiration; and during speech, again, from reasons which may be inferred from what has been stated above, the rhythm is reversed,

STRUCTURE OF THE ORGANS OF SPEECH. 167

the inspiration, namely, being short and the expiration long.

The retreating current of air which is to be employed in speech can, therefore, be modified in a great variety of ways by the manner in which the inspiratory act or the relaxation of the inspiratory muscles is regulated. The expiratory act itself can, however, also be modified by voluntary muscular activity. The expulsion of the air from the lungs is not entirely due to the elasticity described above, but may be reinforced by muscular activity. In quiet breathing this is due to the abdominal muscles, in stronger breathing more directly to the expiratory muscles acting upon the walls of the thorax. When these muscles are called into play, the strength and rapidity of the current of air is increased on the one hand, and on the other the emptying of the lungs is more fully performed than would be possible from the force of elasticity alone. By this means a singer is enabled at any time to hold back the current and so avoid taking breath at unsuitable times. It is, again, within our power to separate the single expiratory act into a number of smaller parts, by suddenly stopping a powerful expiration due to muscular activity, then allowing it to go on, then again stopping it, and so on, the single expiratory act being thus divided into as many short explosive expirations as we please. This gives the singer the power of producing a series of distinctly separated tones—that is to say, of singing "staccato." And then, again, a continuous current of breath can, by a corresponding regulation of the activity of the muscles, be made alternately strong and weak, quick and slow, and thus occasion an increase or decrease in the power of the voice.

All those muscles which directly or indirectly effect

the modifications of the current of air which we have just described, are excited to their activity by motor-nerves, which arise in the spinal canal; these nerves, moreover, may be divided into three groups, one of which, it is true, only contains a single nerve.

(1) The phrenic or diaphragmatic nerve.
(2) The dorsal nerves.
(3) Branches of the brachial plexus.

The *phrenic nerve,* passing from the spinal canal in the upper part of the neck, is the motor-nerve for the diaphragm; its activity occasions ordinary quiet breathing.

The *dorsal nerves* enter the region of the chest from the spinal canal, and are distributed among the intercostal cartilages and the abdominal muscles; they effect the stronger inspiratory and expiratory acts.

The *nerves of the brachial plexus* escape from the spinal canal in the lower region of the neck, and afterwards divide to supply all the parts of the arm, and also the great muscles which pass from the trunk to the arm; when the arm has been fixed to some external object, they help, in cases of great want of breath, to raise the thorax a degree higher.

As long as these nerves can perform their functions in a normal manner, the processes described above, and the modifications of those processes, are carried on without interruption. As soon, however, as any disturbing cause appears, whether a general affection of the whole nervous system or merely a local derangement, the breathing apparatus, and therefore the expiratory current, will suffer, partly from the affected nerves being themselves disturbed, and partly from the will being deprived of its influence. Thus general nervous excitement occasions quick breathing movements, or a convulsive cessation of these movements; rapid speech is, therefore, the effect of this nervous excitement, while the stoppages in the speech observed at such times may be partially attributed to the check sustained by the breath. It is, again, a well-known fact, that if the chest or hands are cold, a numbness may be produced, the result of which will be a halting trembling voice.

We must include in the apparatus for the production of sound not only the motor-nerves, which act upon the muscles of these apparatus, but also the sensory nerves, which render the skin forming their external covering capable of receiving impressions. These sensory nerves have a twofold importance with regard to their apparatus and their functions. In the first place, they possess the characteristics of all sensory nerves belonging to the skin—that, namely, of imparting the intelligence of the contact of the surface of the skin with any foreign body, and thereby giving warning of, and affording protection from, external injury; in many parts of these apparatus, indeed, the arrangement is such that the usual circuitous path to the exercise of volition through a conscious sensation is unnecessary when an injurious foreign body or a detrimental irritation is to be removed, but the contact of the foreign body or the irritating object is sufficient to create a so-called "reflex action," the purpose of which is to remove the irritating body. The air-passages, strictly speaking, are specially remarkable in this respect. To show the truth of this assertion, we need only recall the fact that when irritating vapours or foreign bodies (when swallowed) enter the larynx they immediately give rise to violent coughing, and any irritation of the inner surface of the nose is followed by a sneeze. A second characteristic of the sensory nerves, which is of importance to the organs of speech, is that they control the activity of the muscles. The excitation which they receive from the tension or wrinkling of the skin they transmit as a sensation to the brain, and thus bring intelligence of the completion of any muscular action; and on the other hand, when contact is sought by any muscular movement, they indicate when and to what degree the contact has taken place. Cases have been known in which persons suffering from an affection of the sensory nerves of the hand have been unable to take firm hold of anything, because these nerves could give them no intimation that contact had taken place with an external object; again, we have all experienced that uncertainty of gait which arises from the foot being " asleep," the cause of which is that we are not conscious of the foot being in contact with the ground. In the same manner an affection of the sensory nerves of the tongue will occasion uncertainty in speech, because no intimation is given of its contact with the different parts of the mouth—for instance, with the teeth in the pronunciation of *t*, by which means alone perfect speech can be produced.

The nerves, sensory as well as motor, of the organs of speech, may be divided into two well-defined groups, separated from each other by the narrow opening between the pillars of the soft palate (the isthmus of the fauces). The anterior group consists of four nerves, the *trifacial (trigeminus), olfactory, facial,* and *inferior maxillary;* the posterior group, on the contrary, is composed of four nerves, which are so intimately connected as to almost constitute a single nerve: they are the *pneumogastric (nervus vagus),* the *spinal accessory,* the *glosso-pharyngeal,* and the *hypoglossal.*

Of the anterior group, the *olfactory* and *trifacial* are sensory nerves; the *facial* and *inferior maxillary* motor-nerves.

STRUCTURE OF THE ORGANS OF SPEECH.

The *olfactory* nerve is distributed to the chamber of smell in the nasal cavity, and produces the sensation of smell.

The *trifacial* nerve is the common sensory nerve for the integument and mucous membranes of the face; it leaves the cranial cavity where it arises from the brain in three branches, whence its name—*trigeminus*. The first branch passes through the orbit to the integument of the forehead, and to the outer and inner surface of the dorsum of the nose. The second branch is distributed upon the superior maxillary bone in the integument of the face between the eyes and the mouth; internally it supplies the mucous membrane of the air-passage of the nasal cavity, and the mucous membrane of the hard and soft palate. The third branch is distributed upon the lower jaw, and supplies the integument of the face below the orifice of the mouth; internally it supplies the mucous membrane of the cheeks and the floor of the cavity of the mouth with the tongue; in the hindermost part of the tongue, however, the *glosso-pharyngeal*, of the posterior group, appears as the nerve of taste (gustatory nerve).

The *inferior maxillary* is the motor-nerve for the so-called muscles of mastication, and for the oral diaphragm with the anterior belly of the digastric muscle.

The *facial* nerve produces the activity of the muscles of the integument of the face, especially therefore of the muscles of the nose and mouth.

The nerves, the combination of which forms the posterior group, are distributed on either side of the *pneumo-gastric*, which acts as sensory nerve to the mucous membrane of the pharynx, larynx, œsophagus, and windpipe; in the pharynx it is supplemented by the *glosso-pharyngeal*, part of which also enters the tongue as a gustatory nerve. Part of the *spinal accessory* blends with both nerves as a motor-nerve, its other parts being distributed to the region of the neck. This intermixture gives rise to those motor-nerve branches which the *pneumogastric* supplies to the muscles of the pharynx and larynx.

The hypoglossal is the motor-nerve for the muscles of the tongue and of the hyoid bone.

CHAPTER II.

THE RELATION BETWEEN THE ORGANS OF SPEECH AND THE FORMATION OF SOUND.

Unusual Forms of the Respiratory Mechanism.

The most important condition for perfect and normal speech is a perfect and undisturbed action of the respiratory mechanism; that is to say, a quick inspiration should follow, with the greatest possible regularity, a long easy expiration. It seems right, therefore, to devote a few words to those disturbances of the respiratory mechanism, which either destroy perfect speech or render the exercise of it impossible for the time. We cannot, of course, here allude to those disturbances which owe their existence to serious diseases, such as heart-complaint, hydro-thorax, etc., but can only mention those which appear as passing disturbances of an otherwise perfect respiratory mechanism. Since, therefore, in these cases, the condition of the mechanical apparatus is perfect, they will only be considered in connection with the form and manner in which it is employed. The employment of the respiratory apparatus is, however, synonymous with the application of its proper muscular activity. But since the irritation of muscles must always proceed from their motor-nerves, it follows that all these disturbances must be referred to unusual or abnormal excitation of the nerves then in action, whether such a condition of excitation has arisen voluntarily or from unforeseen circumstances.

The disturbances in question naturally fall into two divisions, in the one of which inspiration, in the other expiration, if not alone, yet certainly in a great measure alone, assumes an unusual form.

As disturbances of the normal form of inspiration, we have the phenomena which are known as—

> Hiccough,
> Gaping, and
> Stammering.

Of these forms the simplest is the *hiccough*, which is merely produced by violent inspiration, arising from a convulsive contraction of the diaphragm. The ensuing expiration then takes place quietly. The inspired air can, moreover, enter principally either through the mouth or the nose, or through both equally, and in each case the accompanying noise is different. A contraction of the glottis may also take place at the same time, and in this case the entering stream of air creates in passing through the vocal chords a sharp clear tone. In any case the hiccough arises from over-irritation of the nerves of the diaphragm, the cause of which we know to be either psychical conditions or overfilling of the stomach. The influence of the latter is undoubtedly due to the fact that the overladen stomach resists to a greater or less extent the fall of the diaphragm; the contractions of the diaphragm become, therefore, necessarily more laboured, and occasionally, like other over-irritated muscles, assume a convulsive character. Frequently, however, the hiccough appears as a sign of the general over-irritation of the nervous system in hysteria, and, probably from the same reason, it may not uncommonly be observed in otherwise healthy young persons, particularly children.

ABNORMAL FORM OF RESPIRATION. 175

The above explanation of hiccough as a convulsive contraction of the diaphragm is further confirmed by the manner in which it may be stopped. It is, namely, only necessary to allow an exceedingly protracted and, finally, forcible expiration to follow a long and quiet inspiration. The slow inspiration, especially when it is chiefly performed by the wall of the chest, prevents the phrenic nerve from being too powerfully irritated, while the long expiration gives the phrenic nerve time to recover from its over-irritation. A single trial of this remedy will often stop a troublesome attack of hiccough.

Gaping also arises from a convulsive form of inspiration, which, however, is not so short and violent as in the hiccough. In the latter, moreover, those muscles which raise the wall of the chest are at once brought into prominent action, while further a rapid contraction of the diaphragm is necessary before the climax can be reached, after which a somewhat rapid fall of the thorax produces a quick expiration. The important part which is played by the rise of the chest is particularly shown by the fact that in very violent gaping the head is thrown backward, and the shoulders raised, in addition to which even the arms are sometimes stretched upwards. During the gaping inspiratory process the mouth is opened spasmodically, the external pterygoid muscle and the group of the muscles of the hyoid bone drawing the lower from the upper jaw; at the same time the soft palate is spasmodically raised and closes the air-passage of the nose. The whole phenomenon seems an indication of strong desire for air, and the existence of this desire under those circumstances in which gaping is generally observed—sleepiness, for instance, or weariness—may be perfectly explained as follows: such circumstances are accompanied by a general inactivity of the nervous system, which shows itself in a weak respiratory action, insufficient for the body when awake, so that after a time a more or less marked desire for air must arise, the demand for which is announced by gaping.

The root of that defect in speaking which we call *stammering* lies also in spasmodic inspiration, and so resembles the hiccough, that here, as in the latter, the diaphragm is subject to spasmodic contraction. While, however, in the hiccough a short convulsive spasm causes a short violent inspiration, after which expiration proceeds with perfect freedom, in stammering a long contractile spasm of the diaphragm takes place, which as long as it continues prevents expiration. As, however, the possibility of speech depends upon the existence of this issuing stream of air, it is impossible for a person suffering from such a spasm to produce any sound. This ineffectual and therefore exaggerated effort even in this case to create some sound with the aid of the organs of the mouth and throat, gives rise to distressed grimaces, and this distressed expression must necessarily be augmented by the fact that, by so delaying expiration, a want of breath is felt and the circulation of the blood interrupted. When at length the spasm ceases and is followed by a quick expiration, this appearance entirely disappears, and the natural condition is restored till again destroyed by a fresh spasm. This phenomenon, as far as it is connected with a defect in speech, we are accustomed to call stammering. The defect in speech is, however, a phenomenon which only at times accompanies the spasm in the diaphragm, being due to an attempt to speak during the spasm. There may be no attempt to speak, and yet the cause of the phenomenon (the spasm in the diaphragm) may be experienced; in this case it will not cause stammering, but will either, if there is just then no occasion for speaking, be quite imperceptible to the observer, or, if the persons affected give up the ineffectual effort to produce a sound, only appear as an inability to speak. It is well known that great physical excitement—as, for example, surprise—will occasion attacks of stammering, and the same cause will in certain persons give rise to a passing inability to speak. If, now, as appears from the above, stammering is only an occasionally observed symptom of a long contractile spasm in the diaphragm, it must be clear that all attempts to cure stammering by exercising the organs of the mouth and throat must be unsuccessful, and that this defect can only be efficiently treated by following those rules which were given above for the treatment of hiccough. A quiet, unhurried inspiration must be followed by an expiration as slow and long as possible, the issuing stream being either employed in speech or not. In this manner the motor-nerves of the diaphragm can most effectually recover from their state of over-irritation and return to their normal condition. We must, moreover, be careful not to fall into the common error of confounding *stuttering* with *stammering*. In stuttering, the process of breathing is quite normal, and the defective speech only arises from inaptitude in the formation of sound; this defect in speech is, therefore, peculiar to children, idiots, and persons suffering from apoplexy.

As an abnormal form of expiration, we might mention in the first place obstruction of expiration. This, however, is not quite correct, for there is a kind of obstruction of expiration which is intentionally produced by entirely closing the glottis, the effect of which is, either to influence the abdominal viscera by means of the depressed diaphragm, as in straining, or, by bracing up the chest for labour requiring great exertion—as, for instance, lifting a weight—to afford certain muscles a firmer basis for operation; this kind of obstruction does not, however, concern us here. There is another kind, again, which is caused by a long contractile spasm in the diaphragm, and this being only a secondary peculiarity of a defective inspiration, has already been described. The altered forms of expiration which really belong to our subject are—

    Sneezing,
    Coughing,
    Laughing, and
    Sighing.

Of these, the simplest is that which attracts our attention as *sneezing*. Just as the hiccough depends upon a single violent spasm during inspiration, so the sneeze is due to a single violent spasm during expiration, generally of the abdominal muscles, but when very violent of the other expiratory muscles also. It is a reflex action which occurs after an irritation of the mucous membrane of the air-passages of the nose. A few slight contractions of the abdominal muscles are at first suppressed by some short inspirations rapidly following each other without any intervening expirations; then, however, follows a vigorous contraction of the abdominal muscles, by means of which the stream of air is violently driven out through the mouth and nose. In its passage through the nose the air produces a well-known noise, which may, however, be connected with a sound produced in the vocal chords. We recognize the same peculiarity, though the action is voluntarily and less violently performed in " blowing the nose."

Coughing and *laughing* are also due to a spasmodic contraction of the expiratory muscles, generally of the abdominal muscles, and only in violent cases are the other

ABNORMAL FORMS OF RESPIRATION. 179

expiratory muscles contracted. They differ from sneezing only in this respect that, while in the latter the act of expiration is accomplished by a single violent action, it is here characterized by a number of separate impulses of the expiratory muscles with small intervening pauses. In long-continued coughing or laughing, short inspirations, which, on account of their shortness and violence, often approach the verge of hiccoughing, are taken between the separate expirations modified as described above. *Coughing* most closely resembles sneezing, not only as regards its origin, but also as regards its execution. It is, for instance, a reflex action which follows an irritation of the air-passages, particularly of the windpipe and the larynx, but also of the pharynx and the nasal cavity. The accompanying expiratory impulses may attain great violence, so as in this respect to resemble the single impulse of sneezing. While, however, in sneezing, the stream of air escapes, as a rule, through the nose, in coughing it escapes through the cavity of the mouth, which is separated by the raised soft palate from the nasal cavity, and enlarged by dropping the lower jaw and by the depression of the floor of the cavity, the tongue at the same time being pushed forward. The stream of air, in its passage through the mouth, merely produces a breathing sound, which, however, is generally accompanied by a sound, shrill or deep as the case may be, produced by the vocal chords, the glottis being as a rule spasmodically contracted. Performed voluntarily and with less violence, coughing assumes the form known to us as "clearing the throat." In *laughing*, the separate expiratory impulses are not so violent, and the stream of air passes either through the fairly open mouth, or, when the mouth is shut, through the nose. The stream of air produced by laughing is heard merely as a breathing or blowing noise; this, however, may be accompanied by a sound, either high or low, loud or weak, originating in the vocal chords. In the latter case, the stream of air which from time to time is quickly inspired during prolonged laughter, as is also the case in coughing, may produce a clear, shrill tone in that organ which is specially adapted for tones, namely, in the glottis.

Connected with coughing and laughing on account of a similar disturbance of the breathing apparatus, is *sighing*. In the latter, the air contained in the lungs is, in a single act of expiration, either at once or with several consecutive efforts hastily expelled, and escapes either through the mouth or nose. The breathing noise which is thus produced is often accompanied by a shrill tone originating in the vocal chords, in which, on its passage through the nasal cavity, nasal resonance can be distinctly recognized. Considered more closely, a material difference may be observed between these two kinds of sighing. The isolated sigh which appears as a single act of expiration is to be attributed less to the *activity* of the expiratory muscles than to a sudden cessation of that muscular activity, which, as has been already shown, regulates, by retarding, the issuing stream of air; the elastic forces of expiration assume, therefore, absolute power, and drive out the air with greater rapidity. When the sigh is repeated by fits in single expiratory acts, as happens, for instance, in violent crying, the stream of air is, on the contrary, driven out by small, weak muscular impulses, so that, as far as mechanism is concerned, there is a considerable resemblance with laughing and coughing, which accounts for the fact that it is often difficult with a crying child, when it is beginning to be comforted, to decide whether it is still sighing or beginning to laugh. This similarity becomes still more

ABNORMAL FORMS OF RESPIRATION. 181

striking, when we find that if this kind of sighing is continued for any length of time, it will be interrupted by short inspirations, which shows a similarity to sobbing.

Those disturbances of the respiratory mechanism, which impede or prevent the proper use of the stream of air for speech, are therefore either disturbances of the normal form of inspiration, or of the normal form of expiration.

The disturbances of *inspiration* are the hiccough, gaping, and stammering. The disturbance

> In the case of the hiccough is—a single violent spasm of the diaphragm.
>
> In the case of gaping—a slighter spasmodic activity of the muscles of the chest and diaphragm.
>
> In the case of stammering—a more prolonged spasm of the diaphragm.

The disturbances of *expiration* are sneezing, coughing, laughing, and sighing. The disturbance

> In the case of sneezing is—a single violent contraction of the expiratory muscles.
>
> In the case of coughing and laughing—a resolution of a single act of expiration into a series of more or less violent expiratory impulses.
>
> In the case of sighing—similar resolution of a single act of expiration into very slight impulses, or the undisturbed action of the force of elasticity acting during expiration.

The Respiratory Noises.

It is well known that a current of air, in passing through a tube or over an edge, will produce a kind of sound, which, if the vibrations of the air, or of the body set in motion by the current of air, are rhythmically regular, is called a *tone* (in the musical sense); if, however, the vibration is not rhythmical, the intervals of time between the separate waves being irregular, the result is termed a *noise*.

We should assume beforehand that the breath, in passing through the air-passages, would produce such kinds of tone and noise, as its course lies partly through more or less elastic tubes, partly across variously constructed prominent edges. And, in fact, it does so to a great extent, though we find, further, that the noises greatly predominate, because the conditions for the production of musical sound are much more restricted.

In quiet breathing no such noises are perceptible. This, however, is at once explained by the fact that loud and perceptible noises can only be produced by a strong or rapid current of air, whether the latter be strong throughout, or only locally so from the necessity of forcing itself through a narrow opening. In ordinary quiet breathing, however, gentle and slow currents of air pass through sufficiently wide spaces, and thus leave the conditions for the formation of a noise unfulfilled. Nevertheless, the current of breath does not pass quite noiselessly through the air-passages, and of this we may easily convince ourselves by placing the ear or the stethoscope upon proper parts of the body. By these means, even in the quietest breathing, the current of air can be heard entering and returning through the nasal orifices, the larynx, and the windpipe; and by placing them upon the chest, the noise of the passing current can be heard in the ramifications of the bronchial tubes in the lungs. It is this fact which has given rise to the use of the stethoscope by the physician. The form and the mobility of the spaces through which this current passes must necessarily give the distinctive character to the noise, and thus it is possible to decide, from the character of the noise, the form and mobility of the spaces in question; and thus the physician is able to form an opinion, from the respiratory noise which the stethoscope enables him to hear, upon the healthy state of the lungs, or to detect a state of disease, such as obstructions, accumulation of mucus, cavities in the lungs, etc.

Now, although it is perfectly true that the process of breathing is generally accomplished in a manner imperceptible to those standing near, yet it often happens that a person in the vicinity will perceive it to be accompanied by very audible noises. Even the hurried breathing of a person who is excited or out of breath gives rise to a blowing sound of greater or less intensity, which we are accustomed to call "panting." A continued contraction of the air-passages may also cause the process of breathing to be always accompanied by a more or less perceptible kind of noise, as, for example, the local contraction of the windpipe by bronchocele. A similar effect is also produced by a passing obstruction of the orifices of the air-passages, such as, for instance, is caused by an accumulation of mucus in the nose or larynx.

Similar effects may also be observed when, from some passing change in the shape of the cavity, the course of the air in quiet breathing is interrupted. The most generally known and, at the same time, the most interesting forms of this species of noise, are *snoring* and *groaning*.

Snoring is a peculiar noise which is generally observed to accompany inspiration as well as expiration, particularly in sleep. The conditions necessary for its production are that the breath should be drawn through the mouth with the soft palate and tongue in a given position. The soft palate, namely, must be drawn or have fallen back in such a manner that the posterior entrance to the nasal cavity, if not altogether closed, is at least obstructed; the posterior and middle divisions of the tongue are at the same time drawn or have fallen back so far that there only remains a narrow opening between it and the soft palate. It is by the air being forced through this opening that the noise is produced. Similar noises are also produced when, with a closed mouth, the air is forced between the soft palate, which has been drawn or has fallen back, and the posterior wall of the pharynx into the nasal cavity. It is worthy of remark that with a strong current of air, perhaps accompanied by the corresponding position of the soft palate, a rattling noise may be heard in addition to the snoring, which has its origin in a vibration of the soft palate.

Groaning is a noise which is produced when, after the larynx has been perfectly closed by bringing the vocal chords and the arytenoid cartilages into contact (whether spasmodically or as a voluntary action with the object of holding the breath), the current of air, which has in this manner been interrupted, is suddenly resumed. The noise thus produced consists of two elements, which we must be careful to distinguish. The first, namely, is a clicking sound, and the other an explosive sound, somewhat resembling a slight report. Into the origin of the latter element we need not here inquire. The "report" with which the sudden expansion of a compressed mass of air is connected has long been a well-known phenomenon. The former, however, the clicking element, we must discuss more closely. When two contiguous bodies are suddenly separated, the outer air will rush in from all sides to fill up the space thus produced between the two bodies. In dry bodies, which even when in contact always leave a small intermediary space through which the air may pass, this separation may be accomplished without any perceptible sound. It is different, however, in objects which, united by a slightly fluid substance, exhibit a strong mutual adhesion, or, if we may use the term, attachment; in this case the adhesion will resist the separating force till the latter has become strong enough to overcome it. The moment the adhesion ceases, the separation, on account of the greater force employed, takes place so suddenly that the air rushes in from all sides with such rapidity that the masses of air thus brought into collision strike against each other with a clear tone. Thus if the tongue, which has previously been pressed against the hard palate, is suddenly released from this position, a very loud tone of this description is produced, which is commonly called "clicking." A similar tone may be observed upon a sudden separation of the lips, if they have been moistened and tightly pressed together, and even the finger-tips, if moistened, will upon separation give rise to a similar sound. We cannot be mistaken, therefore, in saying that a sudden removal of the arytenoid cartilage and the vocal chord of the one side from the corresponding parts of the other side must also be connected with a similar clicking sound, as all the conditions for its production are present. In the *groan*, therefore, we recognize a noise which is composed of an explosive noise and a clicking noise. It cannot, however, be denied that the latter element plays but a very small part in the noise of groaning, and that it can scarcely be experimentally demonstrated. It appeared, however, not to be without interest to employ this opportunity to show that the peculiarities of the explosive sound which can be produced by the organs of speech not only correspond with the report of a pop-gun, but also comprise the clicking element described above.

It should further be remarked, in connection with what has been said above, that different noises are found to accompany the modifications of the respiratory mechanism (sneezing, coughing, hiccough, etc.) discussed in a previous section. As, however, they are connected with other than the normal relations of the respiratory movements, they cannot be taken into consideration here.

We have in this section become acquainted with three species of noise produced by the organs of speech: panting, snoring, and groaning. The subject is one of great interest, inasmuch as we find each to arise in a different manner.

In panting, a rapid current of air passes through the open air-passages.

In snoring, the current of air forces its way through a long, narrow opening, and causes, under certain conditions, such a vibration of the walls as to give rise to a series of low, rattling, explosive sounds.

In groaning, the noise is produced by the sudden release of a hitherto confined current of air.

Thus we have become acquainted with three typical forms of noise, and also with a secondary form. If we look more closely we shall find that these are the only possible fundamental forms of noise in the air-passages, and that it is possible voluntarily to call forth the conditions necessary for their production. Therefore, again, noises, developed from these three fundamental forms, are employed as articulate sounds, and we shall see presently that the whole group of the so-called consonants originate in this manner.

The Formation of Tone in the Air-Passages.

The above considerations will have convinced us that the respiratory process may give rise to a variety of noises, and we shall have further obtained an intimation that a certain class of these noises, voluntarily produced, may be the basis of the formation of articulate sounds. In articulate sounds we find, moreover, a second, very important element, which is characteristic of audible speech, namely, *tone*, in a musical sense. We have still, therefore, to discover under what conditions the latter can be produced in the air-passages.

The only condition which we could expect to meet with in the air-passages is the escape of the air through a narrow opening furnished with elastic walls. Now, this condition we find is really fulfilled at four points. Commencing posteriorly, we may enumerate the possible formation of such fissures as follows:—

Between the vocal chords of the larynx.

Between the soft palate and the root of the tongue.

Between the apex of the tongue and the upper row of teeth.

Between the two lips.

Of these four possible formations, that existing between the soft palate and the root of the tongue is scarcely worthy of consideration, for the yielding soft palate is not capable of forming an opening the edges of which are as sharply defined as those necessary for the production of a pure musical sound. A fissure at this point may, indeed, produce vibrations of the soft palate, but on account of the size and want of elasticity of the soft palate they are necessarily ample and irregular, and thus only produce that burring rattling noise which we recognize as an element of snoring.

The sound produced by the fissure between the apex of the tongue and the incisor teeth of the upper jaw is purer and more distinct, and furnishes sounds of undeniable musical value. To produce these, the anterior portion of the tongue, formed into a groove in the middle, must be brought into contact with the anterior portion of the hard palate in such a manner that the point of the tongue lightly covers the entire posterior surface of the incisors to their free extremity. The expelled air thus passes, following the furrow on the back of the tongue, through the fissure between the tip of the tongue and the free extremity of the teeth, and a whistling sound is produced, which becomes higher when the tongue is pressed flatter towards the roof of the mouth, and lower when, by means of a deep furrow along the back of the tongue, the centre line of the tongue is depressed, though at the same time the lateral edges must remain in contact with the palate. This tone, however, exercises but little influence on the formation of speech, because it never attains any power, and also, as we shall presently see, because its position is too forward. It is only employed in "hissing," though also sometimes in a low whistle.

The tone formed by the *lips* owes its origin to the projection of both lips, the lateral portions being at the same time pressed together, so that the air is forced through the middle portion of the lips which have thus been brought into slight contact. In this manner a whistling sound is produced, which becomes higher if the lower jaw is slightly dropped and the tongue raised; lower, on the contrary, when the jaw is dropped still

FORMATION OF TONE.

more and the tongue depressed. Here, again, as in the previous case, the current of air is led by a kind of furrow along the back of the tongue directly to the fissure which is to produce the sound. It is well known that the whistling sound created in this manner may attain very considerable strength, and is also capable of a fair amount of modification as regards height and depth. However, this form is unadapted for speech, because, being produced so far forward, it cannot easily combine with other speech-sounds, and because, from the same reason, it cannot combine with noises, which, as we shall presently show, is of great importance in the formation of articulate sounds. We all know how well, on the contrary, this kind of whistle is adapted to act as a signal, and often assumes the character of a small musical performance.

Of the four above-mentioned possible methods of producing tone, we have now only to consider the last, that, namely, by the *vocal chords of the larynx*, the only one which is adapted for the formation of articulate sounds. Although it will require special demonstration to show how the tones produced by the larynx take part in the formation of articulate sounds, yet a few words are necessary here, if only to explain why the several kinds of true musical tones just discussed cannot be included in the elements of speech. A tone, the origin of which is very forward, is capable of no other modification than that of pitch given in its production. A tone, on the contrary, which is produced far back in the air-passages, such as the tone produced by the larynx, is capable of considerable modification by the resonance of the secondary cavities of the mouth and nose, and has also the power, while the current of air upon which it is carried is passing through the mouth, of mingling with the different noises which may be created in the latter, and both these properties prove to be important elements in the formation of the series of sounds which are employed in speech.

The Larynx as an Apparatus for producing Tone.

Turning our attention again to the minute anatomical description of the larynx which has been given in a previous section, we must now discover how far it may be regarded as an apparatus for producing tone, or, if we prefer the expression, as a musical instrument.

In this respect the most important part of the larynx is formed by the *vocal plates*, which, converging upward in a concave form, cause a local contraction of the upper part of the windpipe; they terminate in edges which pass horizontally from before backwards, and are called the *vocal chords*. Their outer surface is covered in such a manner by the thyro-arytenoid muscle and cellular tissue, that the mucous membrane which lines the windpipe passes outwards in a horizontal direction above the vocal chords, as far as the latter are concerned in the production of tone. The fissure lying between the vocal chords (the *glottis*) is, therefore, really formed by two protuberances projecting on either side, which in a vertical cross-section present a triangular appearance, and are so situated, with their sharp edges in juxtaposition, as to enclose between them the glottis (cf. Fig. 24). From below, therefore, the entrance to the glottis presents the appearance of a wedge; from above, on the contrary, that of a fissure in a level surface. The above only refers to that portion of the edges of the vocal plates which is really employed in the production of tone, to the larger anterior division, namely; for the smaller posterior division into which the arytenoid cartilages are inserted is not free, but is attached as a border of the so-called *glottis respiratoria* to the vertical lateral walls of the superior cavity of the larynx. This difference will be at once understood by a glance at the internal wall of the larynx. We shall there see, namely, that above the line which marks the edge of the vocal plate, in the posterior portion the wall rises smoothly upwards, whilst in front a deep indentation of the lateral wall (the ventricles of Morgagni) leaves the edge of the vocal plate perfectly free.

The substance of the vocal plates is a strong elastic tisue, which may be most aptly compared with india-rubber, and is therefore peculiarly well adapted for being thrown into vibration by a passing current of air. The vocal plates may on this account alone be compared to the reeds of certain musical instruments, which from this fundamental peculiarity are sometimes called " reed-instruments." There is, however, an important difference in these reed-instruments which we must not pass over. The reeds (free vibrators) of the instruments used in music are, namely, thin strips of metal or wood, which, attached merely by a narrow edge, execute oscillations like those of a pendulum, in which the point of attachment may be compared to that of the pendulum. With such reeds the vocal chords cannot be compared, as they differ from them both in material and arrangement. Their material is a soft, elastic membrane, the elasticity of which has no power to assert itself; and in this it differs from the strip of wood or metal, if it is only attached at one end. A membrane of this kind can only become elastic, and be employed for the production of tone, when it is stretched between at least two points. Stretched membranes of this kind are not employed in musical instruments; though we meet with them in children's musical toys, when they are blown upon at the edge that is parallel to their surface. Another instance is the tone produced by blowing upon a leaf or blade of grass held between the lips. Such stretched membranous plates have, again, more resemblance to a stretched string, as they vibrate throughout their entire length between two opposite points; we might almost describe them as membranous strings, and compare their tones, as far as principle is concerned, to the Æolian harp.

The pendular oscillation of a free point characterizes the reed of a musical instrument. If we wish to imitate these peculiarities in a membranous material, we can only do so by fastening an elastic membrane under the necessary tension in such a manner that it shall only offer *one* free edge; as, for example, when stretched over the half of the opening of a tube. When blown upon at right angles to the surface of the membrane, the free edge will perform vibrations the plane of which lies at right angles to the plane of the membrane, and thus far resemble the vibrations of a reed. To what extent the free edge thus attached at either end will at the same time perform vibrations like those of a stretched string, need not here be discussed. On account of their similarity to a reed, membranes when arranged in the above manner are generally termed *membranous reeds*.

The best way to construct such membranous reeds is to place two membranes of this kind opposite each other in such a manner that their free edges shall almost touch; a stream of air driven through the narrow slit thus formed will consequently strike the two membranes simultaneously. For the production of a pure tone we need scarcely say that it is necessary that the material and tension of the two membranes should be perfectly similar. Now, the vocal apparatus of the larynx consists of two membranous reeds attached in the manner described above. It may on this account be successfully imitated in two ways. Firstly, we may so close the opening of a tube with two sheets of indiarubber, the free edges of which lie opposite to each other, so that the slit thus formed between them, which is to represent the glottis, lies across the diameter of the mouth of the tube. Secondly, a thin and tolerably wide indiarubber tubing may be drawn over an open wooden tube, so that about 2–3 cm. (·78–1·17 inch) of the indiarubber tube may extend beyond the wooden one; by gently stretching two diametrically opposite points of the free circumference of the indiarubber tube the latter is drawn into a long narrow opening. The second kind of imitation, from its representation of the wedge-shaped entrance to the tone-producing slit, is the more accurate; the former is, on the contrary, better adapted in every way for experiments upon the laws of the formation of sound by such membranous reeds.

Musical instruments in which durability and precision of tone are required cannot, of course, be prepared from such sheets of indiarubber, or indeed from any kind of elastic membranes. Instruments constructed upon the reed principle are, therefore, provided with the more durable and reliable reeds of metal or wood. Still, however, the elastic membranous reeds offer an advantage which can never be attained by metal or any kind of rigid reed. Every metal, namely, can only produce one tone, and therefore a reed-instrument must be provided with as many reeds as the number of tones to be produced by the whole instrument, an arrangement which may be seen at any time in an harmonium. With a single pair of such membranous elastic reeds a great number of tones may, on the contrary, be produced, as greater tension will occasion higher tones, less tension lower tones. As, therefore, the vocal plates of the larynx are such a pair of membranous elastic reeds, they possess the advantage of being able alone to produce a relatively large numbers of tones regulated merely by the degree of tension into which they are brought by muscular activity. The compass of the scale which the larynx is capable of producing is generally considered to consist of from two to two and a half octaves; more practised individuals may increase it; highly educated singers, indeed, will sometimes have a compass of from two and a half to three octaves; and the celebrated singer Catalini is said to have had at her command a compass of more than three and a half octaves.

Now, in order that the tone-producing current of air may have sufficient influence upon the edges which are to be set in vibration, the slit between the two must be as narrow as possible; in a wider slit a quantity of useless air would pass through. If, then, a tone is to be produced in the larynx, it is especially necessary that the two vocal chords, strictly speaking, should be drawn together as closely as possible. In this mutual advance they are thrown out of the state of rest which characterizes them when placed at a greater distance in the process of breathing, by the two following muscles—the thyro-arytenoid and the lateral crico-arytenoid.

These muscles cause the arytenoid cartilages to rotate in such a manner as to approximate their vocal processes (cf. Fig. 12). Now, since the posterior extremities of the vocal chords are attached to these processes, it follows that they also must be approximated, since at their anterior extremities upon the thyroid cartilage they already are in close juxtaposition. There is, however, a difference in the action of these muscles. The thyro-arytenoid muscle, for instance, from being attached at a higher level to the arytenoid cartilage, draws the upper portion of this cartilage more powerfully forwards and downwards, and the arytenoid cartilage is thus made to rotate in such a manner upon a horizontal axis that its vocal process is pressed downwards. When the glottis, therefore, is adjusted by the activity of the thyro-arytenoid muscle, it lies lower than when the vocal chords are in a state of rest. When, however, the glottis is adjusted by the crico-arytenoid muscle, its position is higher, because this muscle acts upon the muscular processes of the arytenoid cartilage which are situated beyond the cricoid cartilage, and draws them down forwards; the principal portion of the arytenoid cartilage, which is situated within the cricoid cartilage, is thus forced to rise, and the glottis so adjusted consequently lies higher (cf. Figs. 15 and 16). It should, however, be remembered that this change in position does not affect the whole of the glottis, but only the posterior portion, the anterior attachment of the vocal chords with the thyroid cartilage representing a fixed point, at least as regards the effect of the movement of the arytenoid cartilage upon the vocal chords. It would thus be more correct to say the thyro-arytenoid muscle, in adjusting the glottis, gives it such an inclination that its posterior end lies lower than its anterior end; the lateral crico-arytenoid muscle, also employed in the formation of the glottis, causes, on the contrary, a different inclination, raising the posterior extremity higher than the anterior. Whether the above-mentioned peculiarity has any influence upon the tone produced, is uncertain, but such an influence is at least probable, when we find that the positions described must affect the current of air which comes in contact with the vocal chords in two different ways. In the first place, the increased height of the central part of the glottis, which is caused by the lateral crico-arytenoid muscle, must produce a more gradual convergence of the side walls of the lower laryngeal cavity; the current of air can, therefore, glide onwards with little interruption to strike with its full force upon the vocal chords. The position given to the glottis by the thyro-arytenoid muscle must, on the contrary, produce a more rapid convergence of the side walls of the lower laryngeal cavity, because the centre of the glottis lies at a lower level, and the effect of the current of air must, therefore, be partly expended upon the side walls before it reaches the vocal chords in which they terminate (cf. Fig. 21). In the second place, the current of air rising vertically through the windpipe will traverse the plane of the vocal chords in a direction which will differ with the position of the latter. If we represent this ascending current of air by a line drawn upwards to the centre of the glottis, we shall find that this line forms, when the thyro-arytenoid muscle is in action, an acute angle with the anterior half of the glottis, but, when the lateral crico-arytenoid is in action, an obtuse one. It seems scarcely probable that such differences in the direction in which the current of air strikes the vocal chords can be without influence upon the tone produced.

The mere adjustment of the glottis is not, however, sufficient to give the vocal chords the power of producing tone; the air ascending the windpipe must be forced to pass through the glottis, arranged in such a manner that the current may strike against the vocal chords with its full strength; and, to ensure this end, all side passages, by means of which it could escape the glottis, must be closed. Such a side passage is the *glottis respiratoria*, which is bounded on either side by the arytenoid cartilages, and appears when the vocal chords are under tension as a triangular opening. It is impossible that this opening should be closed directly, but indirectly it is easily accomplished. When, for instance, the vocal processes are approximated, the whole of the anterior edges of the arytenoid cartilages are drawn towards each other, and lie close together, still further supported by the spring-like action of the cartilages of Santorini at their apices; since, moreover, the space between the posterior edges of the arytenoid cartilages is closed by the transverse arytenoid muscle, and by the mucous membrane with which the latter is covered, a cap or lid is thus formed over the *glottis respiratoria* which effectually prevents the escape of the current of air. Again, it is possible that the mutual approximation of the arytenoid cartilages, and perhaps, also, the simultaneous contraction of the transverse arytenoid muscle, may force a fold of the mucous membrane which covers the anterior surface of the latter into the above-mentioned cavity, and so further assist in its closure. We must not overlook the fact that this closure at the same time causes a narrowing of the air-passage from behind forwards, or rather, to speak more correctly, such a shortening of the orifice that the remaining part of the latter, namely, the glottis properly so called, must form a still sharper angle with the windpipe—a circumstance which must have a considerable influence upon the velocity, and consequently upon the force of the current of air passing through the glottis.

In the tone-producing apparatus just described, the windpipe may be considered as the "porte-vent," and the pharynx, with the cavities of the mouth and nose which connect it with the outer air, as the "resonance tube." The tone-producing apparatus of the larynx may, therefore, be described as a *vibrating reed*, with a simple porte-vent and a resonance tube, which, at first simple, is afterwards divided into two, and further possesses the power, by a special adaptation of the soft palate, of directing the current of air either through both portions of the resonance tube, or according to choice through one of the two alone.

The *force of the current of air* which throws the vocal chords into vibration cannot be accurately estimated, as we have no means of calculating its intensity in the moment of passage. We shall, however, be justified in saying that the pressure of the air in the windpipe must be considerably increased at the moment of exit, and that, particularly during speech, the pressure upon the air in the windpipe must be greater, because the opening through which it escapes is confined. It is evident, however, that this pressure does not depend entirely upon the relations just mentioned, but also upon the contractible force of the expiratory muscles. Experience agrees with experiment, and fully justifies this statement.

The force by which, in breathing, the air is driven out of the lungs when the entire glottis is open, consists, as we have already seen, of two elements, namely—

(1) The elastic pressure of the expanded tissue of the lungs.
(2) The activity of the expiratory muscles.

The importance of the first element was established by Donders through the following experiment: he placed in the windpipe of a human corpse a manometer, and then opened the cavities of the chest by an incision between the ribs; the lungs sank immediately from their own elasticity, and the expelled current of air caused the mercury in the manometer to rise 6 mm. (·23 inch = pressure of 80–90 mm., or 3·12–3·51 inches, of water). The lungs were then filled with air through the windpipe to their utmost extent, and again by means of the manometer the force was observed with which the air was driven out through the elasticity of the tissue of the lungs; the manometer registered a pressure of 30 mm. (1·17 inch), or 420 mm. (16·38 inches) of water. These experiments give on the one hand a result higher than the maximum of that pressure which during expiration can be effected by the elasticity of the lungs alone, and, on the other hand, they show that even in the most perfect expiration, such as may be observed in a corpse, there is still a residue of elastic power in the lungs sufficient to support 6 mm. of mercury (or 80–90 mm. of water).

These numerical values are not, however, perfectly true for ordinary respiration, as in inspiration the maximum of expansion for the lungs is not generally attained, and as regards expiration, the air is never expelled from the lungs by elasticity to the extent observed in a corpse, though, on the other hand, it may be more completely expelled in the living subject by muscular exertion.

Valentin, again, experimented upon the force of the expired current of air by allowing several persons to breathe, with the nose closed, upon a manometer (*pneumatometer*) placed in front of the mouth. It appeared that the ordinary easy expiratory stream had a pressure of 4–5 mm. of mercury (·15–·19 inch), or of about 60 mm. (2·3 inches) of water; in more forced breathing, however, a pressure of 10 mm. (·39 inch) of mercury, or 140 mm. (5·76 inches) of water.

The most powerful expiration of a weak person

registered 38 mm. (1·48 inch) of mercury, or 532 mm. (20·75 inches) of water. The effect produced by very powerful lungs was as much as 266, 290, and even 326 mm. of mercury (10·37, 11·46, 12·7 inches), or 3724, 4116, 4564 mm. (136, 160, 172 inches) of water. We find from these experiments that in the ordinary process of breathing, or even when it is slightly forced, we by no means employ the elasticity of the lungs to its full extent, because we do not carry the repletion of the lungs to its maximum. We learn, however, at the same time, that the muscular power employed in the most powerful act of expiration may in strong persons exceed the elastic activity of the lungs by a pressure of from 3000 to 4000 mm. of water. The mean strength of the expired stream of the three persons giving the highest results was equal to a pressure of 4135 mm. Now, if we assume that the preceding inspiration was as deep as possible, we must deduct from this result a pressure of 420 mm. (16·4 inches) of water as the action of the elasticity of the lungs, and we shall then find that a pressure of 3715 mm. (135·8 inches of water) will express the muscular force employed in expiration.

That the pressure of air in the windpipe should be greater during the adjustment of the glottis and the production of a tone is at once obvious upon physical grounds, but cannot, from reasons which are equally clear, be proved by experiment. We must, therefore, be satisfied with the results of the experiments which Cagniard-Latour performed upon a person who had a fistula on the windpipe, *i.e.* an abnormal orifice of the windpipe upon the anterior surface of the throat, such as are made in tracheotomy, as, for example, when a child is suffering from croup. Cagniard-Latour placed a manometer in this fistula, and found—

When a middle note was sung, a pressure of 160 mm. (6·24 inches) of water.

When a higher note was sung with the same force, a pressure of 200 mm. (7·8 inches) of water.

When a loud call was given, a pressure of 945 mm. (36·8 inches) of water.

If we compare these figures with the result of Valentin's experiments, according to which the pressure of the expired current of air in the windpipe during quiet respiration is about 60 mm (2·34 inches) of water, we find that—

(1) During the production of tone, the pressure of air in the windpipe is perceptibly increased.

(2) During the production of higher tones the pressure of air is greater than during the production of lower tones.

(3) It is also greater when a loud shout is given.

In the last case the pressure of the air is, as we see from a comparison of the results, fifteen or sixteen times greater than in tranquil respiration.

The Pitch of Tones.—The tones which can be produced by the vibrating reeds of the larynx, when acted upon by the current of air streaming through the glottis, are capable of considerable variation as regards pitch. The limits between which the human larynx has the power of producing tones is about four octaves, namely, from E to c'''; the greatest limits ever attained are an $F_{\prime}$ of a singer named Fischer, and an f''' of a *prima donna* named Sessi, a distance therefore of five octaves. A single larynx is never, however, in possession of such a compass; indeed, it becomes remarkable if it exceeds two or two and a half octaves. Three or three and a half octaves, as the compass of a single individual, is regarded in the history of music as an extraordinary occurrence. Every person has

his own compass somewhere in the scale of four octaves;
moreover, the various compasses have been arranged in
four classes, into which the individual compasses fall
according to their places in the scale.

The bass voice has a compass from E to f'.
The tenor ,, ,, c to c''.
The alto ,, ,, f to f''.
The soprano ,, ,, c' to c'''.

According to another calculation, the bass voice
extends from D to $f^\sharp$, tenor from c to a', alto from g to e'',
and soprano from c' to a''. In this division, however,
nothing is said of the possibility of an individual compass exceeding the limits of the class to which it belongs
in either an upward or downward direction.

These four classes, moreover, differ not only in the
position which they hold in the possible range of four
octaves, but also in the special quality of tone which is
peculiar to each class of voice, and which may be
referred to the corresponding structure of the larynx.

The difference in the pitch of tones is due in the first
place to the number of vibrations performed by the vocal
chords in a given time; the greater the number of vibrations, the higher is the tone produced. While E is produced by 80 vibrations in the second, 1024 vibrations
are required in the same period to give c'''. Estimated
by the number of vibrations performed by the vocal
chords in a given time, the bass voice may be described
as belonging to that class the tones of which are produced by 80 to 342 vibrations; the tenor in the same
manner is characterized by 128 to 512 vibrations, the
alto by 171 to 684, and the soprano by 256 to 1024
vibrations.

When, therefore, the question is asked by what means
the pitch of a tone is estimated, the answer will clearly

FORMATION OF TONE IN THE LARYNX.

be that the conditions must be discovered under which a greater or less number of vibrations of the tone-producer—in the case of the larynx, the vocal chords—will be created.

It is now known that the pitch of a tone is due to the following causes:—

(1) A stout, firm substance will give a deep tone. Thus the thick, substantial vocal chords are as well adapted to produce a deep tone, as thick strings. This fact cannot, indeed, be verified by direct observation, though at the same time it is supported by universal experience. For instance, when the larynx is affected by catarrh, the voice is perceptibly lower, the explanation of which lies in the fact that under these conditions the mucous membrane covering the vocal chords is swollen, thus increasing their size. The accompanying impure sound (hoarseness, inequality) of the voice is caused by the ill-fitting edges of the glottis, made soft and uneven by the swollen mucous membrane. This peculiarity is particularly striking when permanent catarrh has caused permanent thickening and hardening (induration) of the mucous membrane; the rough bass of a confirmed drinker is due to this cause.

(2) Long strings give deeper tones than shorter ones of the same thickness. Long vocal chords must, therefore, produce deeper tones than shorter chords. The truth of this assertion is shown by the well-known fact that men speak in a lower voice than women, the former as a rule being bass or tenor, the latter alto or soprano. A comparison of the male and female larynx at once explains this peculiarity; we find, namely, that the size of the male larynx greatly exceeds that of the female, especially as regards length, the ratio between the length of the male and female larynx being 3:2. Again, a child, from

the undeveloped state of its larynx, speaks in a high register. At the age of puberty the development of the larynx commences and proceeds somewhat rapidly. The irregularity which is peculiar to the voice at this period is well known, the latter then being familiarly described as "cracking" or "breaking." This period is much less marked in girls than in boys, the fully developed larynx in their case differing relatively but little from the child's—being, in fact, about the size of a boy's before the age of puberty. If the perfect development of an individual is retarded by castration, the larynx will retain its youthful form, and consequently the high register. The knowledge of this fact has given rise to a shameful practice for procuring high voices in choirs.

The two properties just mentioned decide in the first place the height of the register peculiar to the larynx; in addition to this, however, we find a power to produce a certain number of notes of different pitch. We have now to discover the conditions upon which the production of tones of different pitch by a single pair of vocal chords depends. Physical laws would lead us to assume that these conditions must be occasioned by changes in the tension of the vocal chords, and this supposition we shall find confirmed by the experiments which have been made upon the larynx.

Tension of the vocal chords can, however, be attained in two different ways, namely—

(1) By the chords being stretched in the direction of their length, whether this is done at both ends, or at one end only, the other being fixed.

(2) By the action of the current of air, which forces the vocal chords in a direction vertical to their position when at rest.

Direct tension of each vocal chord is produced to

some extent by the mere adjustment of the glottis. Before adjustment the entire vocal chord from the thyroid to the cricoid cartilage forms a straight line; after adjustment, on the contrary, it forms an angle projecting inwards, the apex of which angle lies in the vocal process of the arytenoid cartilage. The line bent thus into an angle must obviously be longer than the straight line; the vocal chord must therefore have been stretched to attain this greater length (cf. Figs. 15 and 16). As, however, the arytenoid cartilage, on account of its want of elasticity, occasions no tension in that part of the vocal chord with which it is in contact, and as the portion of the chord which is situated between the arytenoid and cricoid cartilages (generally called the *crico-arytenoid ligament*) is very short, while that situated between the arytenoid and thyroid cartilages (the vocal chord in the more limited sense, or *thyro-arytenoid ligament*) is considerably longer, it follows that the angle produced by the adjustment must belong principally to the latter division. If we consider further that in adjustment by the *thyro-arytenoid* muscle the vocal process of the arytenoid is at the same time pressed down, and in adjustment by the lateral *crico-arytenoid* muscle is raised, we shall see that there must also be an angle in the vocal chord when viewed from the side, the summit of which will be directed downwards in the first, upwards in the second adjustment (cf. Figs. 15 and 16). The effect upon the tension of the actual vocal chord will be the same in this case as in that of the first-mentioned angle, which is apparent only from above. Thus the mere adjustment of the glottis has some influence upon the tension of the vocal chords, partly through the approximation of the vocal process of the arytenoid cartilages, and partly through their depression or elevation.

The *crico-thyroid* muscle has, however, a more direct influence upon the tension of the vocal chord. In the anatomical description of the larynx it was shown how the thyroid cartilage articulates by its inferior horns with the sides of the cricoid cartilage, and how this attachment permits it both to move forward, and also to rotate upon a horizontal axis passing between the articulations of both sides. It was shown, further, how both these movements must be produced by the *crico-thyroid* muscle, and that they were necessarily accompanied by tension of the vocal chords (cf. Fig. 9). We need not, therefore, say more upon this point, further than to remark that we may in the living subject distinctly recognize the influence of the *crico-thyroid* muscle upon the tension of the vocal chords, and therefore in the production of the higher tones. The depression of the thyroid cartilage, for instance, must cause the lower border of the latter to be approximated to the upper border of the cricoid cartilage. This part of the larynx can, however, be felt through the skin without any difficulty; and if the finger is placed upon the spot while a high note is sung, the described approximation of the two cartilages will be distinctly felt, and we shall be assured that the necessary tension has taken place.

Tension of the vocal chords is also produced by the stretching action of the *thyro-arytenoid* (in some cases the lateral *crico-arytenoid*) and the *crico-thyroid* muscles. The former effects the tension by a pull upon the posterior end of the actual vocal chord, drawing inwards and downwards the vocal process of the arytenoid cartilage. (If the *lateral crico-arytenoid* is the adjusting muscle, then this movement is directed inwards and upwards, the effect as regards tension being the same.) The *crico-thyroid* muscle, on the contrary, occasions tension by stretching the anterior end of the vocal chords, as it draws their point of attachment with the thyroid cartilage forwards and downwards.

The second species of tension experienced by the vocal chords is caused by the current of air which is forced between them. When, for instance, the ascending current presses against the vocal chords, they yield before it and bulge out into a curved line. As, however, the arc is longer than its chord, the vocal chord must necessarily be stretched and drawn out. The stronger the current of air, the greater will be the curvature; and the greater the curvature, the greater also the tension which it occasions; a greater tension, however, also produces a higher tone. Thus we find that the pitch of the tone depends upon the strength of the expiratory pressure, whether this pressure is produced from a feeling of pain, or intentionally for the purpose of creating a higher tone. For this reason the voice of a person speaking in violent anger will often rise suddenly to an exceedingly high pitch; singers, again, are obliged to use such effort in producing forced high notes, that they lose the power of modulation, and are thus very liable to turn the note into a scream. This fact, moreover, considered from different points of view, explains another interesting peculiarity connected with singing. When great pressure is put upon the current of air in the windpipe, it naturally passes out quickly, and the reserve of air is soon exhausted; low notes, therefore, which are produced by a more gentle action upon the vocal chords, can be held longer than those forced high notes.

Now, although the laws described above, which attribute the difference in the pitch of tones to the degree of tension to which the vocal chords are subjected, are in perfect harmony with the first principles of physics, and therefore require no further confirmation, yet it is interesting to find that they have been proved by direct experiment with special reference to the larynx. Johannes Müller, who has won a deserved reputation by his work upon the formation of tone in the larynx, experimented upon a larynx which had been removed from a male subject; he adjusted the glottis by connecting the arytenoid cartilages, and then attached a thread to the thyroid cartilage. By taking the thread over a pulley and fastening a small scale to its free end, he was able, by placing different weights in the scale, to vary the tension of the vocal chords. The tone produced by the various degrees of tension was then tested by blowing in each case upon the vocal chords with as nearly as possible the same force, the precaution being taken to compare the tone answering to each degree of tension with the notes of a piano. It would take too long if we were to give the whole series obtained by Müller in this manner; the following extracts from his experiments must, therefore, suffice:—

"By gradually increasing the weight which held the vocal chords in tension from 7 to 540 grm. ($\frac{1}{4}$–19 oz.), he succeeded in producing the entire series of tones and semitones from $a\sharp$ to $d\sharp'''$.

"When the tension was small, a small increase in the weight (7·3 grm. = ·22 oz.) was sufficient to raise the pitch of the tone a semitone.

"When the tension was greater, the addition required rose to 43 grm. = 1·52 oz."

We shall more readily understand these experiments, and, what is still more essential, the conclusions to be drawn from them, if we compare in a few cases the weights necessary to increase the tension so as to raise the tone one octave.

FORMATION OF TONE IN THE LARYNX.

Tone.	Tension.	Tone.	Tension.	Tone.	Tension.
$a\sharp$	7 grm.	$d\sharp'$	41 grm.	b	15 grm.
$a\sharp'$	88 ,,	$d\sharp''$	142 ,,	b'	95 ,,
$a\sharp''$	325 ,,	$d\sharp'''$	540 ,,	b''	366 ,,

If, on the other hand, we compare the degrees of tension and their results, we find that a gradual increase in the weight from 7 to 277 grm. will raise the pitch of the tone from $a\sharp$ to a'', but beyond that a further addition of 263 to 540 grm. will only raise the pitch to $d\sharp'''$.

Müller then reversed the process; that is to say, attached the scale and its weights in such a manner as to draw the thyroid cartilages backwards and so relax the vocal chords; in this manner he was able, by gradual relaxation of the vocal chords obtained by increasing the weight from 4 to 56 grm., with a constant pressure of air to lower the note from $d\sharp'$ to B.

Thus, by merely altering the tension of the same pair of vocal chords, he was able, with a constant pressure of air, to obtain a compass of more than three octaves, from B to $d\sharp'''$.

Müller further succeeded in showing by direct experiment the influence exercised by a variation in the *force* of the pressure of air. He again adjusted a larynx in the manner described above, and while maintaining the same degree of tension, varied the force of the pressure of air. In three experiments which he carried out upon this principle, gradually blowing more strongly upon the vocal chords the tension of which remained constant, he succeeded in raising the pitch of the tone produced from $d\sharp$ to a, from g to $c\sharp'$, and from g' to e''; he was able, therefore, counting semitones, to force out from six to nine tones above that which was characteristic of the tension under ordinary circumstances. He further remarked particularly that the quality of such forced tones was greatly inferior to that of tones of the same pitch, produced entirely by direct tension of the vocal chords, and this was especially true of those tones which, where the tension of the vocal chords was at its maximum, could be forced out by increasing the pressure of air; he describes them as unmusical and screaming.

According to the laws of physics a difference in the length of the porte-vent, or the resonance tube, or both, should, through the resonance which is inherent to them, exercise an influence upon the pitch of a tone; this, however, cannot be proved in the human organ of speech. There is, indeed, a fact which directly contradicts this theory, namely, that when high tones are produced the larynx rises, thus lengthening the porte-vent, or the windpipe, while theoretically we should consider the lengthening of the porte-vent as one of the conditions for the production of low tones. This seeming contradiction is, however, explained when we remember that the walls of those parts adjoining the larynx, as porte-vent and resonance tube, are too soft and yielding for their resonance to have any perceptible effect upon the remarkably powerful tone of the vocal chords.

Chest and Head Notes.—The notes which the human voice is capable of producing are of two kinds, and so are generally divided into chest and head notes (*falsetto*). The latter, as a rule, have a higher pitch, but both are further characterized by a peculiar quality. Now, as the formation of the tones employed in speech must be primarily referred to the vocal chords in the larynx, we are justified in assuming that the peculiarities in question are caused by different action of the vocal chords during the production of tone. Direct observation upon the living subject is of little assistance in showing how far

FORMATION OF TONE IN THE LARYNX.

we are right in this supposition; as we merely find that chest-notes produce a much greater vibration, particularly of the walls of the chest, while falsetto notes are accompanied by an elevation of the larynx and by a considerable increase of exertion. We are therefore forced to fall back upon experiments upon removed larynxes, and shall have the more confidence in them, as we have already found such experiments to be entirely satisfactory in explaining the production of musical notes by the voice.

From these experiments it appears that chest-notes are always produced when the entire vocal plates are thrown into vibration, and that, on the contrary, head-notes are produced when only the sharp edges of the vocal chords vibrate. This fact may be proved by observing the action of the vocal chords during the production of a tone. The result of these experiments so far has been to show that the vibration which is limited to the extreme edges of the vocal chords arises when, with a somewhat more widely open glottis, the vocal chords are highly stretched, and a strong rush of air then passes rapidly through them which can only cause their edges to vibrate by friction; during the production of chest-notes, on the contrary, the vocal chords are relaxed and their edges lie nearer together, so that the whole of the vocal plates are forced to vibrate like valves. These greater vibrations of the entire vocal plates call forth a corresponding increase in the resonance of the windpipe and its ramifications, which has given rise to the terms "chest-note, chest-voice."

From the manner in which it thus appears that head-notes are produced, it should follow that they require a greater supply of air than chest-notes, the air in the former case passing with greater rapidity through a larger opening; this agrees with the fact that head-notes cannot be held as long as chest-notes, while on the other hand this very agreement is greatly in favour of the view we have taken of the production of head-notes.

The Quality of the Voice.—The tones created in the larynx have, besides their pitch and division into chest and head notes, a peculiar *quality* (*clang*), which characterizes them as tones of the human vocal organs. This quality, like that of all musical instruments, is chiefly dependent upon the structure of the whole apparatus as regards both material and form. Variations in the character of these two factors impart to each individual voice an individual " quality." They, namely, determine the composition of the different resonances, and the manner in which they blend to form the compound tone, which is the cause of the peculiar "quality."

The most important point in connection with this part of the subject is the size and condition of the cartilage of the larynx, if, that is to say, it is in a normal condition, or shows any signs of a change in its texture (such as ossification). It is also of the greatest importance to consider the resonance of the cavities of the windpipe and of the mouth and nose, which, again, depends upon the form of the walls and upon the extent of these cavities. We have already remarked, in passing, the part which the resonance of the air in the windpipe plays in the production of chest-notes, therefore we shall now only draw attention to the fact that the resonance of the air in the cavities of the mouth and nose has a considerable effect upon the quality of a tone; for when both mouth and nose serve as exits for the air, the quality of the tone differs from that produced when either of these orifices are closed. When the mouth is closed we have a nasal quality, which is used intentionally for certain sounds, but sometimes, from habit or from some defect in the palate, a person can use no other, or, as we say, "speaks through his nose." The resonance of these cavities will, moreover, be effected by their size and shape in each particular instance, while even comparatively unimportant circumstances, such, for instance, as the loss of a few double teeth, will have a perceptible effect upon the quality of the voice.

It would be almost impossible to enumerate all the causes upon which this difference in "quality" depends; and such an attempt would, moreover, possess little interest. It is enough to know that herein lie the reasons of the quality of the human voice as such, and of the quality peculiar to each individual.

If we consider, further, that the existence of a particular register depends upon the corresponding formation of the tone-producing apparatus, and that this formation also possesses the conditions necessary for a peculiar quality, we shall see how it is that the four principal registers—bass, tenor, alto, and soprano—not only differ in their position in the scale, but also in the quality which is peculiar to each.

Intensity of Tone; Crescendo and Decrescendo.—The intensity of a tone depends partly upon the forces immediately concerned in its production, partly upon the accessory circumstance of resonance. A loud tone requires a strong pressure of air and healthy vocal chords capable of performing vibrations; with such vocal chords the tone will be louder, in proportion to the force with which the air is expelled by the expiratory muscles, as we have seen from Cagniard-Latour's experiments with the manometer, which for a shout showed a pressure five times greater than that for ordinary singing. The resonance of the air contained in the windpipe and lungs, and of the walls of the chest, the resonance of the air in the cavities of the mouth and nose, and the resonance of the component parts of the larynx and especially of the walls of the air-passages, are all so many means for reinforcing the tone, the intensity of which depends, therefore, upon the degree of perfection to which this resonance can be brought. A spacious thorax, a spacious nasal cavity, and a large larynx, each of course, in a healthy condition, will contribute materially towards the production of powerful tones.

A weak voice is occasioned, on the one hand, by any affection of the mucous membrane which covers the vocal chords (catarrh, for instance), or by muscular weakness which prevents the possibility of a powerful expiration; and, on the other hand, by disease of the lungs, which diminishes their capacity for containing air and producing resonance; and, indeed, by any circumstance which prevents powerful resonance in the above-mentioned parts.

Another interesting question is the possibility of giving a crescendo or decrescendo effect to a tone sustained at the same pitch. We have already seen that the pitch of a tone is primarily dependent upon the tension of the vocal chords, but that with the same degree of tension a slight expiratory effort will produce a low tone, a strong one, on the contrary, a high tone. We know, further, that if a given tone is to become *forte*, the current of air must be increased in strength, and that if, on the contrary, we change it to *piano*, the current must be weakened. The tone should therefore become higher when *forte*, lower when *piano*. As, however, it is possible to pass from *piano* to *forte* without altering the pitch of the tone, there must be some means of correcting the effect of the difference in the strength of the current of air. This counteracting influence can only arise from

FORMATION OF TONE IN THE LARYNX.

the muscles of the larynx, which, as the tones become *forte*, will be relaxed, when it becomes *piano* will, on the contrary, be more highly stretched, so that in both cases the difference in tension will correct the variations which would be caused by the difference in the strength of the current of air.

Let us now glance back, and we shall find that although there are present many conditions which render possible the production of tones (in a strictly musical sense) in the air-passages, yet that of all these the tone-producing power of the larynx is the only one which is fully adapted for the formation of articulate sounds.

In the larynx, moreover, we have a musical apparatus of a peculiar kind, which may, indeed, be generally compared to a vibrating reed, but which differs in many respects from the reeds employed in musical instruments.

The tone is here produced by a moist membrane composed of elastic tissue (the vocal plate), which by means of organic change is always in a condition to produce tone, and therefore does not suffer from continued use, as, for instance, is necessarily the case with the indiarubber plates, by means of which we can construct a musical apparatus upon the same principle. While with the reeds used in musical instruments a separate pipe is necessary for each tone, the material of the vocal chords is such that the vibrating reeds of the larynx can be employed in the creation of a large series of tones, embracing from two to two and a half octaves.

This is rendered possible by the faculty which the portion of the vocal plates principally employed in the production of tone (the vocal chords) possesses of receiving different degrees of tension, partly by the immediate action of muscles which pull them in the direction of their length, and partly by the degree of force with which the current of air is driven against them. These two kinds of tension act simultaneously, so that the absolute degree of tension distinctive of a particular pitch may be caused by a different division of the two forces. Thus it is possible if, as in a note sung *forte*, one force producing the tension (the pressure of air) is too great, by diminishing the other (muscular activity) to maintain an equal tension, and therefore the same pitch.

By varying the action of the vocal chords we are able to obtain two *registers* of musical notes, the *register* of chest-notes and the *register* of head-notes, the latter being somewhat higher than the former.

The resonance in the passages through which the air is supplied (the windpipe, etc.), and in those which carry it away (the cavities of the mouth and nose), corresponding to the porte-vent and resonance tube of a reed-instrument, serve partly to reinforce the tone, and partly to give to it the peculiar quality characteristic of the human voice.

The quality of the voice can be modified by changing the form of the resonance tube, especially the very adaptable cavity of the mouth, in different ways.

The larynx, therefore, in spite of its diminutive size and simple construction, must be regarded as one of the most perfect and comprehensive of musical instruments, and superior in action to any artificial musical instrument.

Another fact is interesting, namely, that the entire larynx, and particularly the space between the vocal chords, merely serves under ordinary circumstances as a free passage for the current of air employed in respiration, and that a single slight muscular action is sufficient to adjust the vocal chords for the production of musical tones, and so to change a free air-passage into an inimitable musical apparatus.

Voice and Speech.

In the last section we showed that the air, in its passage through the breathing apparatus, is capable of producing different sounds, which sometimes assume the character of a noise, sometimes that of a tone (in a restricted sense). We further traced these sounds to their origin, and found that those which are caused by the inspired current of air are not of frequent occurrence, and are rather to be regarded as peculiar and accidental phenomena; those, on the contrary, which are produced by the expired current of air occur more frequently, and are more varied in nature; then, again, they are more easily uttered and sustained because there is less direct muscular activity required for the creation of the expiratory current than for the inspiratory current, expiration being to a certain extent merely an involuntary reaction after the effort of inspiration.

This peculiarity of expiratory sounds is the reason why they are to a great extent employed in the means of communication characteristic of man, that is, in articulate speech. We say to a great extent, for by no means are all sounds employed which can be created by the expiratory current in the above-mentioned manner, but only those which can be easily uttered, and possess the advantage of being easily combined so as to form those combinations of sounds which we call "words." Again, this choice is by no means universally the same or a constant rule for all races of men; very generally speaking, it is true that the same sounds are universally used in the formation of speech; if, however, we look more closely, we find that each race, or even smaller fractions of the human species, offers not inconsiderable differences, arising in some cases from special modification of these primary sounds, in others to a use of particular sounds which are only met with in certain languages or dialects. As an example of the first kind of variation, we may mention the many different pronunciations of the vowel *A*; of the second, the comparatively limited distribution of the English sound *th*. That, moreover, this possibility of easy utterance and easy combination of sounds which we have given above as the motive in their choice is a very relative one, we know from personal experience, when, in learning a foreign language, we have been obliged to master those sounds or modifications of sounds which are peculiar to it. Practice from earliest youth is here, as in so many cases, the only foundation for the term " easy."

The sounds employed in the formation of speech are, however, by no means either pure noises or pure tones; ordinary speech is much rather composed to a great extent of a mixture of noise and tone. In whispering only is tone almost excluded. It is the combination of these two elements in the formation of sound to which is generally applied the term "voice." * Thus the voice represents the "tone-quality" of what is uttered, and we may speak of a voice as being musical, strong, etc. The voice is, therefore, quite independent of speech, and may equally be employed for unintelligible sounds and for most pathetic speech. A singer's fame depends upon his power of modulating his voice, and we all know how

---

* The term "voice" (Stimme) is here used in a different sense to the sense generally applied to it in English phonetics, where it is used for the sound produced by the vibration of the vocal chords. For the latter the author uses *tone* (Ton), which word is retained.—Tr.

seldom a word when sung can be rendered merely as a word without drawing severe criticism upon the singer. We speak, therefore, and with justice, of the voice of birds, etc.

"Speech," on the contrary, is the creation of combinations of sounds, by means of which we render ourselves intelligible, and are able to communicate with others; and, in a wider sense, the combination of separate compound sounds (words) into sentences, etc. The conception of "speech," therefore, infers an intelligible meaning in what is spoken, and is consequently quite independent of the conception of "voice," it being immaterial whether it is uttered in a musical or an unmusical voice. In this sense we talk of a person speaking well, vulgarly or with great enthusiasm, and also use these expressions with regard to written or printed speeches, which shows still more plainly the independence of the conception of "speech" from that of "voice."

It is important that we should be quite clear about the difference between these two conceptions, for they are not always as clearly differentiated as they should be. Thus we often hear the remark that the Italian is a beautiful language, because it has such a musical sound, when evidently only the voice-quality of the Italian language is implied.

Since, therefore, we are now proceeding to consider the elements of speech—that is to say, articulate sounds with reference to their creation and mutual relation—we shall not, after what has been said above upon the choice of articulate sounds, confine ourselves to a single alphabet. We should in that case be as deserving of blame as a person who would attempt to explain the mechanism of walking or grasping from the observation of a single individual. Just as a true demonstration of the movements of walking and grasping depends upon a thorough investigation of each joint of the arm and leg, which will account for every variety of walking and grasping; so for our purpose must we explain every mechanism and apparatus which assist in the formation of articulate sounds, that we may thus become acquainted with the whole range of possible articulate sounds, and distinguish those which are actually in use. We may, however, without in any way injuring our subject, pay particular attention to the more familiar languages of Europe.

Reciprocal Closure of the Cavities of the Mouth and Nose.

Of the two means of exit open to the expiratory current of air, that of the cavity of the nose is, under normal conditions, only employed in the mechanism of respiration. The passage through the cavity of the mouth, though under unusual circumstances also forming a passage for the breath, is, on the contrary, generally employed when the current of air is used for the creation of speech. The cavity of the nose, however, serves also as a passage for the air in certain articulate sounds. We shall, therefore, proceed to examine by what mechanism the current of air is driven through one or other of these passages.

A general explanation is at once given in the peculiar adjustment of the soft palate, which, when at rest, hangs vertically downwards, closing from behind the cavity of the mouth and leaving the entrance to the nasal cavity free; when raised, however, till it lies horizontally, the floor of the nasal cavity is continued to the posterior wall of the pharynx: thus the entrance to it is closed, while that of the cavity of the mouth is left perfectly open. This relation is sufficiently shown by the two views given in Fig. 6. In both, *a* represents the nasal cavity, *b* the cavity of the mouth, *d* the windpipe with the larynx, and *f* the soft palate; in *A* the soft palate is hanging down and closes the cavity of the mouth, in *B* it is raised and closes that of the nose. This sketch, though correct as regards the leading points, is a very rough one, and would require to be much developed and filled in before it could be called a perfect representation. The idea we gain from this figure is far too much that of a door opening at different angles, while the soft palate is a yielding, pliable structure, by which an opening can be closed in many other ways than by that which is alone possible with a rigid board.

There are in the human organism several such valves, so arranged that, under certain relations, they close an otherwise open passage. The principle is the same in all, for each consists of an arched plate or lip, which when effecting the closure does not touch the opposite side with its free edge only, but with a considerable extent of its convex surface. The advantage of this arrangement is that the greater the pressure upon the concave side of the arch the more perfect will be the contact, provided, of course, that the valve cannot go back too far, which in every case we find, from some special provision, to be impossible. The valves in the cavities of the heart and in the veins are provided with an exceedingly simple check, the principle of which is precisely the same as that of the soft palate.

In the anatomical section we compared the soft palate to the blinds of a bay window, the middle one of which is broad and drawn only a little way down, while the narrow side blinds reach to the bottom of the window. The broad middle portion is the soft palate, strictly speaking, and the narrow hanging sides the pillars of the fauces. Now, in each of these three pillars there is a muscle (the *pharyngo-palatine m.*) which draws down the soft palate and thus effects many important changes; but in the question now before us we may undoubtedly regard them as checks of the descriptions mentioned above, which, when the soft palate is employed to close the cavities of the mouth and nose, prevent it from springing back too far.

We must, moreover, examine the two portions into which the soft palate is still further divided if we wish to obtain an accurate acquaintance with its mechanism. These two parts may be termed the upper and the lower part; the former is that which adjoins the posterior border of the hard palate, the latter that which terminates in a free edge. Viewed externally, no division is visible between the parts, but it is shown very plainly in the internal structure by the arrangement of the muscles. Two pairs of muscles enter the soft palate from above in such a manner, that each, consisting of a right and a left hand muscle, forms a loop, the broad summit of which spreads out in the soft palate. One is formed by the *tensor veli* muscle, and belongs specially to the upper part of the soft-palate; the other by the *levator veli*, which, together with the *pharyngo-palatine* of the pillars of the fauces, is chiefly spread throughout the lower part of the soft palate.

The elevation of the soft palate is principally effected by the *tensor palati* muscle, notwithstanding the apparent contradiction offered by the name of the muscle. The form, namely, of this muscle is very peculiar. Springing from the side of the pterygoid processes of the sphenoid bone which skirts the posterior nares, it passes with its tendon through a notch situated at the base of the inner plate of this process into that portion of the soft palate which is contiguous to the posterior border of the hard palate, and there joining the corresponding muscle of the other side, forms the above-mentioned loop. The portion of this loop lying behind the hard palate is only formed of the tendons of both muscles, and indeed in such a manner that they together constitute a broad aponeurosis, the anterior border of which is firmly attached to the posterior border of the hard palate. When now the two *tensor palati* act simultaneously this membrane is pulled obliquely, and so forms a continuation of the arch of the hard palate in the direction of the posterior wall of the pharynx. A horizontal wall of division is thus to a certain extent created between that portion of the nose and the cavity of the mouth adjoining the pharynx, and the most important part of the closure of the nasal cavity to the current of air effected, only a proportionately small gap being left between the posterior wall of the pharynx which lies upon the vertebral column, and the upper portion of the soft palate now stretched into a horizontal position. This gap is filled by the lower portion of the soft palate being drawn into it by the *levator palati* muscle. An arch is thus formed upwards and backwards, resting against the posterior wall of the pharynx, the free edge, which touches more lightly, passing into the pillars of the fauces.

Passavant[*] was the first to show that this mechanism is not the sole agent in the closure of the nasal cavity, but that the posterior wall of the pharynx comes into contact with the elevated soft palate by means of a projecting fold against which the soft palate rests. To understand the cause of this protuberance we must

---

[*] G. Passavant, Ueber die Verschliessung des Schlundes beim Sprechen (Frankfurt a. M., Sauerländer, 1863), und Virchow's Archiv, Bd. XLVI., s. 1-31.

remember that the pharynx is surrounded by three constrictor muscles, each of which may be compared to a loop with a fixed point of attachment. The first and inferior constrictor has its origin in the larynx, the middle one in the hyoid bone, and they both spread out backwards to such an extent as to entirely cover the sides and back of the portion of the pharynx bordered by the larynx and the oral cavity; they are thus peculiarly well adapted to produce a contraction of that portion of the larynx through which the food passes in the act of swallowing, in which consequently they play an important part. The action of the superior constrictor is different. It arises from the posterior margin of the internal pterygoid plate, therefore at the side of the posterior nares, and also from the inner surface of the inferior maxillary bone under the last molar teeth. Between these two points of origin a middle portion may be observed, consisting of fibres which are an immediate continuation of the buccinator. This superior constrictor is very different in construction to the two others, not expanding as it passes backwards, and so enclosing the nasal portion of the pharynx as a band of scarcely 2 cm. (·78 inch) in width. The action should, therefore, only affect this portion of the pharynx, which is really the case, as it draws forwards the above-mentioned protuberance of the posterior wall of the pharynx, almost upon the same level as the base of the nasal cavity, and, because some of its fibres run upwards, at the same time draws it downwards. It is obvious that the raised portion of the soft palate must, by contact with this protuberance, accomplish the closure of the nasal cavity with great precision. We must not, however, forget that with such properties the superior constrictor cannot be considered as a muscle employed in swallowing, but as one of those which form part of the mechanism of speech.

The truth of this assertion may be shown in many ways.

Passavant was able to prove the existence of this protuberance upon the posterior wall of the pharynx by direct observation upon a subject born with such a high palate that the upper part of the pharynx was quite visible. He was even able to take its dimensions; he estimated it as raised from 5–6 mm. (·19–·23 inch) above the surface of the pharyngeal wall, and as from 9–12 mm. (·35–·47 inch) in length. It is remarkable that a fact so important for the investigation of the mechanism of speech should have hitherto met with no further consideration, although it was published as long ago as 1863.

The fact of the perfect closure of the nasal cavity by the soft palate in speech was, after much controversy, first experimentally demonstrated by Czermak.* His experiments prove this closure first in the case of the pure (not nasal) vowels, and then for the consonants, of course with the exception of the resonants (m, n, ng), which are still often regarded as consonants. He first showed that the elevation of the soft palate differed with the utterance of each vowel, the greatest elevation occurring with the vowel i (ee in see), and that the elevation gradually diminished when the vowels were uttered in the following order:—i, u, o, e, a.† This he proved in the following manner. A thin wire was bent twice at right angles in the same plane; to one end a small ball of wax was attached, and the wire was then pushed through the nose till the wax ball lay upon the

* Ueber das Verhalten des weichen Gaumens beim Hervorbringen der reinen Vocale. (Sitzungsberichte der wiener Akademie — mathematisch-naturwissenschaftliche Klasse —, Bd. XXIV., S. 4. März, 1857.)

† It should be remembered that the vowels mentioned are in every case the German vowels. The English equivalents are—for i, ee in see; e, a in pay; o, o in no; u, oo in $poor$; a, a in $father$.—Tr.

posterior surface of the soft palate; the other end of the wire hung as an indicator before the mouth. The vowels were then uttered in the following order—*a, e, o, u, i*—and the indicator rose for each, attaining the greatest elevation with *i*; the order of the vowels was then reversed, and the indicator gradually sank, till, when *a* was no longer audible, it resumed its former vertical position. He was afterwards * able to make even closer observations. For instance, in a surgical operation conducted by Professor Schuh at Vienna, the face of the patient was so opened that the posterior surface of the soft palate could be seen, and Czermak experimented upon it with Schuh and Brücke. He thus discovered that in uttering the vowel *i* the soft palate was raised to such a height that its posterior (in the act of raising, the upper) surface lay at an angle of about ten degrees above the plane of the floor of the nasal cavity; when *u* was uttered the point at which the soft palate came into contact with the wall of the pharynx lay 6 mm. (·23 inch) lower; for *o* and *e* it fell again 6 mm., and when *a* was uttered there was only a slight elevation in a backward direction of the surface of the soft palate.

Czermak further demonstrated in several ways that the closure, which is effected by the elevated soft palate, is a very complete one. In his first treatise he mentions the following experiment upon himself. While uttering the vowel *i* he had some water poured through a small tube into the hindermost part of the nasal cavity; this water remained there and did not flow down into the lower part of the pharynx: this was also the case when the vowels *u, o,* and *e* were uttered, the water only entering the pharynx when he uttered the vowel *a*. The

---

* Czermak, Bemerkung über die Bildung einiger Sprachlaute, in: Untersuchungen zur Naturlehre des Menschen und der Thiere (published by Moleschott), V., 1.

closure had, therefore, been sufficient to support the weight of the superincumbent water till the vowel *a* was uttered, when it became too weak to answer that purpose. That, however, there was a closure even in the latter case has been shown by Passavant * in another manner. He repeated Czermak's experiment, using, however, milk instead of water, the advantage being that milk could be more easily seen, by reason of its white colour, when escaping down the pharynx. The result of the experiment was the same as when Czermak tried it. He resorted, however, to another method, to discover whether the escape which accompanied the utterance of the vowel *a* arose from imperfect closure, or from the weight of the fluid forcing open a closure which otherwise would have been perfect. A wire, of the thickness of a strong thread, was bent at right angles, and carefully introduced into the nose till one end could be seen through the open mouth hanging down below the free margin of the soft palate, the other end projecting from the nose. Upon moving the latter, the end hanging down the pharynx could be distinctly seen to move slightly from side to side; when, however, the vowel *a* was uttered it was no longer possible to produce this motion, which shows that the contact between the soft palate and the posterior wall of the pharynx is so perfect when the vowel *a* is uttered that a wire of the thickness of a thread will be held fast. Although the above-mentioned facts are quite sufficient to prove that when the vowels are uttered an air-tight closure of the nasal cavity takes place, still Czermak † did not consider a further experimental proof to be superfluous. For instance, while he was uttering the vowels, he held a mirror or a polished steel blade before

---

* Ueber die Verschliessung des Schlundkopfes, S. 13–14.
† Bemerkungen über die Bildung einiger Sprachlaute, S. 2.

his nose, and found no moisture upon its surface—a sign that no air could have passed through the nasal cavity, which must, therefore, have been entirely isolated from the current of air. This experiment also was tried by Passavant with the same result.

We must not omit to mention that from Passavant's observation it appeared that in some exceptional cases there was a small gap between the soft palate and the wall of the pharynx during the utterance of *a, o, u*, which did not affect the purity of the sounds.

As, however, we are not here discussing the formation of the separate articulate sounds, but merely the laws for the isolation of the nasal cavity during the production of pure oral sounds, we need not at present extend our remarks beyond the general laws just laid down for the vowels. Still it is a fact too important to be omitted that Czermak, and after him Passavant, have shown that there is the same isolation of the nasal cavity for the oral consonants.

We are, therefore, perfectly justified in saying *that during the production of all pure oral sounds, whether vowels or consonants, the nasal cavity is entirely shut off from the expiratory current of air.*

These facts would lead us to expect a similar exclusion of the mouth from the current of air during the production of nasal sounds, and this we shall find to be the case. The nasal sounds which are employed in ordinary speech are the nasal modifications of the vowels so general in French and German, and the so-called resonants, *m, n, ng*, or semi-vowels, as they have been termed. Now, as the soft palate, when at rest, hangs down before the posterior opening of the mouth like a valve till it touches the root of the tongue, we have the necessary provision for the isolation of the mouth, and any special apparatus is apparently unnecessary, although we may well imagine that as such nasal sounds only occur occasionally in speech, and since in speech the soft palate is generally raised to effect the closure of the nasal cavity, so, when the mouth is to be isolated for the formation of a single sound, it must be temporarily drawn by some special muscular action into that position which it always assumes when at rest.

There can be no question as to the fact that in nasal sounds the current of air passes through the nasal cavity. The point may be argued, however, whether this isolating closure of the mouth is only effected by a temporary resumption of the state of rest, or whether a special closing action is not rather the cause. Direct observation by looking into the open mouth is impossible, since the mechanism necessary to produce the sounds acts so as to close the aperture of the mouth. The question may, however, be solved in another manner, for besides our knowledge of the theoretical possibility of such actions, it is possible to make observations upon ourselves and to follow them out upon others.

Muscular sensation gives evidence of two movements during the formation of the nasal vowels, namely—
(1) A movement of the soft palate downwards and forwards;
(2) A movement of the tongue backwards and upwards.

The inference to be drawn from these movements is clear; close contact must, for instance, be formed between the soft palate thus drawn down forwards and the tongue drawn towards it backwards, the result of which will be a perfect isolation of the mouth. That such a complete isolation really takes place in the nasal vowels is shown in the well-known defect in a foreigner's pronunciation of the French nasal vowels; for though he pronounces the vowel itself rightly, he adds a *k* to the end of it. Now, as this is an explosive sound formed by the root of the tongue and the soft palate, its appearance here is a proof that contact between these two parts is broken at the end of the vowel, and therefore that such a contact must have existed during the utterance of the vowel. The defect merely arises from this liberation being performed audibly; it is most noticeably in the nasal *a*—as, for instance, " departemank."

Since, however, we are not here considering the formation of the separate articulate sounds, but merely the mechanism employed in the closure of the mouth, we need not enter into the discussion as to whether, and to what extent, such a complete closure of the mouth is necessary in all nasal sounds; we may be satisfied with having ascertained the fact, *that an absolute isolation of the mouth from the expiratory current is possible through special muscular action, and may be regarded as part of the mechanism of speech.*

The Nasal Cavity.

From what has been said in the preceding section, it appears that we have the power of allowing the air which has ascended from the larynx into the pharynx to escape either through the nasal or through the oral cavity, and at the same time it was shown that the course of the current differed with the different articulate sounds.

The nasal cavity is of the two the most simple in construction, being formed of immoveable, rigid walls; its influence on the formation of articulate sounds is, therefore, uniform.

CLOSURE OF THE NASAL CAVITY. 231

The formation of independent noises or tones—that is to say, of any which could be employed as articulate sounds—is rendered impossible by such a construction. The only sounds which a normal nasal cavity is capable of producing are—

(1) A blowing sound, when the current of air is driven through the open nasal cavity with considerable force—a noise generally called snorting.

(2) A hissing sound connected with a more or less pronounced whistling tone; it is produced at the nostrils, and requires that the nostrils should be pressed together so as to leave only a narrow slit, as in blowing the nose.

As, however, the latter sound can only be created with the help of the finger, and the former possesses no value as an articulate sound, they need not occupy our attention any longer.

We can here only consider the air-passage, properly so called, of the nasal cavity, because it alone forms the channel of the current of air. This space may be roughly described as funnel-shaped, and its lower wall (the hard palate) as horizontal in the usual position of the head. The upper wall starts from the posterior nares and rises, following the concavity of the middle turbinated bone, gradually upwards, and is at its anterior extremity about half as high again above the floor of the cavity as it was at the posterior nares. The anterior extremity of the space thus marked out by the middle turbinated bone lies in close proximity to the hollow side of the dorsum of the nose, against which, consequently, the current of air must strike, after which it is forced almost at right angles through the narrow opening of the nostril, through which it finds its way into the open air. A general idea of the form of this cavity may be easily obtained by making a funnel of paper, completely closing the wide end and piercing a small hole immediately below it. The inner wall of each nasal air-passage is formed by the straight septum of the nose, and is therefore also straight; the outer wall, on the contrary, bulges out considerably, so that in a horizontal section the narrowest parts are before and behind, and the widest in the middle (cf. Fig. 31). In this widest part the passage is imperfectly divided into two parts by the so-called lower turbinated bone.

We must, however, observe further that these walls of the air-passage are not perfectly air-tight, but are pierced by canals and orifices leading into side chambers. A narrow slit upon the inner side of the roof between the septum and the free edge of the middle turbinated bone leads into the long narrow space which is lined with the olfactory mucous membrane, and also opens into the hollow side of the dorsum of the nose. Near the posterior nares the spheno-ethmoidal sinus leads to the sphenoidal cells, and the superior ethmoidal fissure (at first united with the spheno-ethmoidal sinus) to the posterior ethmoidal cells. At about the middle of the outer side wall the inferior ethmoidal fissure leads to the anterior ethmoidal cells and to the frontal sinuses. In the same fissure, or separated from it, an aperture leads to the antrum, and behind the back part of the inferior turbinated bone lies the considerable opening of the Eustachian tube, which leads into the tympanum and its side chambers.

Thus the air-passage, with its two narrow openings and intermediate greater width, possesses the general form of a resonator, and there can be no doubt but that it has a corresponding influence, and that the tones with which the air passing through it vibrates are strengthened by its resonance. The larger the nasal cavity the more powerful the resonance, and, consequently, the reinforcement experienced by the tone.

Resonance being the only influence exercised by the nasal cavity upon the formation of articulate sounds, it follows that all nasal sounds—that is to say, all sounds passing through the nasal cavity—must be accompanied by tone, being produced in the larynx and reinforced by resonance in the nasal cavity. In consequence of the peculiarity of the walls of the nasal cavity, it appears that sounds uttered with the nasal resonance, particularly the nasal vowels, are fuller and more ample than the same sounds when strengthened by the resonance of the cavity of the mouth. The general impression of fulness and richness conveyed by the French language arises from its wealth in nasal vowels; and it is for this reason that second-rate tragic actors like to give a nasal resonance to all the vowels in the pathetic speeches of their heroic parts.

We have still to consider whether, and how far, the side chambers of the nose, among which we may include the chamber of the organ of smell, take part in the production of this resonance.

That they do so in a certain indirect manner there can be no doubt. The manner in which they are arranged causes the bony walls enclosing the upper and outer side of the air-passage to be extremely thin, and, moreover, to occupy such a position as to have the air-chamber of the air-passage on one side and the air-chambers of the side chambers, particularly the ethmoidal cells and the antrum, upon the other. Now, since the septum which forms the inner wall of the air-passage is also very thin, it follows that the greater part of the walls of the air-passage are peculiarly well fitted to take up musical vibrations, and thereby to reinforce the resonance. The floor of the nasal cavity, the hard palate, also takes part in this reinforcement, but differs from the other walls in its thin places being little exposed to the surface.

This kind of participation in the resonance of the nasal cavity cannot, however, be claimed for the other side chambers (frontal sinuses and sphenoidal cells), as they lie too far off. However, since these cavities are of some size, and it is, moreover, possible that all these secondary cavities may exercise a common influence upon the importance of the nasal cavity, it will be well to look for a relation to the air-passage of the nasal cavity which will be common to all the secondary cavities. From this point of view it is a remarkable fact that the approach to all these side chambers is free to the returning, but not to the entering, current of air. This curious circumstance has been already alluded to in the anatomical section and explained, as showing that the side chambers must serve to warm the entering air. Without interfering with this view of the value of the side chambers, we may see in this peculiarity an evidence that by this means the air contained in the side chambers is able to take a more direct part in the resonance of the nasal cavity, the easy approach to the side chambers for the returning stream of air rendering it possible for the latter to impart musical vibrations to the air, and also to the walls of the side chambers. It is, however, further possible that the resonance of the nasal cavity may be transmitted to all the bones of the skull, and so find its way to the air of these air-chambers.

The air of the chamber of the organ of smell can, through its narrow connection with the air-passage, come into direct contact with the vibrations of the air contained in the latter. It is not, however, immediately open to the returning current of air.

If, therefore, we attribute this importance to the side chambers we have *in the nasal cavity an exceedingly comprehensive resonance apparatus, the influence of which upon the formation of articulate sounds must necessarily be very important.*

The nasal resonance is an essential and characteristic component of certain articulate sounds, particularly in the languages nearly related to us, of the French nasal vowels and of the so-called resonants, the sounds, namely, which we call *m, n, g.*

Is its participation in the formation of articulate sounds to be limited to this? The difficulty of this question is increased by the impossibility of solving it by direct experiment. We shall, however, see our way more clearly to the answer if we approach the question from another side. The resonance of the cavity of the mouth plays a very important part in the formation of all other articulate sounds, while the air is prevented from directly entering the cavity of the nose. If, therefore, the resonance of the nasal cavity is to take part in the formation of these other articulate sounds, it can only do so by the resonance of the cavity of the mouth being transmitted to the nasal cavity. There can be no doubt as to the possibility of this process, for, on the one hand, the vibrations could be transmitted through the soft palate to the nasal cavity, and, on the other hand, the hard palate which vibrates with the resonance of the mouth may impart its vibrations to the air of the nasal cavity. Should this prove to be the case, a difference will be found between the resonance thus transmitted from the cavity of the mouth to that of the nose and that which occurs when the entire current of air passes through the nose; for in the first case the air present in the nasal cavity is a quiescent layer, in the second a moving current. The relation, therefore, of the nasal cavity must, if it really takes part in the resonance of the cavity of the mouth, be similar to the relation of the side chambers of the nasal cavity to the cavity itself, as they also are filled with a quiescent layer of air, which, separated from the air-passage by thin walls, is thrown into sympathetic vibrations with the resonance produced in the latter.

We shall, therefore, without further hesitation, adopt the view *that the resonance of the nasal cavity also plays a part in the formation of non-nasal articulate sounds;* that, however, it then only appears as a *reinforcement of the resonance of the cavity of the mouth,* and does not assume the specific character which distinguishes nasal sounds.

The directly excited nasal resonance does, however, sometimes play an immediate part in the formation of all articulate sounds, giving to the latter the character to which we apply the term "nasal twang."

The general conception of this mode of speaking is by no means scientifically correct, the ordinary acceptation of the term "nasal twang" embracing every species of pronunciation in which the nasal element asserts itself with undue prominence. It may, however, arise from two different causes; firstly through a stoppage of the nasal cavity, or secondly through insufficient opening of the nasal passage.

The closure of the nasal passage can be accomplished in different ways. After the voluntary closure of the nostrils by pressure with the finger, the most common example is the obstruction of the passage by a foreign body, such as accumulated mucus, polypus, etc. The effect of such a stoppage is twofold. One result is purely mechanical. During certain series of sounds, in which the ascending air cannot escape with sufficient rapidity through the lips, an accumulation is produced at the back of the cavity of the mouth; when the air-passage is in its normal condition this accumulation is not evident, because from the frequent removal of the soft palate in continuous speech the air can easily escape through the nasal cavity. When, however, the means of exit is closed in that direction, the accumulation becomes unpleasantly perceptible, and must be reduced in bulk through the passage of the cavity of the mouth, which causes, however, a temporary obstruction in the flow of speech. Czermak* mentions a very remarkable example in the case of a girl whose soft palate had so grown into the posterior wall of the pharynx that the entrance to the nasal cavity was completely closed. The obstruction of the nasal cavity acts, secondly, upon the pronunciation by altering the resonance, for in the formation of nasal sounds the air is entrapped in a closed space, being in the end obliged also to escape through the cavity of the mouth; the nasal sounds are, therefore, formed imperfectly and falsely. Finally, there is no doubt that the alteration in the form of the cavity has a very considerable modifying influence upon the part taken by the resonance of the nose in that of the mouth. The same disturbance is also produced, though in a less degree, by the partial obstruction of the nasal cavity which is experienced during a "cold in the head" from the swollen condition of the mucous membrane and from its increased secretion.

* Bemerkungen über die Bildung einiger Sprachlaute, in: Untersuchungen zur Naturlehre u. s. w. (published by Moleschott), V., 6.

The improper escape of air through the nasal cavity is most striking in persons suffering from that defect known as "cleft palate," especially when the division is continued into the hard palate. This defect naturally renders a perfect closure of the nasal cavity impossible, and therefore a portion of the air must escape through the nose during the formation of all articulate sounds, thus imparting a nasal intonation to the whole manner of speaking. The escape of air will naturally be especially great in those sounds, the formation of which depends upon a compression of air in the cavity of the mouth; in attempting to form such sounds as, for instance, *b* or *p*, the air may be heard escaping through the nose with a distinct blowing noise. It is evident that a good pronunciation may thus be prevented in many ways; now, however, we are not concerned in examining them more closely.

A nasal twang may be often observed unaccompanied by any such grave defect, though it is always caused by insufficient contact between the soft palate and the posterior wall of the pharynx, a portion of the current of air being thus allowed to escape into the nasal cavity. This imperfect closure may be due to such unimportant causes as a too severe tension of the soft palate, which is prejudicial to its mobility, or swollen tonsils, which impede the elevation of the soft palate; or it may only arise from a bad habit of not raising the soft palate sufficiently —a habit which may be peculiar to an individual, or may extend as a peculiarity in dialect over a considerable area.

It has already been observed that in individual cases the contact between the soft palate and the wall of the pharynx may be somewhat imperfect without being prejudicial to the formation of articulate sounds. That the

CLOSURE OF THE NASAL CAVITY. 239

effect of a very imperfect contact will be a nasal twang is, however, an ascertained fact. It will, therefore, be interesting to know to what extent this contact may be broken without injuring the articulation. The experiments of Passavant* will give us the wished-for information. He first discovered the fact that the soft palate might be removed a certain distance from the posterior wall of the pharynx without interfering with the articulation, but that when once this limit is passed a nasal intonation ensues. He proved this in the following manner:—A thread was, with the help of a small tube, so passed behind the soft palate, that one end protruded through the nostrils and the other through the mouth. When the pure vowels were uttered, the thread was found to be held fast by the soft palate. Both ends of the thread were then pulled, thus removing the soft palate from the wall of the pharynx; the vowels were again uttered, the soft palate being gradually removed from the wall of the pharynx; at first no change was observed, but at a certain point the nasal intonation became suddenly perceptible.

In order to gain more accurate information about this distance, Passavant made the following experiment:—Pieces of indiarubber tubing 5 cm. (1·95 inch) long were placed behind the soft palate in such a manner that when the latter was raised they would be pressed against the posterior wall of the pharynx. For the better adjustment of the tube a thread was fastened at either end, one protruding from the nose, the other from the mouth. The experiment was made with three tubes, the first of which had a sectional area of 3·14 sq. mm. (·0048 sq. inch), the second 12·46 sq. mm., and the third 28·27 sq. mm. The two first tubes produced no differ-

* Ueber die Verschliessung des Schlundes beim Sprechen, S. 15–16.

ence. When the third was adjusted the nasal intonation was observed in a number of consonants, but not in the vowels. Thus the "nasal twang" in this case began to appear with an aperture of, roughly speaking, about 30 sq. mm. (·045 sq. inch).

A case observed by Brücke* shows, moreover, that it is possible for speech to be produced with tolerable purity when the soft palate is entirely wanting. As this was only accomplished with the aid of a special appliance, it cannot, however instructive it may be in itself, have any bearing upon the question before us.

The Cavity of the Mouth.

The cavity of the mouth differs essentially from that of the nose, in its walls being less rigid and its construction more mobile. Except the hard palate and the alveolar processes of the two jaws, the walls are all yielding, and as they are further lined or acted upon by muscles they are extremely mobile, thus enabling the cavity of the mouth to assume a great variety of forms. Still it so far resembles the nasal cavity that it is a cavity which has a low posterior entrance between the soft palate and the root of the tongue, which is still further contracted by the pillars of the fauces on either side, and that anteriorly it has also a narrow opening, while the middle portion is of much greater dimensions. Thus the cavity of the mouth has, like the nasal cavity, the form of a resonator, and the air contained in it is capable of essentially reinforcing sound by resonance. This resonance, however, can never be as strong as that

---

* Nachschrift zu Kudelka's Abhandlung. (Sitzungsberichte der wiener Akademie — mathematisch-naturwissenschaftliche Klasse — Bd. XXVIII., S. 71.)

of the nasal cavity, because its soft walls cannot so readily take it up as the thin, bony walls of the nasal cavity. The influence exercised by the close proximity of the nasal cavity in reinforcing the resonance of the cavity of the mouth has already been discussed.

The shape of the cavity of the mouth, when in its quiescent condition with the jaws closed, may be described as a short oval enclosed by four walls; *i.e.* (1) the floor, (2) the roof formed by the hard palate and the soft palate, and (3) and (4) the two side walls formed by the cheeks.

This form is, moreover, subject to important modifications.

Thus, in the first place, the alveolar processes of the jaws as well as the teeth project far into the cavity just at the boundary between the roof and the side walls, and between the floor and the side walls. They form upon the upper as also upon the lower jaw a parabolic curve, which lies almost parallel with the lateral and anterior periphery of the cavity of the mouth, leaving, however, the back part of the latter free. The hindermost part of the cavity of the mouth is, therefore, uniform, but the greater middle and anterior divisions are separated by the highly projecting alveolar processes and teeth into two spaces, one of which (the *cavum buccarum*, or cavity of the cheeks) is situated between the teeth and the alveolar processes, with their coating of mucous membrane (the gums) on the one side, and the cheeks on the other. The second space (the cavity of the mouth, strictly speaking, or the *oral cavity*) is, on the contrary, bounded by the alveolar processes and teeth of both jaws. When the teeth are closed, there is no communication between the two spaces, except that which still remains between the teeth; both are, however, direct continuations of the posterior undefined division of the cavity of the mouth, and are, therefore, placed in direct communication with each other through the passage to the latter behind the hindermost teeth. The cavity of the cheeks may be roughly divided into two, or rather three parts; firstly into the space between the molar teeth and the cheeks, and secondly into that between the incisors and the lips: the first may be considered as the *cavity of the cheeks* proper, the latter the *cavity of the lips*.

As in the following investigations considerable importance will attach to these divisions, it will be well to mention them again, that the terms used in future may convey a distinct idea of the part intended.

The whole cavity between the soft palate and the lips is called *the cavity of the mouth*.

The undefined back portion of the latter, between the soft palate and the hindermost molar teeth, *the posterior cavity of the mouth*.

The space enclosed by the teeth, the inner cavity of the mouth, or *oral cavity*.

The space between the molar teeth and the cheeks, *the cavity of the cheeks*.

The space between the incisors and the lips, *the cavity of the lips*.

The posterior cavity of the mouth is bordered on either side by the ascending portion of the lower jaw, and by the *internal pterygoid muscle* lining its inner surface. It is, therefore, no wider than the oral cavity, and the transition from its lateral wall to the inner surface of the cheeks is accomplished by a sudden bend outwards between the posterior margin of the ascending portion of the lower jaw and the last molar teeth. The oral cavity follows as a direct continuation of the posterior cavity, while the cavity of the cheeks is situated on either side outside the molar teeth. In front of the oral cavity, and separated from it by the incisors, lies the cavity of the lips. It is worthy of remark, that when the teeth are closed the cavity of the lips is not so entirely separated from the oral cavity as are the cavities of the cheeks; for the molar teeth of the upper jaw close exactly upon those of the lower jaw, shutting off the cavity of the cheeks with great precision; but when the teeth are closed, the incisors, on the contrary, of the upper jaw overlap those of the lower jaw, leaving between the two rows of incisors an almost vertical fissure, which thus connects the oral cavity with the cavity of the lips.

It follows, from the relative positions of the spaces of the cavity of the mouth, that the air passing under the soft palate into the oral cavity passes out through the cavity of the lips, while the cavity of the cheeks merely occupies a lateral position. This fact becomes the more striking when we remember that, before using the cavity of the mouth as an air-passage, the obstruction produced by the overlapping of the incisors is removed by opening the jaws, and that when this is done the cheeks are drawn tightly over the molar teeth, by which means the cavity of the cheeks is either entirely or partially destroyed.

Before investigating the important modifications in the form of the cavity of the mouth caused by the tongue, it will be well to consider the various ways, besides the one just given as typical, in which the cavity of the mouth may be used as an air-passage and their relation to the sounds produced.

The most necessary condition for the adaptation of the cavity of the mouth as an air-passage is that the lips should either be actually opened, or so lightly closed that the stream of air can easily break the contact. We shall presently consider the various noises which may be produced by the air passing through the lips, and need now, therefore, make no further remark on the subject.

It is possible to allow the air to pass only through the passage just described when the teeth are closed, if the cheeks are drawn closely across the molar teeth by the *buccinator muscle*. The air then streams through the slit between the two rows of incisors with a hissing noise.

If the tension of the cheeks is diminished by drawing back the corners of the mouth, the stream of air can also pass through the cavities of the cheeks; and, indeed, the greater portion will follow that course, if a strong expiratory effort drives forward such a mass of air that the oral cavity is filled to excess, and the air which cannot escape through the fissure between the rows of incisors rushes through the outlet afforded by the cavities of the cheeks. A stream of air taking this direction gives rise to a rushing noise in the cheeks, sometimes scarcely perceptible, but which may be very loud when produced by a strong current of air. In the latter form it is employed to mimic violent anger.

When the teeth are separated, the current of air can pass out unhindered. The cavity of the cheeks may at the same time be either destroyed by pressing the cheeks upon the molar teeth, or retained by drawing back the angles of the mouth. In both cases the air passes through with a scarcely perceptible breathing sound, or, if the current is strong, with a louder blowing noise.

If the lips are sufficiently compressed, the cavities of the cheeks may be fully expanded by the expired current of air either with closed or open teeth, and the air can

CLOSURE OF THE CAVITY OF THE MOUTH. 245

only be driven through the narrow aperture of the mouth by the help of the buccinator muscle. No characteristic noises, except those caused by the compression of the lips, are, however, occasioned.

The most important modification in the form of the cavity of the mouth is, however, produced by the elevation of the *tongue* from the floor of the cavity.

It has already been observed in the anatomical section that the chief part of the substance of the tongue consists of a bundle of muscular fibres, which raises the mucous membrane forming the floor of the cavity of the mouth into a long fold from the hyoid bone to the lower jaw. Some of these fibres are quite free, and traverse the tongue partly in a longitudinal, partly in a transverse direction. These muscles have the power of altering the shape of the tongue in a great variety of ways, forcing it to become short and thick, long and thin, or bending it towards either side. The other fibres of the tongue are the terminations of three muscles, with fixed points of origin—the *genio-hyo-glossus*, the *hyo-glossus*, and the *stylo-glossus*—the fibres of which spread out in the substance of the tongue, and mingle with its inherent fibres mentioned above. The action of these muscles serves principally to alter the position of the entire tongue, by drawing it upwards, downwards, forwards, backwards, or to either side; as a secondary action they also influence its outward conformation by strengthening the action of the inherent muscular fibres of the tongue. Again, irrespective of the actions of the muscles just mentioned, the tongue is subject to considerable elevation or depression from the diaphragmatic muscles of the floor of the cavity of the mouth, namely—the *genio-hyoid*, the *stylo-hyoid*, the *mylo-hyoid*, and the *digastric*—through the united action of which it is forced upwards; and from the muscles which draw down the hyoid bone—the *sterno-hyoid*, the *sterno-thyroid*, the *thyro-hyoid*, and the *omo-hyoid*—the combined actions of which draw down the hyoid bone, and with it the floor of the cavity of the mouth.

The body of the tongue lies as a thick fold upon the entire floor of the posterior cavity of the mouth and the oral cavity. The posterior portion, or root, is thinner, and forms the floor of the posterior cavity of the mouth; in the oral cavity it is slightly raised from the floor, standing apparently upon a short, thick stem, somewhat resembling that of a mushroom; the foremost part, or tip, is, on the contrary, much more free and mobile. The hindermost part of the under surface of the free tip is attached to the internal surface of the lower jaw by a small longitudinal fold of the mucous membrane, the *frenum linguæ*, and similar bands, the *glosso-epiglottic ligaments*, unite the root of the tongue with the upper surface of the epiglottis.

When at rest the tongue fills almost the whole space included in the posterior cavity of the mouth and the oral cavity, lying lightly against the teeth on either side, and at least touching the soft palate above, thus leaving only a narrow fissure between its surface and the hard palate. But even in this circumscribed position it can display its extraordinary power of mobility, for with its tip it can touch almost any point of the roof and lateral walls of the oral cavity as well as the fore part of the floor.

It can exercise its mobility most strikingly, however, when the jaws are separated and the mouth opened; for then the tip commands the whole of the cavities of the cheeks and of the lips, and, protruding beyond the lips, can even touch the outer surface of both, and also the skin of the cheeks adjoining the angles of the mouth.

We need not here speak of the influence exercised by the tongue in its variety of shape and position upon the expiratory current passing through the cavity of the mouth, as we shall have to allude to it more fully when discussing the formation of articulate sounds.

For the same reason we shall defer the examination of the posterior closure, effected by the soft palate and the root of the tongue, and the anterior closure by the lips, with their characteristic peculiarities—those, at least, which have not already been mentioned.

The Superior Cavity of the Larynx and the Pharynx.

Having now gained some acquaintance with the cavities of the nose and mouth in regard to their relation to the expired current of air, it remains for us to examine from the same point of view the passage which the air has to ascend when leaving the glottis, before it can enter one of the two cavities, which are of such importance when it is to be employed in the formation of articulate sounds.

We need scarcely say that this course pursued by the the current is first through the superior cavity of the larynx, from which it passes into the pharynx, and thence either into the cavity of the mouth or the nasal cavity.

The general conformation of the *superior cavity of the larynx* is the same as we have noticed in the cavities of the mouth and nose. It is a broad cavity with a narrow entrance, the glottis; and a narrow exit, the pharyngeal opening of the larynx. This is the structure of a resonator. We shall, therefore, be justified in asserting that as soon as a tone is formed in the glottis it is reinforced by the resonance of the superior cavity of the larynx. This space, moreover, is to some extent complicated by the so-called ventricles of the larynx. In the anatomical section these cavities have already been described as pouches situated immediately above either vocal chord in the side wall of the superior larynx; as, moreover, they are called into existence by the tension of the vocal chords, strictly speaking, the effect they produce is to give to the vocal chord a sharp edge, which places it at once in a position to be employed as an apparatus for the production of tone. We must, however, further regard them as air-chambers situated immediately above the vocal chords, and shall give the more importance to this view when we observe that these pouches are greater than is necessary merely for the liberation of the vocal chords. They commence, namely, upon the inner surface of the upper cavity of the larynx as a narrow crevice, perhaps 3 mm. (·117 inch) high, the ends of which are rounded off both behind and before. Within this crevice, however, these cavities are formed in such a manner in the anterior portion of the mucous membrane lining the upper cavity of the larynx, that their upper margin is in front near the thyroid cartilage 10–12 mm. (·39–·47 inch) above the vocal chord, descending backwards till their posterior end rests upon the arch of the vocal chord. The width of these ventricles from within outwards is about 5 mm. (·195 inch). The space enclosed by the ventricles is, therefore, considerable; and when they are fully expanded, the mucous membrane, in the fore part of which they are situated, is so forced into the superior cavity of the larynx that this portion of it is rather narrower, and only attains its full dimensions above the

THE SUPERIOR CAVITY OF THE LARYNX. 249

level of the ventricles. We may well suppose that part of the air ascending from the glottis laden with musical vibrations will be caught in these ventricles, and there produce a reinforcing resonance. This, however, is not all. These ventricles are in direct contact with the mucous membrane; there is, therefore, between them and the cavity of the upper larynx a thin band composed of a fold of mucous membrane, the lower margin of which forms the upper lip of the entrance into the ventricles. This margin is inaptly termed the *superior vocal chord*. Now, when the ventricle is expanded by the stream of air which rushes into it, this band is stretched, and in this condition is exactly fitted to take part in resonance vibrations.

We are, therefore, justified in saying *that we have in the ventricles another reinforcing apparatus which has special reference to the superior cavity of the larynx*, irrespective of its importance as giving free room to the vocal chords. This cannot, indeed, be proved by experiment, several experiments upon the " superior vocal chords " having produced no satisfactory results. We must, therefore, at present be content with the above theoretical deduction.

The *pharyngeal orifice* of the superior cavity of the larynx is almost vertical. The air issuing from it does not, therefore, pass directly upwards, but first strikes against the posterior wall of the lowest portion of the pharynx—that, namely, which is in contact with the vertebral column, following which it necessarily rises upwards. The air is, however, in some measure directed upwards by the conformation of the pharyngeal orifice of the larynx. This orifice is widest at its upper end, which lies at some distance from the vertebral column, the sides being there pushed apart by the epiglottis. The greater part of the current of air will, therefore, escape through this upper portion, and necessarily take an upward direction—the more so as the inferior surface of the epiglottis is concave from side to side, and its free margin curved forwards. These peculiarities give to the current of air issuing from the pharyngeal orifice of the superior cavity of the larynx a more upward direction than from the position of this orifice we should be led to expect.

If the soft palate is depressed, the current of air strikes the base of the skull at the arched roof of the pharynx and then passes into the nasal cavity.

If, on the other hand, the soft palate is raised, and the nasal portion of the pharynx consequently cut off, the current of air strikes against the lower surface of the soft palate and passes into the cavity of the mouth.

CHAPTER III.

THE FORMATION OF ARTICULATE SOUNDS.

Articulate Sounds.

If, with our knowledge of the structure of the organs of speech and the physical properties with which they are endowed, we now proceed to inquire into the origin of articulate sounds, we find that our natural impulse is first to seek an explanation of the articulate sounds in general use, and then to find their equivalents in the letters of our alphabet. It has, however, been already observed in the section upon voice and speech that the task is by no means such a simple one, and the way was also indicated by which alone we can obtain a true comprehension of articulate sounds.

If, from the standpoint there taken, we disapproved of any investigation confined to a certain number of articulate sounds as resting upon a wrong foundation, we must here even more emphatically protest against the idea that the letters in our alphabet at all correspond with the number of articulate sounds which we employ. Setting aside altogether differences of dialect, and confining ourselves entirely to the so-called true pronunciation, we find that our alphabet is nothing more than an arbitrary collection of letters, in which, on the one hand, several letters represent the same sound, and on the

THE ORGANS OF SPEECH.

other hand, several sounds which exist as pure elements of speech are not represented at all by a special letter, but must be expressed by a combination of letters, while compound sounds, on the contrary, are given in a single letter. The English and French languages are particularly wanting in this correspondence between articulate sounds and the letters of the alphabet, but even the German language, which in this respect has fewer imperfections, affords sufficient proof of the truth of the remark made above.

Thus in the German alphabet we find two letters which do not represent a simple sound, but stand for a compound one, namely, *x* for *ks* or *gs*, and *z* for *ts* or *ds*.

Again, we find as different letters for the same sound, *k*, *q*, and *c* (before *a*, etc.), *f* and *v*, *i* and *y*.

C before *i*, moreover, represents the same compound sound which is expressed by *z;* in words from other languages *t* has the same peculiarity.

The letters *c*, *q*, *v*, *y*, *x*, and *z* might, therefore, be dispensed with, as there are no articulate sounds which especially correspond to them. If we strike out these letters we have nineteen left, which, however, do not represent all the simple articulate sounds which we make use of, and we are obliged to form combinations of letters for simple articulate sounds. The sound *sch* is only expressed by those three letters, the guttural resonant by *ng*, and by *ch* two different sounds formed between the tongue and the palate, one of which is produced more forwards (as in *ich*), the other being more guttural (as in *ach*).

We might prolong this criticism upon the letters of the alphabet; it would, however, be of little interest, for what has been said will suffice to show that the alphabet cannot be regarded as proportionate to the number and variety of our articulate sounds.

In spite of the incongruities which it is easy to see must be the consequence of this state of things, it is nevertheless the general practice to regard the alphabet as the representative of our store of articulate sounds, and thus we find that in most grammars the alphabet is given instead of an enumeration of articulate sounds.

This error gives rise to a still greater one. It is, for instance, most natural that an effort should be made to divide articulate sounds into a number of groups so as to review them more easily; but in doing so attention has been paid only to the general impression which the sounds corresponding to the different letters make upon the ear, and the sounds are divided into—

(1) Vowels:

a, e, i, o, u.

(2) Consonants:

(*a*) *semivowels*—

liquids: *l, m, n, r.*
spirants: *f, h, j, s, v.*

(*b*) *mutes*—

tenues: *c, k, q, p, t.*
mediæ: *g, b, d.*
aspirates: *ch, ph, th.*

The only reference to the physiological origin of sounds is generally the following division:—

labials: *b, p, ph, f, m, v.*
dentals: *d, t, th, l, n, r, s.*
gutturals: *g, c, k, q, ch, h, j.*

A critical analysis of these two methods of classification, which are those commonly adopted in grammars, would take up much time to no purpose, and may therefore with advantage be passed over.

The physiological method of classification is the only one by which we can obtain, from a general survey, a true insight into the character of articulate sounds. And this may be done in two ways. We may, on the one hand, confine our attention to a certain series of articulate sounds—for instance, those of the German language—and then inquire into the cause of the production of the separate sounds, the influence exerted by the position of the mouth, the tongue, etc., and form categories of such sounds as are produced under the same or similar conditions. The investigation may be extended in this direction by studying the dialectic variations of the various sounds. This manner of dealing with the question undoubtedly tends merely to the explanation of a certain number of sounds without obtaining any satisfactory general point of view. Dialects and foreign languages will, therefore, always offer fresh fields for investigation, and thus it is impossible for the method to attain anything like completeness.

The other method of physiologically classifying articulate sounds is founded upon the means which the so-called organs of speech present for the production of such sounds as may serve for articulate sounds. Its object is as far as possible to assign a place in a previously completed system to every species of sound which can be created by the organs of speech. Like every investigation conducted on the *à priori* principle, it cannot dispense with a knowledge of the relations with which it deals—in this case a knowledge of the articulate sounds really in use, which knowledge, however, merely affords convenient landmarks. The system once perfected, all articulate sounds in use will be found there, or at least may be at once inserted in their proper place.

We shall now endeavour to give the leading features

of such a system, at least so far as it is compatible with our present knowledge.

The Elements of Articulate Sounds.

The articulate sound is not a simple phenomenon, but is composed of various elements, which are intimately blended together into the apparently uniform whole, which we call an articulate sound.

The simple elements are of three kinds, namely—

> Tone,*
> Noise,
> Resonance.

The difference between articulate sounds is partly due to the different degrees in which one of these elements participates in the production of the entire articulate sound, partly to the character or property of that particular element.

Giving a wider significance to the term resonance than it is generally understood to possess, we may assert that with one exception, which will be mentioned presently, *resonance plays a part in the formation of all articulate sounds*. We must now explain and account for this wider significance.

By resonance is generally understood the phenomenon of a second body performing sympathetic vibrations with the body originally made to vibrate. The result is that the sympathetic vibrations of the secondary body produce a special impression upon the organ of hearing. It may follow from the properties of the body performing the secondary vibrations that the effect upon the ear

---

* German, *ton*. The term "tone" is retained for the sound produced by the vibration of the vocal chords instead of the usual English term "voice."—Tr.

will be the same as that produced by the body performing the primary vibrations, in which case they will blend to form a single impression, the former merely reinforcing the latter. It may, however, happen that the body performing the secondary vibrations is unable to reproduce the primary vibrations perfectly, and then its vibrations make a different impression upon the ear. We need not, however, inquire more closely into these peculiarities, as they do not immediately concern the question before us. The impression upon the ear produced by vibrations assumes the character of a *tone* (musical sound) when the vibrations are regular or synchronous, and when a sufficient number of separate vibrations take place in a given interval. If either of these conditions is not fulfilled, the impression of *noise* is made upon the ear. We generally consider resonance in connection with tones, because the laws by which it is governed here receive the truest development, and because, again, it derives its greatest importance from its connection with tones. We must not, however, overlook the fact that those vibrations which only give rise to noises have the power, as we know from experience, of causing secondary vibrations; at the same time it must be confessed that this species of resonance has not been much investigated. We may, therefore, give a somewhat wider interpretation to the term resonance than it is generally understood to possess, and distinguish between *tone-resonance* and *noise-resonance*.

Articulate sounds will, therefore, fall into one of the three following categories according to the character of their composition from the above-mentioned elements:—
  (1) Tones,
  (2) Noises,
  (3) Mixed sounds, or combinations of tone and noise.

THE FORMATION OF ARTICULATE SOUNDS. 257

The formation of the tone, and also of any particular noise, is always connected with a certain part of the air-passage, and the accompanying resonance is as perceptible in that part of the air-passage which conducts the air to the larynx (the "porte-vent") as in that which carries it off (the resonance tube).

It has already been shown at what parts of the air-passage the production of true tones is possible, and at the same time it was observed that only those tones which, among the possible methods of production, are produced in the larynx, can be employed for the formation of articulate sounds. The character of the laryngeal tone, except as regards its division into chest and falsetto notes, is always the same, for differences in pitch and intensity are of no consequence when it is considered merely as a tone; but when the tone produced in the larynx, carried onwards by the current of air, is accompanied by different kinds of resonance, it becomes so changed that it can give rise to a whole series of articulate sounds. This modifying resonance, however, as has been already shown, is effected both by the cavity of the mouth and the nasal cavity, and thus the tone-sounds may be still further divided into—

(1) Resonants of the cavity of the mouth, *pure vowels*: *a, e, i, o, u*.

(2) Resonants of the nasal cavity with the mouth open, *nasal vowels*; with the mouth shut, *resonants*: *m, n, ng*.

The last division is founded upon the participation of the cavity of the mouth in the resonance of the nose, when the mouth may either be open, as in the pure vowels, or closed at different points (the lips, teeth, or palate), so that the part of the cavity lying behind the point of closure takes part directly in the resonance.

s

As regards the noises which are created in the air-passages, we have already pointed out the more unusual forms, which, moreover, cannot be employed in the formation of articulate sounds. We have now, therefore, only to consider those which are easily and voluntarily produced, and consequently suitable to be employed as elements of speech.

Now, since every noise caused by a stream of air is due to some obstruction of that current, it is clear that the rigid walls of the nasal cavity offer no facility for the voluntary creation of different noises. We have also seen that the only noise which can be created in a normal nasal cavity is "snorting," which is caused by the friction of a strong rapid current of air against the walls of the nasal cavity.

Thus, in explaining the cause of noises in the air-passages, we need only turn our attention to the larynx and the cavity of the mouth, and perhaps also to the laryngeal and oral portions of the pharynx, for the great mobility of these parts affords every facility for the most varied obstruction to the current of air.

Let us first consider under what conditions a current of air can create a noise in a long, narrow chamber of variable form, and we shall find—

(1) If the cavity, though at one point narrower, is so wide open that the current of air meets with no obstruction of importance, a gentle, quiet current will pass through noiselessly; but when a stronger current is impelled through the cavity with increased rapidity, a fricative noise, due to its friction upon the walls of the cavity, and corresponding in loudness to the force of the current, will be created.

(2) If the cavity is so narrowed at one point that the current of air in passing is very much compressed, the

friction of the air upon this part of the walls produces, with a slight effort, a *rushing* noise, with a stronger effort, a *hissing* noise.

(8) If two opposite parts of the walls are so approximated that they come into slight contact, then, if the surfaces thus brought into contact are large, the current of air will force a passage for itself, and, as long as it continues, will keep this narrow passage open, streaming through it with a hissing noise; this form of noise is undoubtedly merely a modification of the previous one. If, however, one or both of the surfaces in contact are small, and the retreating portion of the wall adjoining the surface in contact is shaped like a lip, then the advancing air will be compressed behind the barrier till it is able to break through it, forcing the valve-like obstruction on one side, and so creating the necessary outlet. As soon as this is done the valve returns by its elasticity to its former position, which it maintains till the pressure of the accumulated air is again great enough to overcome the obstruction, and this process is repeated with great rapidity as long as the current lasts. Whenever the barrier is broken through, the suddenly expanding air rushes outwards with an explosive sound, which is weak if the resistance has been slight, but more audible when it is greater. The rapid succession of these explosions conveys the impression of a *rattling* or *burring* noise. If the intervals between these escapes of air are so small that the vibrations of the obstructing plate follow each other with great rapidity, we have the conditions necessary for the production of a musical sound—as, for instance, is the case in the vocal chords. We are now, however, only investigating the conditions for the creation of *noise*, and need, therefore, say no more on that subject, especially as we have already considered it at some length.

(4) If two opposite portions of the walls are so firmly pressed together that they entirely cut off the current of air, no noise can be produced. But if the two surfaces are suddenly parted, a noise ensues. If the obstruction is merely *removed* without any pressure from the current of air, by separating the surfaces in contact, a *clicking* noise is heard, the origin of which has already been explained in connection with "groaning" in the section upon respiratory noises. If, on the contrary, the pressure of the advancing current of air is so great that it *breaks through* the obstruction, the expansion of the suddenly issuing air gives rise to an *explosive* noise. If the barrier is *raised* while the air is pressing upon it, a noise ensues which is a mixture of the clicking and the explosive elements. When the force of the current of air is considerable, the latter, when weak the former, predominates.

(5) A similar *explosive* noise is created when the air passing through a cavity is suddenly entirely stopped. The cause of this noise is, however, different. It is, namely, the result of the succeeding portion of the current of air striking upon that which has been suddenly checked in its progress, and which, thus brought to a standstill, receives the shock of the air following upon it. The stronger the current of air that has met with this check the greater will be the concussion between the two divisions of air, or, to use a familiar expression, the clapping sound. A distinct effect may also be produced by the contact which takes place between the obstructing portions of the walls. By observing sounds which are formed in this manner—t and p, for instance—we find that this noise, as represented in its full value in the formation of articulate sounds, is accompanied by a slight explosive noise caused by the relaxation of the muscles effecting the closure.

The different noises which have just been described are all employed in the formation of articulate sounds, and form the groundwork of the so-called consonants, with the exception of the sounds *m*, *n*, *ng*, which are generally included among the consonants by grammarians. It will not, however, be possible to give an account of all the consonants which are possible or even in use, but, to make what follows more intelligible in describing the different noises, examples will be taken from the consonants with which we are most familiar. Noises (*strepitus*) fall naturally into two groups from the time of their duration—into those which may be prolonged for some time (*continui*), and into those which are momentary, being merely the result of a sudden action (*repentini*). The two kinds of noises may be further subdivided according to the manner in which they are produced.

The noises employed in the formation of articulate sounds may, therefore, be classified as follows :—

I. *Strepitus continuus*.

  (1) *Str. cont. spirans*.

      Example: *h*, the air passing through the open mouth.

  (2) *Str. cont. stridulus*.

      Example: *ch* (in *ach*, German, or *loch*, Scotch.—Tr.), the air being forced through a narrow opening between the palate and the dorsum of the tongue.

  (3) *Str. cont. vibrans*.

      Example: lingual *r*, when the current of air is driven between the upper incisors and the apex of the tongue, which lies against them.

II. *Strepitus repentinus.*
  (1) *Str. rep. avulsivus.*
      Example: the peculiar clicking noise of the Hottentots produced by suddenly withdrawing the anterior part of the tongue from the hard palate, occasionally employed by us when we suddenly separate the lips to form the whispered *p*.
  (2) *Str. rep. explosivus.*
      Example: *t*, when the current of air breaks through the obstruction formed by the contact of the tongue with the upper incisors; also *p*, when the closure of the lips is suddenly forced by the current of air, as in *pa*.
  (3) *Str. rep. occlusivus.*
      Example: *p*, produced by suddenly closing the mouth during the passage of a current of air, as in *ap*.

The examples given in this classification show that all the noises described above as possible are actually employed in the formation of articulate sounds. Glancing at the list, we see at once that the movements necessary for the production of these noises have that in common that they are based upon the approximation or separation of opposite parts of the air-passages. When, therefore, we come to investigate the various forms which can be assumed in the production of these noises, our aim will be to discover those localities at which the different approximations and separations take place.

The parts which are situated below the tongue need not here be taken into consideration, as the current of air which enters the cavity of the mouth between the pillars of the fauces is carried forwards upon the dorsum of the root of the tongue, and therefore must find its way out along the upper surface of the tongue. Still, when the tongue is raised, thus blocking up the natural path, the current of air is obliged to force its way along the sides of the tongue and pass out between the lower surface of the tongue and the teeth of the lower jaw, and in doing so creates a hissing, fricative noise. This way is, however, not so direct as that along the dorsum of the tongue, and cannot, like the latter, allow the full strength of the current of air to pass, the course being further impeded by the teeth, and especially the teeth of the lower jaw. The current of air which occasionally passes below the tongue cannot, therefore, be of much importance in the formation of articulate sounds; this, however, is not the case with the obstructions alluded to, which have an important effect upon the clearness and distinctness of the utterance, for in the formation of many articulate sounds, especially those in which the front part of the tongue is raised, they produce a division of the current of air. This applies particularly to the incisors of the lower jaw, a want of clearness and decision in the utterance being very noticeable when these teeth are absent.

We shall, therefore, regard the current of air which passes over the tongue as alone adapted to take part in the formation of articulate sounds—a view which is supported by the fact that the tongue in all its relations belongs to the floor of the cavity of the mouth. At the same time, we must not forget that an effect may occasionally be contributed by the escape of the air beneath the tongue.

If now we follow the passage of the air with reference to the localities of possible contraction and expansion, and the effect upon the formation of articulate sounds, we shall have to point out three regions as of special interest from our present point of view, namely—

The larynx,
The oral cavity, and
The cavity of the lips.

We find the larynx adapted for contraction through the two lateral protuberances, the free margins of which constitute the vocal chords. We know that the space between the vocal chords can, on the one hand, be so expanded by muscular action, that, as in ordinary breathing, a gentle current of air can pass through quite noiselessly, and that, on the other hand, by the same means a perfect closure may be effected, so that, for instance, in holding the breath, the exit of the air is entirely suspended. A number of noises are possible from this arrangement. A *strepitus continuus spirans* must ensue when (1) a violent stream of air passes between the glottis opened to its fullest extent, and (2) when the vocal chords are so closely approximated as to offer an obstruction to the current of air, though without affording the conditions necessary for the production of tone. The *strepitus continuus stridulus* is not possible because the surfaces of the vocal chords brought into contact are too narrow, and therefore more adapted for the production of tone; on the other hand, the production of a *strepitus continuus vibrans* is possible when the glottis is adjusted, but not sufficiently so as to produce a tone. As regards the *strepitus repentinus*, we have already shown how both the *strepitus explosivus* and the *strepitus avulsivus* take part in the "groan." It seems probable, however, that the *strepitus avulsivus* can be heard independently, for if the breath is held for some time, and then, without allowing the expiratory current to escape, the closure is destroyed, a slight click is heard, which is most easily explained if we regard it as a *strepitus avulsivus*. A *strepitus occlusivus* also seems possible in the larynx, for if a current of air, especially if toneless,* is allowed to pass through the larynx, and then suddenly stopped, as in holding the breath, a small clapping sound is heard which may be explained in this manner.

In the oral cavity a long surface is presented both by the roof and floor. The two surfaces may be perfectly separated by removing the lower jaw from the upper, and can then again be gradually approximated till the jaws meet. In the formation of noise the greater or less separation of the two surfaces is alone of interest, because the opportunity is there given for a *strepitus continuus spirans*. The modifications of which the cavity of the mouth is capable when the jaws are closed will be considered in the remarks upon the cavity of the mouth. Although the oral cavity as a whole has little influence upon the noises available for speech, yet it acquires great importance from the fact that it is composed of several parts, all of which play a prominent part in the formation of noise.

The roof of the oral cavity consists of three parts—the soft palate, the hard palate, and the alveolar process with the teeth. In considering the third division, we may confine our attention to the incisor teeth and the corresponding portion of the alveolar process, as they alone lie in the direct path of the current of air. The molar teeth, and the part of the alveolar process into which they are inserted, may be regarded as the lateral parts of the hard palate. Opposite to these parts we have, indeed, only the tongue, which, however, from the wonderful power it possesses of changing both form and

* German, *tonlos*, unaccompanied by tone; the general term in English is "unvocal," "unvoiced."—Tr.

position, may equally well be divided into three parts, which will correspond to those of the roof. The root of the tongue is situated opposite to the soft palate, the middle part of the tongue opposite the hard palate, while the front part (apex) is situated opposite the alveolar process and the teeth. We cannot, of course, assign any distinct boundaries to these three divisions of the tongue—a remark which, moreover, applies equally to the divisions of the roof.

Turning our attention first to the expansions of the oral cavity, we find in the first place, setting aside the general expansion effected by the depression of the lower jaw alluded to above, that in the roof of the back part a local expansion may be produced by the elevation of the soft palate; it has, however, been already observed that the expansion in this case is not of so much importance as the closure of the nasal cavity. But whatever its value in this respect, it is of no assistance in the formation of noise, and need not, therefore, detain us here. This is also the case with the local expansions which can be created by the depression of the entire tongue or of separate parts of the tongue. We may, therefore, at once proceed to the *contractions*.

It is clear that a contraction at any of the three places which can allow of the production of a *strepitus continuus spirans* could have no other effect than to modify the noise generally in the oral cavity. We may, therefore, at once investigate the more complete closures.

The entire length of the tongue may be so approximated to the roof of the oral cavity as to give the conditions necessary for *strepitus continuus stridulus*. The lower jaw must at the same time be widely separated from the upper jaw, and the tongue raised to a great height, almost as in the act of swallowing. The noise created by the stream of air under these circumstances is a rough, blowing sound, which, however, from insufficient opening of the mouth, is not powerful. It is very difficult to obtain the necessary position of the parts in question; the result will be most easily attained with the head bent downwards. There is less difficulty in effecting a closure at one of the three above-mentioned places; each closure, moreover, gives rise to a distinct noise, and these three noises are such important factors of speech that it will be simpler at once to give the corresponding articulate sound, instead of entering into a long description. The *strepitus continuus stridulus* between the root of the tongue and the soft palate, is the sound of *ch* in *ach;* that between the middle of the tongue and the soft palate the sound of *ch* in *ich*;* and that between the apex of the tongue and the alveolar arch the sound of *s*.

A *strepitus continuus vibrans* can only be produced by the posterior and anterior of the three points of closure; in the first case by the margin of the soft palate and the uvula, in the second by the moveable tip of the tongue. Both noises give rise to an *r*. It is further an interesting fact that the membranous character of the soft palate inclines it to vibrate as a whole in the formation of the above-mentioned noise *ach*, which sometimes causes an *r* to intermingle with the *ach*.

As regards the various forms of the *strepitus repentinus*, we find that the *str. rep. avulsivus* may be formed at the three points of closure, the result being the clicking sound. It is produced with the greatest ease by the tip of the tongue and the alveolar portion of the hard palate, being more difficult with the middle of

---

* These two sounds will be explained more fully presently, but to avoid the long description necessary to distinguish them, they will always be referred to as *ach* and *ich*.

the tongue and the hard palate, as modifications arise from the situation of the closure to be broken through; it may, namely, lie between the apex of the tongue and the incisors, or between the apex of the tongue and a more backward part of the hard palate, or between the *lower* surface of the foremost part of the tongue and different parts of the hard palate. The latter modification is characterized by a duller sound. The *str. rep. avulsivus* of the most backward of the three points of closure differs in the manner of its production from those of the anterior points, for here it would appear to be the soft palate that is moved or suddenly detached —a view which is founded partly upon the sensation accompanying the act, and partly upon the fact that the root of the tongue is brought against the more solid and immoveable part of the soft palate. This noise is not easy to make; it may, however, be acquired with a little practice, when the sound will resemble a weak, tolerably clear click.

Whilst the more easily produced clicking sounds are only employed to a very limited extent as articulate sounds (by the Hottentots), although they are often heard as a sort of interjection of doubt or displeasure, the *strepitus repentinus explosivus* has a very wide application in the formation of articulate sounds; it is heard, when formed at the posterior point of closure between the root of the tongue and the soft palate, as a dull *k*, at the middle point as a clear *k*, and at the foremost point between the apex of the tongue and the alveolar portion of the palate, as *t*.

The only point at which the quick, strong muscular action necessary for the production of the *strepitus rep. occlusivus* appears to be possible is the anterior point of closure; it here appears as *t*.

Just as the closure of the oral cavity is effected at three different points, so that of the lips varies in character; and, indeed, here we have four different points of closure: (1) by the contact of the two lips, (2) by the contact of the lower lip with the incisors of the upper jaw, (3) by the contact of the upper lip with the incisors of the lower jaw, (4) by the contact of the tongue with the upper lip. A fifth form, by the contact of the tongue with the lower lip, does not belong to the question before us, as the current of air cannot pass between them.

The wide opening of the lips, which is one of the conditions for the production of a *strepitus continuus spirans*, calls for no particular remark here. It accompanies the depression of the lower jaw in the production of this *strepitus* in the oral cavity, and has, therefore, no special peculiarity. The opening of the lips has undoubtedly a very important effect in the formation of articulate sounds, but not in the department of noises; its influence is asserted in the formation of vowels, and will, therefore, be more fully entered into in connection with the latter.

The *str. cont. stridulus* may be produced in two ways by the lips: either, namely, the air may be allowed to pass between the entire length of the lips, or only between the middle portions. The noise is softer and weaker in the first case than in the second. The *strepitus vibrans*, which it is possible to make between the lips, is, from the size and thickness of the lips, very difficult to produce, and is not so sharp and clear as the vibrating noise of the oral cavity; it is, therefore, never employed as an articulate sound.

All the forms of the *strepitus repentinus* can be produced by the lips, and have already been given as examples; we need not, therefore, allude to them again.

The three other forms of the closure of the lips, when only one lip creates the closure with the opposite row of teeth, or the upper lip with the apex of the tongue, have no special influence upon the formation of noise, and only differ from the closure formed by both lips in the sound being less full and characteristic.

The noises formed in the air-passages may, therefore, be classified according to the localities in which they are produced, as—

  I. *Strepitus laryngeus*
      produced in the glottis.
 II. *Strepitus oralis*
      produced in the oral cavity,
  (1) *strepitus oralis* strictly speaking
      the entire oral cavity taking part,
  (2) *strepitus gutturalis*
      between the root of the tongue and the soft palate,
  (3) *strepitus palatinus*
      between the middle of the tongue and the hard palate,
  (4) *strepitus dentalis*
      between the apex of the tongue and the alveolar part of the palate corresponding to the incisors.
III. *Strepitus labialis*
  (1) *strepitus labialis* strictly speaking
      between the two lips,
  (2) and (3) two forms of the *strepitus dento-labialis*
      between one lip and the opposite incisors,
  (4) *strepitus linguo-labialis*
      between the apex of the tongue and the upper

THE FORMATION OF ARTICULATE SOUNDS. 271

lip; partially replacing the *strepitus dentalis* when the upper incisors are absent.

We have already shown which of the noises enumerated above can be produced at these different places. The number of noises which are possible in the air-passages by voluntary muscular activity is, therefore, very considerable, and they appear in great variety even after those have been set aside which are not adapted for the formation of articulate sounds.

We are now in a position to point out the elements which give a distinctive character to the different articulate sounds.

At the commencement of this chapter we showed that a well-defined group is formed by a number of sounds, which we distinguished as "tone-sounds" (musical sounds, tones), because they are merely a laryngeal tone, modified by different forms of resonance.

We now find that a second category may be formed, from the noises which are voluntarily created in the air-passages. These sounds are those which are generally called consonants by grammarians (with the exception of *m, n, ng*). Some of the consonants are formed only by their distinctive noise, as, for instance, *r* (*strepitus vibrans*), while others may be produced in two ways, either as a pure noise or as a noise mixed with tone; in other words, the current of air passing from the larynx into the other air-passages to produce these noises may be either accompanied by tone or it may be toneless. The consonants formed in this manner by the addition of tone are called soft or *mediæ*, while the corresponding consonants (formed by the same noise) which are not accompanied by tone are known as hard or *tenues*. This difference is most striking in the consonants formed by the *strepitus explosivus*, and has, therefore, been observed even in the letters of the alphabet. We find for the toneless explosive sounds the letters p, t, k, and the corresponding tone-sounds b, d, g. It was formerly thought that the difference between the "hard" and "soft" consonants could be explained by regarding the "hard" consonants as the "soft," with the addition of an aspirate, as expressed in letters: $p = b + h$ or bh. The ground for this view was undoubtedly the same which gave rise to the terms "hard" and "soft," the fact, namely, that the toneless explosive sounds are generally uttered with a greater pressure of air.

We have hitherto only considered the characteristics of speech produced by the ordinary voice. There is, however, another kind of speech, which we call *whispering*.

The general idea of whispering is that it is only a peculiar manner of speaking, the object of which is that it should not be audible at any distance, and therefore stands in direct opposition to loud, far-reaching speech. Softness is at once accepted as the characteristic of whispering, and the only difference recognized is that of intensity. If this were so, the distinction between the two ways of speaking would be no more than that between the *piano* and *forte* production of the same note.

It cannot, however, escape the attention of any one endeavouring to discover the true nature of whispering, that this softness is something auxiliary, and that whispering is distinguished from loud speech by a more specific feature, which is at once its characteristic.

We see, moreover, if we look still more closely, that this specific feature is due to an entire absence of tone; that is to say, in whispering the element of tone is entirely excluded from the formation of articulate sounds. It, is therefore, very generally supposed that if tone is not allowed to take part in the formation of articulate sounds a whisper will be produced, and consequently its elements can only comprise the noises which are employed in loud speech.

This conclusion cannot but strike us as extraordinary when we remember that some of the articulate sounds, the vowels and resonants, namely, are entirely founded upon tone. This class of sounds should, therefore, be entirely absent in whispering; and in addition to this, the "soft" consonants could not be pronounced, or would be replaced by the corresponding "hard" consonants.

Now, it is not only possible to produce all the vowels and resonants in a whisper, but also to mark the difference between the "hard" and "soft" consonants. Undisturbed activity must, therefore, be allowed to those relations by which the laryngeal tone is moulded into those sounds. Thus we find that absence of tone cannot be regarded as the characteristic of whispering, but that we must seek some other element which will so stand in the place of tone as to be equally affected by those modifying influences, and thus perfectly replace it as an element of speech.

This substitute for tone must have its origin in the larynx, or its subsequent fate in the air-passages would not be so entirely analogous to that of the tone produced in the larynx. Brücke* takes the very probable view that in whispering a *noise* is formed in the glottis instead of the tone which constitutes an element of loud speech. This noise is no other than that which has been described above as the *strepitus continuus spirans* of the larynx.

* Grundzüge der Physiologie und Systematik der Sprachlaute (Wien, 1856).

This view, which from the present state of our knowledge seems to have most in its favour, leads us to find the characteristic of whispering in the fact that, the mechanism being in other respects the same, the element of tone in loud speech is replaced by a laryngeal noise.

The Vowels.

By "vowels" we understand those articulate sounds, the basis of which consists of a tone produced in the larynx, and in which, the mouth being open, the sonant current of air passes out either directly through the cavity of the mouth alone, or also through the nasal cavity. They approach in many ways very nearly to the consonants, but the sounds most nearly related to them are *n*, *m*, and *ng*, which, like the vowels, are based upon laryngeal tone, and are only distinguished from the latter by the fact that the mouth being shut the current of air which produces them can only escape through the nasal cavity. From this close relationship with the vowels the three sounds have been excluded from the category of consonants, and formed into a separate group, under the name of "resonants." Although, however, this division is entirely justifiable and well founded, the designation "resonants" is not happily chosen, as it seems to imply that the influence of resonance is characteristic of the conformation of these sounds, while the vowels stand in precisely the same relation and are equally indebted to the influence of resonance for their peculiar conformation.

Moreover, the character of this resonance has even occasioned the division of the vowels into two classes: pure vowels and nasal vowels. The resonance of the cavity of the mouth alone is engaged in the formation of the first group, while both the resonance of the nasal cavity and that of the open mouth together contribute to the formation of the nasal vowels.

In the compound resonance of the nasal vowels, that contributed by the nasal cavity must always be the same, the form of that cavity being invariable. The individuality of the different nasal vowels cannot, therefore, be due to the nasal cavity, but must rather be sought for in the resonance of the cavity of the mouth. It is just this, however, which gives individuality to the pure vowels; they, therefore, must be regarded as the typical vowels of which the nasal vowels are modifications. This view will appear the more correct when we find how comparatively limited is the actual application of the nasal vowels.

The Pure Vowels.

In the formation of the pure vowels the nasal cavity is entirely shut off from the cavity of the mouth by the elevation of the soft palate, and moreover, as we have already shown, the closure is most complete in uttering the vowel *i*, and least so in uttering *a*, the intervening degree following in the succession of *a, e, o, u, i*. Although, however, the strength may vary (that is to say, the pressure of the soft palate upon the posterior wall of the pharynx), the closure is always so perfect that the entire current of air can only escape through the cavity of the mouth.

The resonance tube, through which the current of air has to pass after it has been thrown into musical vibration in the larynx, is so formed that the current of air first traverses the superior cavity of the larynx, and then passes through the laryngeal and oral divisions of the pharynx into the cavity of the mouth, from which it finally escapes between the lips. Thus the path marked out for the current of air is by no means straight, but turns off rapidly above the larynx. Ascending vertically through the glottis, the current of air strikes against the lower surface of the epiglottis, and is consequently deflected backwards, so that, after issuing from the pharyngeal opening of the superior cavity of the larynx, it breaks upon the posterior wall of the pharynx, which it then ascends. If now the soft palate is hanging down, the most direct and natural path that it can follow will be through the nasal cavity; if, however, the nasal portion of the pharynx is cut off by the elevation of the soft palate, the current of air will be conducted along its lower surface into the cavity of the mouth. Thus the soft palate not only cuts off the nasal cavity from the current of air, but turns the latter directly into the cavity of the mouth. It follows, further, that the current of air thus deflected will naturally follow the roof of the cavity of the mouth, and, descending at the back of the upper incisors, will flow outwards past their lower margin, and finally through the lips. Thus the current of air, in passing from the glottis to the lower margin of the incisors and the opening of the mouth, describes a large curve along the intervening surfaces described above; opposite to all these surfaces lies the arched dorsum of the tongue, so that we might almost say the current of air, in following these walls, forms an eddy round the dorsum of the tongue from its root to its apex.

The form of this curved resonance tube may be modified in a variety of ways, and so exercise a marked influence upon the resonance of the tone passing through it. These modifications affect the length as well as the width and internal conformation of the resonance tube. The production of the different vowel-sounds rests entirely upon these relations, for the element of tone contained in vowels is the same for all, and can only vary as regards pitch and intensity, and therefore can in no way affect the vowel-sounds as such.

That the resonance tube, by adding its resonance to the tone passing through it, has the power of giving a vowel character to the sound produced which will vary in accordance with its shape, has been shown by Willis in two series of experiments. He attached a resonance tube to a reed instrument with a vibrating reed, and by altering the length of the tube he succeeded in producing a recognizable imitation of the five typical vowels when the reed was thrown into vibrations; the longest resonance tube gave u, the shortest an i, the other vowels resulting from the intermediate lengths. He also attached to the same instrument a wooden funnel, 15 mm. (·58 inch) deep and 75 mm. (2·9 inches) in diameter, as a resonator, by means of which, when the reed sounded, he again produced the five vowels in a recognizable manner, by pushing forward a wooden slip so as gradually to diminish the size of the mouth of the funnel, the smallest opening corresponding to u. Brücke,* who repeated these experiments, found that the vowels produced by the second method were more distinct than those resulting from the first. Although there was no similarity between the vowel-sounds produced by these methods and those of the human voice, yet they were quite sufficient to prove that on the one hand the length of the resonance tube, and on the other the size of its free opening, has a modifying influence upon the general

* Grundzüge der Physiologie und Systematik der Sprachlaute (Wien, 1856), S. 17.

vowel character imparted to the tone by the tube itself, and therefore that the vowels of speech could be *approximately* imitated. The great difference between the material of such artificial apparatus and the human organs of speech naturally puts *perfect* imitation out of the question.

The resonance tube of the glottis may be lengthened at two points—in its most backward position and in its most forward portion; the length of the cavity of the mouth, from the posterior wall of the pharynx to the incisor teeth, must always remain the same. The posterior portion may be lengthened by depressing the larynx; when the depression is slight it is merely slightly drawn away from the hyoid bone, which remains quiescent; as, however, it can only be moved a very short distance from the hyoid bone to which it is attached, when the depression is greater the hyoid bone, and also the root of the tongue, are obliged to descend with it. The anterior portion, the cavity of the lips, can be lengthened by the protrusion of the lips. The increase in the length of the resonance tube attainable by these means may be as much as 2-3 cm. (·78-1·17 inch). On the other hand, the resonance tube may be shortened by elevating the larynx and pressing the lips upon the incisors, to the extent again of 2-3 cm. The difference between the greatest and shortest length of the resonance tube will, therefore, be about 5 cm. (1·95 inch). Such a difference cannot but have an influence upon the pitch of the tone, as a longer resonance tube always creates a deeper tone; consequently, the tone produced in the glottis being the same, *u*, when the resonance tube is at its greatest length, will sound deeper than *i*, when the tube is at its shortest; thus the deepest notes can only be sung upon *u*, the highest upon *i*. This was particularly striking, as regards the *u*, in the bass of the so-called Jubilee Singers, who some time ago went through Europe; he had to sing his lowest note upon *o* in the words "We are rolling," but distinctly sang "We are ruling."

Although it cannot be denied that the length of the resonance tube has an influence upon the characterization of the different vowel-sounds, yet this influence chiefly effects the speech when it is pure and natural; for, though with some effort, *i* may be uttered with a depressed larynx, and *u* with a raised larynx; the sounds, however, as well as being difficult to create, are less pure and clear.

On the other hand, the different conformation of the interior of the cavity of the mouth is of the greatest importance in the differentiation of the vowels.

If, with the mouth fairly opened by the withdrawal of the lower jaw and the tongue lying quiescent upon the floor of the cavity, a tone is created in the glottis, the sound *a* is heard. This being the most simple conformation of the cavity, *a* is regarded as the fundamental vowel.

The modifications of this simple conformation, which are necessary for the production of the other vowels, can only be effected by raising the tongue from the floor of the cavity of the mouth towards the palate, and by bringing the lower jaw towards the upper, thus generally approximating the floor of the cavity to the palate.

Passing at once to the most extreme positions employed in the formation of vowels, we see directly that the closest approximations of the tongue to the palate must be regarded as examples of this kind of conformation, when at the same time the lower jaw is so depressed as to allow the current of air to pass out freely between the incisors. A general approximation of the dorsum of the tongue cannot take place, because even when the mouth is closed it does not quite touch the hard palate; and, moreover, such a general approximation would not materially affect the conformation of the cavity of the mouth, but merely diminish the size of the aperture. A new and characteristic conformation of the cavity of the mouth is only obtained when part of the tongue is so approximated to the palate that a very narrow passage only is left for the air, while the remaining less elevated portion forms with the corresponding portion of the hard palate a considerable cavity, the resonance of which is of the greatest importance in deciding the character of the vowel-sound.

The simplest form of approximation is that of the anterior portion of the tongue to the alveolar process and the anterior portion of the hard palate, because the mouth may retain the moderate degree of opening characteristic of the formation of the vowel a. The lateral edges of the tongue at the same time are brought against the molar teeth of the upper jaw so that only a narrow passage outwards is left along the dorsum of the tongue, though not so narrow as to occasion a fricative noise. In this position of the tongue a cavity of some size is left between the hinder part of the tongue and the elevated soft palate and posterior wall of the pharynx. If now, with this conformation of the cavity of the mouth, a tone is produced in the glottis, it will receive the character of the vowel i, and this i becomes particularly pure and clear if, when it is uttered, the larynx is raised, and the lips, by the retraction of the angles of the mouth, pressed against the incisors.

If, on the contrary, the posterior part of the tongue is so approximated to the soft palate and posterior wall

THE FORMATION OF ARTICULATE SOUNDS. 281

of the pharynx that a narrow passage only is left for the current of air, though not sufficiently narrow to cause a fricative noise, then the air breaks through this cleft into a large cavity which remains between the anterior portion of the tongue and the corresponding portion of the palate. If, with the mouth in this position, a tone is now produced in the glottis, it will receive the vowel-character u. A clear, good u can, however, only be formed when at the same time the larynx is depressed, and the orifice of the mouth altered in a twofold manner; namely, con-

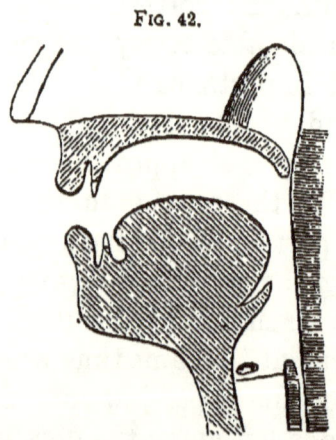

FIG. 42.

Position of the mouth for A.

tracted by the elevation of the lower jaw, and prolonged by the tube-like protrusion of the lips.

We can now understand why the soft palate seems to be most raised when u and i are uttered. Since, in forming u, the current of air must force its way through the narrow space between the tongue and the soft palate, the lateral pressure which it then exercises will force the yielding soft palate upwards; and this is still more the case when, during the formation of i, the exit of the air is hindered in the narrow passage above the anterior portion of the tongue, and it must, therefore, accumulate in the cavity above and behind the root of the tongue. So, again, in *i* the soft palate finds its greatest elevation and its firmest contact with the posterior wall of the pharynx.

Upon comparing these various conformations of the cavity of the mouth with resonators, we find the following characteristics :—

> When *a* (*ah*) is uttered, the cavity of the mouth assumes the form of a large resonator, with a fairly wide inlet, and a very large outlet, which, however, is smaller than the space contained in the cavity of the mouth.

FIG. 43.

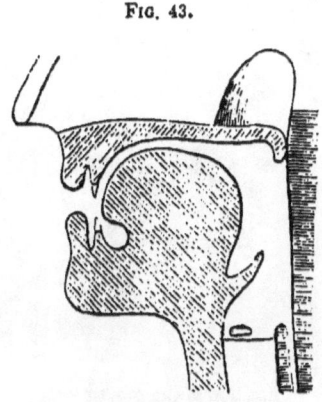

Position of the mouth for *I*.

> When *i* is uttered, the posterior portion of the cavity of the mouth constitutes a smaller resonator, the inlet of which is formed by the orifice of the larynx, and the outlet assumes the form of a long narrow tunnel.

> When *u* is uttered, the anterior portion of the cavity of the mouth forms a small resonator, the inlet to which is a long narrow tunnel, and the outlet more or less contracted.

THE FORMATION OF ARTICULATE SOUNDS. 283

The creation of these three sounds depends entirely upon these conditions, since, if the conditions are fulfilled, the corresponding sounds at once result. These leading features do not, however, fully represent the conformation of the entire air-passage; for, though still giving the first place to those just described, we find several other possible modifications of the air-passages, which are based upon (1) the degree of perfection to which the form of the resonance cavity is carried, (2) the degree of elevation or depression of the larynx, and

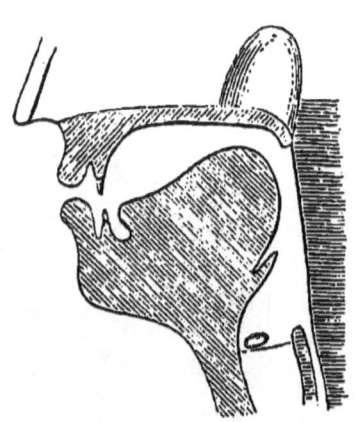

Position of the mouth for *U*.

(3) the different conformation of the orifice of the mouth. Thus the modification of sound produced will vary according as the form of the air-passage is decided by the action of one or more of these factors, and as there can be no limit to the variety of forms thus possible to the air-passage, there is also an equally wide range given for the modification of the three sounds in question, which modifications are partly individual, partly characteristic of certain languages or dialects. We shall presently draw attention to the more important of these

modifications. We have, however, described the conditions under which those modifications arise which ensure the clearest and fullest sound accompanied by the least exertion. To recapitulate briefly, they are—

For *a*, a large orifice to the cavity of the mouth.

For *i*, compression of the lips upon the incisors and elevation of the larynx.

For *u*, tube-like protrusion of the lips and depression of the larynx.

In addition to these three typical positions of the mouth there is a fourth, which in two modifications gives rise to distinctly characterized vowel-sounds. Taking the mouth opened for *a* as a starting-point, we may describe this fourth position as a general contraction of the cavity of the mouth, which is effected by approximating the lower jaw to the upper, and by raising the middle of the dorsum of the tongue towards the palate. The whole of the back of the tongue is thus arched, and runs parallel to the arch of the palate. The cavity, which in this position acts as resonator, is both longer and less capacious. If a tone is produced in the glottis, it will receive from a resonator of this form the vowel-character *e*. This sound is not the clear *e* generally distinguished by this letter, but a dull *e*, often noticed in German dialects; for instance, in the abbreviated form of the infinitive, as *mache, reite,* for *machen, reiten.**
It is called by the French *e fermé*.

The two modifications of this conformation of the cavity of the mouth, which are characterized as giving rise to distinct vowel-sounds, are analogous to the two positions which have been described above as those for *i* and *u*; they are to a certain extent an indication of the latter.

* English equivalents, *a* in *hay* and *e* in *set*.—Tr.

THE FORMATION OF ARTICULATE SOUNDS. 285

In the first modification the tongue is brought more forward, so that the cavity situated between the tongue and the palate is narrower before than behind. This position is similar to that by which *i* is formed, and produces the long, clear *e*. When uttered with perfect purity and clearness, the larynx is slightly raised and the cavity of the lips contracted, though not so much as for *i*.

In the second modification the tongue is drawn more backward, and the apex consequently removed to a greater distance from the incisors. This gives a position

FIG. 45.

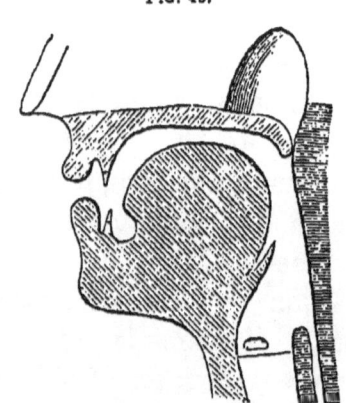

Position of the mouth for *e fermé*.

which is analogous to that for *u*, the posterior half of the cavity being somewhat narrower and the anterior half rather wider. The vowel-character which is thus produced is that of *o*. This *o* will gain in purity and fulness if the larynx is somewhat depressed, and the lips protruded, so as to extend the cavity of the lips, which, however, must not be carried to such an extent as in *u*.

We have so far recognized six different vowel-sounds, each of which is characterized by a special conformation of the cavity of the mouth, *i.e.* of the space between the posterior wall of the pharynx and the incisors. They may be roughly classified as follows :—

    I. The entire cavity of the mouth acting as resonator:
        (1) Wide-open mouth, *a*.
        (2) Half-open mouth, *e fermé*.
    II. Half the cavity of the mouth acting as resonator:
        (1) Anterior half,
            (*a*) Wide open with a narrow inlet, *u*.
            (*b*) Half open with a less narrow inlet, *o*.
        (2) Posterior half,
            (*a*) Wide open with a narrow outlet, *i*.
            (*b*) Half open with a less narrow outlet, *e*.

FIG. 46.

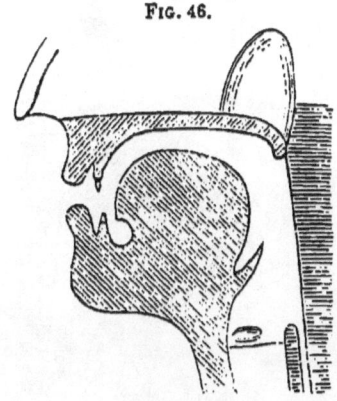

Position of the mouth for the long *E*.

We saw that the vowel-character depends chiefly upon the form of the resonator, but found that, in creating a clear full sound, other secondary conditions must be fulfilled, which consist in variations in the length of the resonance tube; that is to say, of the passage for the current of air from the glottis to the margins of the lips. This increase or decrease in the length of the resonance tube can take place either in the posterior portion of the air-passage—*i.e.* in the division between the vocal chords and the palate—or in the division between the teeth and

THE FORMATION OF ARTICULATE SOUNDS.

the margins of the lips; or, again, in both simultaneously. The sound will be best in the latter case.

The posterior alteration in the length of the resonance tube is effected by the elevation or depression of the larynx. Our observations have shown that in forming full clear vowel-sounds, the ascent of the larynx, beginning with its greatest depression, will correspond with the following succession of vowels:—

u, o, a, e fermé, e, i.

The anterior alteration is effected by the protrusion or retraction of the lips. The several degrees in the

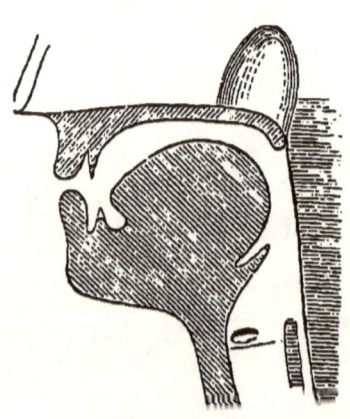

Position of the mouth for *O*.

length of the cavity of the lips, again supposing a full clear sound is to be produced, beginning with the greatest length, correspond to

u, o, a, e fermé, e, i.

We see that the two series of vowels are the same, and thus it appears that a gradual decrease in the length of the resonance tube is necessary for the perfect utterance of those vowels placed in that order.

We have, however, been only studying certain typical forms which are distinguished as being more sharply characterized from the infinite number of possible vowel-sounds. Thus they are susceptible of various modifications, and may therefore be regarded as a foundation for the formation of all possible vowel-sounds. It would be altogether impossible to attempt to mention all the varieties of vowels produced in such a manner, and we must therefore be satisfied with examining the laws upon which these varieties depend. When once these laws are rightly understood, there will be no difficulty, when any new vowel-sound is met with, in recognizing its origin and assigning to it its proper place.

These varieties may, however, arise—
(1) Within the limits of the typical sound itself.
(2) From the transition or mixture of the several types.

For the first class of varieties a single example will suffice, which will further show how necessary it is to distinguish between the primary and secondary conditions necessary for the production of the vowel-sounds mentioned above.

If we only employ the resonance of the cavity of the mouth in uttering an *u*, without either depressing the larynx or protruding the lips, we shall obtain a perfectly distinct *u*, but with no ring in it. If we push forward the lips without depressing the larynx, the *u* will have rather more ring. If we then lower the larynx, the pure full *u* will appear, which we generally regard as the true one. If, with the lips still protruded, we raise the larynx above its ordinary position, we obtain a very clear *u*, which, however, is accompanied by a strong rushing sound; if the lips remain quiescent, not being protruded, the larynx, on the contrary, being depressed, we obtain the English *u* (in *could*), which will be improved if the floor of the cavity of the mouth is still more depressed, thus enlarging the resonance cavity; retaining this increased depression of the floor of the cavity of the mouth, we may raise the larynx above its ordinary position, when we shall obtain a clearer *u*, as it is often heard in English dialectic varieties.

Thus by different combinations of the conditions under which *u* is formed, we obtain no less than six varieties, the greater number of which are in actual use.

The second class of varieties is composed of sounds which have not the pure character of the above-mentioned typical sounds, but partially represent the character of two sounds, thus being intermediate between them.

Such a mixture may arise in two ways: the conformation of the cavity of the mouth may either not agree with any of the types described above, but be intermediate between the conformations belonging to any two types; or the conformation of the cavity of the mouth may be typical, while the secondary conditions either of the conformation of the lips or the position of the lips may not be the true ones, but those corresponding to the formation of another typical sound.

The first of these two categories will be best understood by starting from the position of the mouth serving for *e fermé*. The greatest convexity of the tongue is here so situated that the space between the dorsum of the tongue and the palate are the same in height before and behind that point. If the arch is formed further back, thus approaching to the position for *o*, a dull *oe* results, which will have more of the *o* sound in it the further back the arch of the tongue is removed, and more of the *e* as it has remained nearer to the central position. Both sounds are found in English; for instance, that which approaches to *o* in *but*, and that which resembles *e* in *whet*. If, on the contrary, the convexity of the tongue is brought more forward, so as to approach the position for the pure *e*, the sound gains in clearness, without, however, arriving at the pure *e*. This sound, again, is found in English; for instance, in *yet*.

In the same way we may start from the conformation for *a*, and we shall then find that if the tongue is pushed further back, a different *o* sound mingles with the *a*, which becomes more perceptible as the tongue recedes. This sound is very general. As an *a* with a trace of *o* it appears in the North-German dialects, in Swedish (written *å*), in English (for instance, in *all*, or more nearly in the *a* of *what*); and as an *o* with a trace of *a* in French— for instance, in *encore*. If, on the contrary, the tongue is brought more forward, a broad *ae* is produced, as it is heard, for instance, in the Alemannic dialect; it is also the scornful " Äh ! "

If, when the cavity of the mouth is in the position for *a*, the middle of the tongue is moved towards that for *e fermé*, a dull *ae* is produced, which is often heard in English; as, for instance, in *at*.

In the same way intermediate sounds may be produced between *e* and *i*, and also between *o* and *u*. These series of sounds have not, however, the distinctive character of those mentioned above, but rather appear as dialectic peculiarities of pronunciation; still we may give, as an example of the first intermediate sound, the Alemannic diminutive, which is generally written "*li*," and for the second the Hessian pronunciation of "durch," which has almost the sound of " dorch."

With regard to the second category we may remark, in the first place, that a higher position of the larynx gives a clearer sound to the vowels, and a lower position a duller sound; we can, therefore, by depressing the larynx to the position for *u*, give a dull sound to *i*; and *vice versâ*, if the larynx is raised as it should be for *i*, *u* will be clear.

But that modification of vowel-sounds is more important which is effected by giving a conformation to the cavity of the lips characteristic of a different vowel. The number of intermediate sounds produced in this manner is not very great, but offers much that is interesting.

If, when uttering the pure *e*, the orifice of the mouth is put into the position for *a*, the clear *ae* is heard, as pronounced in German—for instance, in *wählen;* if, on the contrary, the orifice of the mouth is put into the position for *o*, the clear *oe* is heard, also as pronounced in German—for instance, in *Köhler*.

If, in uttering *e*, the orifice of the mouth is shaped as for *u*, the sound *ue* is heard. The sound will, however, be clearer and more distinct if the position for *u* is combined with the utterance of *i*.

The position of the orifice of the mouth for *u* in the utterance of *o* gives to the latter a decided sound of *u*. If, however, we try to combine this position with the utterance of *a*, the result is an unpleasant noise bearing some resemblance to *o*. That a better sound should not be produced under these circumstances is scarcely to be wondered at, as a contraction of the orifice of the mouth must be antagonistic to the character of *a*, which requires the mouth to be widely opened.

The Diphthongs.

By diphthongs we understand a combination of vowel-sounds; but such a combination as will only make a simple impression, or, as we may equally well express it, as shall be monosyllabic. It is often supposed that the character of the diphthong is due to the rapid utterance of the two vowels of which it is composed. This cannot, however, be the right view, for if such were the case any combination of two vowels might become a diphthong, as there is no difficulty in quickly pronouncing any succession of vowels. Yet however quickly the Italian *flauto*, for instance, is pronounced, the diphthong *au* is never heard, but always *fla-u-to* (*trisyllabic*), although in poetry *flau* may be used as a single syllable. The true character of the diphthong must, therefore, be traced to other causes. What these causes are will appear when we have discovered in what way the vowel-combinations constituting real diphthongs are distinguished from other combinations.

In the first place, it must be observed that the two vowel-sounds forming a true diphthong are never of the same value. One of the two is always distinguished by its richer sound and stronger accent. This peculiarity is most striking in cases where the same diphthong is differently pronounced, at one time the first vowel and at another the second predominating in the manner described. An interesting example of this fact is afforded by the different pronunciations of *au* and *ei* which are to be observed in the Swabian dialect. In *Frau*, for instance, the *a* predominates, but in *Maus* the *u;* and thus, again, in *theilen* the *e* predominates (or rather the *a*, as if it were written *thailen*), and in *treiben* the *i*. That we have here a real fundamental difference is shown by the fact that the diphthongs having this distinction suffer a different fate in the various dialects; for instance, the *au* in *Frau* further north, in the Hessian dialect, becomes *a* (*fraa*), but remains unaltered in the Alemannic dialect; on the other hand, the *au* in *Maus* is changed in the Alemannic dialect to an *u* (*Muus*), and remains unaltered in the Hessian dialect; in the same manner *theilen* in the Hessian dialect becomes *thälen*, and *treiben* remains unaltered, while in the Alemannic *theilen* remains unaltered, and *treiben* becomes *trüben*.

We may, if not quite accurately, yet quite intelligibly, designate those diphthongs in which the first sound has more emphasis *trochaic* diphthongs, and those in which the emphasis is laid on the second sound *iambic* diphthongs.

The simplest and therefore the principal class of diphthongs consists of the *trochaic*, in which the second sound is an *i*. It is an important fact that *i* in the second position can form true diphthongs with all the other vowels. We have *ai* (written *ai* or *ei*—*Main, Rhein,* Germ.*), *oi* (written *eu* or *oi*—*Heu,* Germ., *oyster,* Engl.), *ui* (*oui,* French, *pfui,* Germ.), *ei* (with the clear *e*—*pays, paysan* French ; also in the German dialectic pronunciation of the written *ei*), *ei* (with *e fermé, dei,* as in some dialects for *die*). This shows that *i* in the second position amalgamates so easily with all the other vowels as entirely to lose its individuality in the diphthong thus formed. Upon inquiring into the origin of this phenomenon, the simplest explanation appears to lie in the fact that the position of the tongue when at rest is the same as that for the utterance of *i*. Thus, if we utter a vowel and then, without interrupting the current of air, allow the tongue to return to its quiescent position, an *i*-sound will be heard after the vowel, with which, however, from the manner of its production, it will be most intimately connected, the more so as there is no break in the sound during the transition of the tongue from one position to the other, although in the instant of transition its character is somewhat uncertain ; there is, therefore, no appearance

* In English expressed by many combinations: *thy, thine, dye, aisle, buy, guide, height, eye, aye.*—Tr.

of a separating hiatus. In the same manner a *p* may under certain circumstances follow immediately upon an *m*, or a *t* an *n* or *r* without hiatus, resulting merely from the sudden opening of the closure effected between the lips, or between the tongue and the teeth. This explanation, moreover, is supported by the fact that this *i* is often impure, having a sound of *e* in it. The reason for this is at once evident when we remember that the position of the apex of the tongue for *e* and *i* is similar, being merely further back for *e*; the sound of *e* would, therefore, be produced if, when returning to its quiescent position, the apex of the tongue was not sufficiently advanced to produce a pure *i*.

In close connection with this group of diphthongs we have another, which, also trochaic, is peculiar to the guttural dialects (Swabian, Alemannic); we have here, namely, diphthongs, the second sound of which is the *e fermé*, the first *u*, *ue*, or *i*. We may safely assume that in these dialects the tongue when at rest lies more backward, thus corresponding with the position for *e fermé*. The appearance, therefore, of this sound may be regarded as the result of the return of the tongue to its position of rest, as was also the case when *i* appeared as the second sound. Here, again, according to the position of the tongue, we have either a pure *e fermé* or an approach to a pure *e*, an *a*, or *o*. In names or provincial literature, therefore, the second sound is written *a*, *e*, or *o*; for instance, *Bua* (Bub), *Muetter* (Mutter), *Muottathal*, *Flüelen*, *Brienz*, *Liab* (Lieb). The interrogative *wie* also may often be heard pronounced as a diphthong; also the demonstrative pronoun *die* (for *diese*), names of places—*Wien*, etc.

The second class of diphthongs is composed of those which are formed by the combination of the vowels *u*, *a*, and *o*, and which may either be trochaic or iambic. We shall presently show why *i* and *e* cannot be used as first sounds in this class, nor *u* in the iambic form. The following are the diphthongs—*au* (trochaic and iambic), *ou* (trochaic), *uo* (trochaic), *oa* (iambic) : *ao* is difficult to pronounce as a trochaic, easily turning into *au*; *ao* is formed with much greater ease as an iambic, though in neither form does it appear to be in use. As examples, it will be sufficient to mention—for *au* (trochaic), *blau*; for *au* (iambic), *Haus*; for *ou* (trochaic), *dou* (provincialism for *du*); for *uo* (trochaic), *stradicciuola* (Ital.); for *oa* (iambic), *moi* (French). The trochaic *uo* should probably be struck out of this list, as it bears a strong resemblance to the form already mentioned of *u* with *e fermé*. The manner in which these diphthongs are formed will most easily be seen in the case of *au*. Thus, if we examine the origin of *au* attentively, we shall find that it is produced by an *a* being first formed, and that then while it is still sounding the lips are protruded in a tube-like manner, thus giving rise to the *u*-sound, the position of the tongue being unaltered. Thus a tone is created by the resonance of the cavity of the mouth, which first, escaping through the wide-open mouth, sounds as *a*, but which afterwards, from the change in the form of the mouth by the rounded and protruded lips, becomes *u*. Although the influence of the position of the lips is undoubtedly great in the formation of sound, it should always be remembered that the primary sound is formed in the cavity of the mouth, and that it is merely completed or modified by the position of the lips. If the sound formed in the cavity of the mouth is to give an *a* with the *a*-position of the mouth, as well as an *u* with the *u*-position of the mouth, its production cannot correspond to the true *a*-position or *u*-position of the tongue and cavity of the mouth, but it must be an intermediate tone, which can with equal ease become an *a* if the lips are widely separated, or *u* if they are formed into a tube; and if we look closely, we shall find that neither of the two sounds are perfectly pure like the spoken *a* or *u*. That when *au* is uttered an intermediate tone is really formed in the cavity of the mouth, and successively modified into *a* and *u* by the position of the lips, is shown by a comparison with *ou*. The dialectic (Hessian) form *dou* for *du* was the only example given above; here the *o* is not pure, but approaches to *a*, so that the result often resembles *au*, according to the word, or the person speaking; the sound of this diphthong in the dialectic form of the word *Bruder* is more *au*, *Brauder*. Having thus seen that the *a* in *au* is not pure, but nearer to *u*, and finding the transition just alluded to from *au* to *ou*, it appears that the foundation for *au* and *ou* must lie in a dull *a*, which in one case will more resemble *a*, in the other *o*. This further agrees with the fact that *au* and *ou* are sometimes used indifferently in orthography—for instance, *Spandau* and *Spandow*—while *Nassau* is Latinized into *Nassovia*.

We at once see from the above remarks that *oa* must be formed in the same manner; that an impure *a* inclining to *o* must be created in the cavity of the mouth, which by opening the mouth is afterwards changed to *a*. It should, however, be remembered that in the formation of this species of diphthongs only those sounds can be employed between which intermediate forms exist—those sounds, for instance, which assume a different character according to the conformation of the lips. Thus *a*, *o*, *u* can form such combinations with each other, but not with *e* and *i*. On the other hand, we should expect to find a similar relation between *e* and *i*, which is really the case. Among the diphthongs ending in *i*, *ei* was mentioned, in the formation of which a clear *e* takes part (*pays, paysan*); if now we examine the origin of this *ei*, we find that the *e* uttered is very clear, approaching to *i*, to which by a quick retraction of the lips the *i*-character is given. This method of production is, however, the same as that which we have just been discussing; and this *ei* belongs, strictly speaking, more to this category than to the foregoing one. We shall also readily comprehend why, from the great ease with which the tongue assumes the position for the clear *e* and for *i*, this method of formation is not so simple for *ei* and for the diphthongs ending with *i*. These diphthongs do not, however, belong to this class, but rather to that already described, as is further shown by the fact that in forming the *i* the position of the lips remains unaltered.

The third class of diphthongs is the iambic, the first sound of which is an *i* or an *u*. Any of the other vowels may act as a second sound. This class can, however, scarcely be included in the diphthongs, as a consonantal element enters into it, which gives a different character to the combination of sound. Let us endeavour to show this peculiarity in the relation between *i* and *j*, *u* and *w*. If the tongue is laid against the palate as in forming *i*, and a fricative noise is then created either by the closer approximation of the tongue or by an increase in the current of air, the consonant *j* will be heard; if, again, during the formation of *i* the apex of the tongue is quickly drawn backwards into the position, for instance, for *a*, this movement against the current of air will produce, if not a perfect *j*, yet a sound approaching to it, thus giving rise to the consonantal element. The same relation exists between *u* and *w*, the latter being produced by a fricative noise between the protruded lips, and also, though less perfectly, by the rapid retraction of the lips against the current of air. Thus the corresponding consonantal noise is heard when either *i* or *u* are uttered and immediately followed by another vowel, examples of which we see in the Italian *piede, scuola,* the English *water,* and the German *Quelle.* By means of this modification an *i* so placed can be employed in very complex arrangements of vowels, as in the Italian *miei, tuoi, operaio, scrittoio,* etc.; for these complex sounds, when resolved into their elements, are almost *mjei, twoi, operajo, scrittojo,* etc., the *j* and *w*, it is true, being imperfect. On account of this consonantal element the first sounds of these diphthongs, especially at the commencement of a word, are often written as consonants, particularly in English, as in *yonder, year, will, wax,* so that in some the traditional pronunciation alone shows whether it is a true diphthong or not.

The Nasal Vowels.

The nasal vowels are not separate distinct sounds, but merely a modification of the vowel-sounds. This modification is due to the nasal cavity not being cut off by the soft palate during the formation of the vowels, so that the air contained in the cavity can directly participate in the creation of resonance. The only European languages in which their existence is recognized by grammarians are the French and Portuguese. They are, however, very general in dialects, and in this form are often met with even in German. All vowels which are known to us as pure or intermediate vowels can be pronounced as nasal vowels.

If, the posterior orifice of the nasal cavity being open, the current of air is allowed to escape through the cavity of the mouth as well as through the nasal cavity, it follows that the two cavities will each have a distinct resonance, and that we can only hear the nasal vowel when the two resonances reach the ear simultaneously, and blend together to form one impression, in the same way as the different instruments of an orchestra, when played together, produce a single impression.

Adopting this conception of the formation of the nasal vowels, we recognize a mixture of two separate elements, the resonance of the cavity of the mouth, which distinguishes the vowel-sound, and the resonance which, added by the nasal cavity to the laryngeal tone, produces the nasal quality and forms the foundation of the nasal vowels.

In the French nasal sounds acknowledged by grammarians, the soft palate is slightly depressed, so that a considerable portion of the current of air finds its way into the nasal cavity, the resonance thus becoming fuller and more sonorous. The French, as we know, only make general use of *a*, *o*, and *ae* (clear), as nasal vowels (*ae* written *in*, *en*, or *ein*), either at the beginning, in the middle, or at the end of words, as, for instance, *angoisse, avancer, marchand,—incliner, attoindre, marin, payen,—ondée, prononcer, dragon.*

In dialects, or by individuals, either all vowels or a few may be pronounced nasally.

The former arises either from indolence, or from not having the power to raise the soft palate so as to form a pure vowel-sound. The entire speech then assumes a "nasal quality;" as, however, no action is perceptible by which a fuller current of air is conducted into the nasal cavity, a portion of the air merely taking this course by chance, the sounds produced in this manner are not so much sonorous nasal vowels as vowels which, by a more or less strong nasal resonance, are spoilt or rendered impure.

When, as is very generally the case in German dialects, a few only of the vowels are pronounced nasally in speaking, they will almost invariably be found in words or syllables ending in *n*. The nasal vowel-sounds, therefore, generally represent the compound sounds *an, en, in, on, un;* and there is no doubt that they are due to the soft palate during the formation, or even at the commencement, of the vowel-sound, being adjusted for *n*, which, however, is not distinctly uttered. It is to some extent an intermediate sound between the vowel and *n*, produced by uttering the vowel when the soft palate is adjusted for *n*, just as *ue* is an intermediate sound formed by uttering *i* with the lips in the position for *u*. Here, again, as in French, the vowels *a, o*, and *e* are those which are generally pronounced in this manner, though without the same full sound. The nasal *i* and *u* are, however, very commonly met with in the Swabian and Alemannic dialects; as, for instance, in *thun, unverschämt, bin, Win* (*Wein*).

The Resonants.

The term resonants has, since its introduction by Brücke, been understood to express a distinct class of articulate sounds, which, though generally included by grammarians among the consonants, have, when the elements are considered of which they are composed, much greater affinity with the vowels. They are the three sounds *m, n,* and *ng* (as pronounced in German). Grammarians are, however, conscious of some peculiarity in these sounds, and readily allow, if they examine into the character of articulate sounds with any minuteness, that the sounds *m* and *n* (disregarding *ng*) are semivowels. That this distinction is, however, only *felt*, is shown by the circumstance that r and l, and even f, w, h, i, and s, are placed in the same category.

The peculiarity which justifies the separation of the three sounds just mentioned from the list of true consonants, is due to the absence of noise in their formation, they, like vowels, consisting merely of a modification of the laryngeal tone by the varying resonance of the air-passage.

In order better to understand the position in which these sounds stand with regard to the vowels, we will first direct our attention to a particular form of the vowels which is not and cannot be adapted to speech. If we try to utter a nasal vowel, at the same time closing the nostrils, the quality of the nasal vowel will be dull and impure. Moreover, to carry out the experiment successfully, a gentle current of air must be employed, which should not be driven with too great force into the nasal cavity, but allowed freely to escape through the cavity of the mouth. Such impure sounds are sometimes involuntarily produced when the nasal cavity is filled with mucus. We shall be perfectly justified in regarding such a vowel, which can only pass outwards through the cavity of the mouth, as an oral vowel. The dull nasal quality of the vowel is, however, due to part of the current of air employed in its formation being driven into the nasal cavity, from which, the anterior orifice being closed, it is again expelled. The nasal cavity is, therefore, a blind appendage of the air-passage, into which part of the current of air eddies, afterwards again joining the main stream. It is this hollow resonance of the nasal cavity which creates the dull nasal *quality*. The peculiar vowel-character is, however, given by the conformation of the cavity of the mouth, and thus the sound in question is a vowel accompanied by the nasal quality. Unfortunately, it is impossible to show by experiment how this resonance will differ according to the more forward or backward position of the closure of the nasal cavity. Theoretically, however, there can be no doubt that the point at which the closure takes place in the nasal cavity will affect the sound, since the resonance in a deep vessel is different to that in a shallow one.

It is an interesting fact that this same nasal quality is heard if a stronger current of air is employed in the formation of the pure i and the nostrils are closed. The soft palate in i is raised to its greatest height, which causes it to become extremely tense, and enables it to transmit the vibration to the air of the nasal cavity, and so to excite the resonance which is blended with the vowel-sound. This experiment is not so successful with the other vowels; it succeeds best with u, which stands nearest to i as regards the position of the soft palate.

The same peculiarities form the foundation of the three sounds which, as resonants, constitute a separate class of articulate sounds. Their origin, namely, is due to a current of air which, rendered sonant as it issues from the larynx, passes outwards through the nasal cavity; the cavity of the mouth, closed anteriorly, forming a closed expansion, so to speak, at one side of the stream, and mingling its resonance with that of the nasal cavity. The three sounds, therefore, owe their individuality to the point at which the closure of the cavity of the mouth is effected; that is to say, to the depth of the lateral expansion of the air-passage formed by the portion of the cavity of the mouth employed. For m the closure is effected by the lips; for n, by the apex of the tongue and the hard palate; for ng, by the root of the tongue and the soft palate.

THE FORMATION OF ARTICULATE SOUNDS. 303

The form of closure formed by the lips for m is so clearly defined as to render any important modifications of this sound impossible. It is true that even when the lips are closed the form of the cavity of the mouth may be altered in different directions, by expanding or drawing in the cheeks, by protruding or retracting the lips, by more or less firmly closing the jaws; these alterations do not seem, however, materially to affect the character of the m. The only perceptible influence arises from the position of the tongue, the sound of m being more sonorous when the tongue is depressed than when it is elevated. It is, however, difficult to say whether this difference is due entirely to the depression of the tongue, or whether it is not caused by the depression of the larynx, which would almost necessarily accompany that of the tongue, and which would lower the fundamental tone.

The case is different with n, in the formation of which the point of closure is less accurately defined, being in some instances more forward, in others more backward. The most forward point at which the closure can take place is between the apex of the tongue and the incisors of the upper jaw, the most backward that between the dorsum of the tongue and the posterior portion of the hard palate. The farther forward the point of closure the clearer is the sound, the more backward the duller. This may arise from the difference in the capacity of the portion of the cavity of the mouth thus marked off by this varying point of closure; the greater clearness of the n formed by the more forward point of closure may, however, be due to a less complete stoppage of the cavity of the mouth, some air escaping on either side of the tongue, and imparting to the sound something of the clearer character of the oral sounds. This view seems to be supported by the fact that the *m*, which is formed by a still more forward perfect closure, never has the clear quality of the *n* formed by the contact of the apex of the tongue with the teeth.

For *ng* the point of closure is between the root of the tongue and the soft palate. Here again, however, the point at which the closure takes place is not accurately defined, but may be anywhere between the free margin of the soft palate and its attachment with the hard palate. The latter point of contact for *ng* so closely approaches that for *n*, that the sound resulting from this closure contains almost as much *n* as *ng*. Thus a continuous series of resonants may be formed by contact of the tongue with the soft and with the hard palate, which, beginning with the clear *n* by closure at the teeth, passes through the various stages just alluded to, and terminates with the pure, deep *ng* by closure at the free margin of the soft palate. This explains why the sound *ng* is often either not mentioned at all, or merely regarded as a very backward (guttural) *n*. The existence of such transitional forms does not, however, justify us in uniting two typical forms connected by a chain of intermediate forms so that one is regarded as the typical form and the other merely as a modification; if we wished to give a single expression for the two typical forms we should take the middle transitional form, regarding the other forms as special developments of it. We might, therefore, consider the sound *ae* as typical, and the sounds *a* and *e* as modifications in opposite directions; but we could never regard *a* as a variety of *e*. There is another difficulty in explaining the formation of *ng*; when, for instance, it arises from contact between the root of the tongue and the free margin of the soft palate, the cavity of the mouth is entirely cut off from the air-passage, and cannot, therefore, as in the formation of other resonants, form a blind expansion at one side of the air-passage. There is, however, no doubt that a resonance arising from such a relation forms one of the components of *ng*. We must suppose, therefore, that in this case the vibrations are first transmitted to the soft palate, and by the latter to the quiescent layer of air in the cavity of the mouth, just as we explained the participation of the resonance of the nasal cavity in the formation of the pure *i* when the nostrils are closed. If the point of closure is slightly advanced, the portion of the cavity of the mouth opening into the air-passage will still be comparatively small, and we may therefore assume that when *ng* is produced under these conditions the resonance of the cavity of the mouth will still be partly excited by the soft palate. The point at which *ng* passes into *n* should perhaps be considered as marked by the cessation of this action of the soft palate, and the difference between *n* and *ng* will therefore consist less in the difference of the point of closure as in the participation or non-participation of the soft palate in the production of the resonance of the cavity of the mouth.

The Consonants.

The characteristic foundation for the formation of that class of articulate sounds which we call consonants, is supplied by the noises which can be voluntarily created in the air-passages by the current of air passing through them. It has already been shown that the cavity of the mouth alone possesses the power of creating any number of such noises, and that these only are capable of being employed as articulate sounds; we shall now, therefore, devote our attention entirely to the noises belonging to the cavity of the mouth.

Noise alone has no loud quality, but derives its importance from being combined with and interspersed between musical sounds. Hence the name "con-sonants" for the articulate sounds thus founded upon noises. The value of such a consonant will, moreover, be greatly increased if a sonant current of air is employed in its formation. Thus there are consonants with tone and without tone, or, according to the general terminology, *tenues* (without tone) and *mediæ* (with tone). Since, however, with few exceptions, every noise employed as an articulate sound can be uttered either with or without tone, and so assume two forms, it would be better to distinguish a tone-containing and a toneless form or variety of consonants.

The toneless forms of consonants are again commonly called hard consonants, and the forms with tone soft, the difference between which was formerly supposed to be that the hard consonants were connected with an aspirate which was wanting in the soft, so that, for instance, $p = b + h$, that is to say, the (hard) p was produced by uniting b with the aspirate h. Although this view is now generally rejected, being superseded by the distinction given above, yet at the same time it rests upon the perfectly correct observation, that the consonants with tone (soft) are produced by a weaker current of air than those without tone (hard). This fact is the more worthy of attention, since it is not due to chance but to an arrangement which is of absolute necessity. We know that the toneless current of air passes through the wide-open glottis; when, on the contrary, the current is sonant, the glottis must be greatly contracted and adjusted for tone; much less air will, however, pass in a given time through the glottis in its contracted form than when it is wide again; consequently the sonant current of air will be weaker (softer) than the toneless. A consonant with tone can, therefore, never be uttered with so much force as one without tone. On the other hand, the consonant without tone is to some extent obliged to make use of this greater force of utterance; for the consonant with tone, on account of its admixture of tone, is full and sonorous. So, if the toneless consonant, which has no volume (therefore *tenuis*, thin), is to become of equal importance, it must make up by force of utterance what it lacks in tone. Therefore it not only can but must be uttered more forcibly, that is to say, with a stronger current of air, and hence the idea that the addition of a stronger aspiration distinguished the " hard " consonants from the " soft."

We now see, moreover, that the difference between the two forms of consonants is not merely marked by the absence or presence of tone, but that, the fundamental noise being the same, the toneless consonant is as much characterized by a more forcible utterance as the consonant with tone by the admixture of tone. Thus, adhering to the example given above, and β standing for the noise as created by a moderate current of air, the difference just described may be expressed by the formula: $p = \beta +$ increased pressure of air, and $b = \beta +$ tone.

The two sounds h and r may be regarded as the limits of the consonants in these two directions; when used they are both toneless, though from entirely different reasons. We find that h, produced by a current of air escaping through the wide-open mouth upon the walls of which it makes but little fricative noise, combines most readily with tone; but that a sonant current of air, passing through the wide-open mouth, at once assumes the vowel-character *a*, the full sound of which completely annihilates the weak noise *h*. If *h* is to be heard, it must be uttered without tone. It is different with *r*, a full-sounding vibratory noise, which cannot combine with tone, for a sonant current of air has not sufficient force to throw the uvula or the apex of the tongue into vibration.

As we are now about to take a survey of the possible consonants, or those in general use, we must make our so-called alphabet the starting-point, notwithstanding the many deficiencies and inconsistencies which, as we have already remarked, it contains. We must, however, strike out the following superfluous letters before making use of it: *c* (hard, as in *call*) and *q* as being the same sounds as *k*, *v* as being the same sound as *f* or *w*, and *x*, *c* (*ci*), and *z* as not being simple sounds, but the double sounds *ks* and *ts*. We may further strike out *w*, *b*, *d*, *g*, as they are merely modifications of *f*, *p*, *t*, and *k*, made by addition of tone, which we are the more justified in doing as the series is incomplete, there being no letter in our alphabet to represent the modifications of *s* and *ch*.

The remaining consonants may be classified in two ways—either from the nature of their distinctive noise, or from the place where the noise is produced. The first method gives a division into *continuae* and *repentinae;* the latter are generally called *explosivae*, because these sounds predominate in the *repentinae*. The second method employs the terms labiate, dental, and palatal sounds, according as the conditions for their formation are present at either of these three places. Dividing the consonantal noises, therefore, into *labials*, *dentals*, and *gutturals*, we have the following table of noises and the consonants arising from them:—

Strepitus.	Labialis.	Dentalis.	Gutturalis.
1. *continuus*			
spirans	—	h	—
stridulus	f	s	ch
vibrans	r	r	r
2. *repentinus*			
avulsivus	—	clicking sounds	—
explosivus	p (*pa*)	t (*ta*)	k (*ka*)
occlusivus	p (*ap*)	t (*at*)	k (*ak*)

This table is obviously imperfect; for we miss three very characteristic sounds, namely, *l*, *j*, and *sch*. They are generally included among the dentals, but though the apex of the tongue is approximated to the teeth, as in the formation of the dentals, they cannot properly be classified with the latter, for they offer one most important difference, namely, the direction of the current of air. In all the consonants given in the above table, the current of air is confined to the middle line of the cavity of the mouth, or better, the current of air traverses the cavity of the mouth in the direction indicated by the middle line. Thus it passes along the entire length of the dorsum of the tongue, finding an exit between the apex of the tongue and the upper incisors. In the three sounds in question, to which must be added a particular form of *r*, the current of air is impeded by the contact between the apex of the tongue and the incisors; it flows, therefore, over either side of the dorsum of the tongue, and passes out between the lower surface of the tongue and the lower incisors. These four sounds consequently form a separate group, which, as their production is due to the edges of the tongue, may be termed *marginals*.

Those points at which the noise is produced are called the points of articulation, because there the approximation or contact of the opposite portions of the mouth necessary for the formation of the noise takes place, and we therefore distinguish a labial, dental, and a guttural point of articulation. From what has just been said, this number must be increased to four, and the marginal point of articulation added to the three already enumerated.

Again, it may be asked, are we not justified in recognizing a fifth point of articulation in the larynx, that is to say, in the glottis of the larynx? That an *explosive* can undoubtedly be formed here has already been remarked in speaking of the "groan." A *continua stridula* is also possible when a strong, forced expiration is made; this, when the mouth is open, has the sound of a deep, rough *h*, and is in general use as the first sound of a syllable. It is heard distinctly in "panting." The deep English *r* in *are* and *more* may be regarded as a *continua vibrans*, having little of the rattling sound which is generally characteristic of the *r*, but bearing more resemblance to a hoarse breath; it has, therefore, been described as "something between *a* and nothing."

In the following description of the separate consonants the "clicking sounds" (*avulsivae*) are left entirely unnoticed, as a place was assigned to them in the section upon noises, and they are never employed in the languages of civilized peoples.

We need also pay no further attention to *h*, than to remark that when the tongue is depressed almost to the position for *u*, the sound is somewhat duller than when the tongue is more raised.

The Labials.

p, b; f, w.

The labials are remarkable for simplicity in their

THE FORMATION OF ARTICULATE SOUNDS. 311

formation. For the explosive *p* the lips are firmly closed so as to resist the pressure of the current of air which is driven against them by the force of expiration, and further increased in strength by the elevation of the floor of the cavity of the mouth. If now the lips are suddenly opened, either voluntarily or through the pressure of the air accumulated against them, the explosive sound is heard. The sound cannot be produced alone, for the current of air which is thus let loose follows upon it with a breathing sound so closely, that even when it precedes a vowel this breathing sound, though scarcely audible, forms a hiatus between the two. The occlusive *p* has a somewhat different sound, namely, a short and hard one; it cannot, of course, be followed by the breathing sound, if formed with perfect purity. This, however, is very rarely the case. The occlusive *p*, namely, cuts off the current of air with a force which considerably exceeds that with which the lips are brought into a position of rest. It follows, therefore, that a relaxation takes place in the force of closure after the sound is formed, and the air which is compressed by the sudden obstruction breaks through the now powerless closure, and gives rise to a weak explosive *p*. A particular effort is required to avoid this second sound. It is not, however, in any way detrimental to speech, offering, on the contrary, the slight advantage of giving a little more volume to the very soundless occlusive *p*.

In *b* we have the *p* with tone in the explosive as well as in the occlusive form. In the explosive form it is not followed by the breathing sound for many reasons, all of which are based upon the character of the current of air producing the sound, which is weak and with tone. The separation of the lips is, therefore, generally effected by voluntary muscular activity, and the current of air after its momentary obstruction flows rather than bursts out (explodes); the air, therefore, does not follow the sound with such force or in such quantity as in *p*. Then, again, the current of air, being sonant, may be immediately attached to a vowel. For this purpose the cavity of the mouth assumes the position necessary for the formation of the vowel, and the lips are opened at the moment when the tone is produced; if the tone commences before the opening takes place, an *m* is heard before the *b*, this being the resonant formed by closure at the lips. The occlusive *b* is less short and hard than the occlusive *p*, resembling it, however, in being very wanting in volume, and in acquiring more sound from being almost necessarily followed by an explosive *b*. It would almost seem as if the occlusive *b* were altogether without tone, therefore a weak *p*, and only acquired its *b*-character from this attachment to an explosive *b*.

The origin of *f* is due to a fricative noise produced by a current of air escaping through the contracted opening of the mouth. The small orifice may be created by the most different conformation of the lips, an *f* ensuing when the lips are rounded and protruded as well as when they are drawn back and flattened; it can also be formed by allowing the air to escape through one angle of the mouth, or, again, firmly closing the central part of the lips, through both angles. It would be useless to discuss the characteristics of these unimportant varieties of *f*; it will be sufficient to remark that when the floor of the cavity of the mouth is raised and the upper lip protruded a clear *f* is heard; a somewhat duller *f*, on the contrary, when the floor of the cavity of the mouth is depressed and the lower lip protruded beyond the upper.

The German *w* (English *v*) is due to the same causes

as f, of which it is produced by addition of tone, and under similar conditions exhibits the same varieties as those just described for f.

The Dentals.

t, d; s, th (English).

In the formation of the explosive t the air-passage is obstructed by bringing the apex of the tongue against the anterior portion of the hard palate; a partial stoppage is, it is true, sufficient, but of course the better the contact the more complete will be the sound. The apex of the tongue alone is not sufficient for the most perfect contact, but the entire margin of the dorsum of the tongue must be brought into contact with the molar teeth, so that the air becomes compressed in the space between the palate and the dorsum of the tongue. In this case, however, the sudden removal of the tip of the tongue suffices to produce the explosive t. The point at which the apex of the tongue effects this closure is by no means fixed, but varies considerably, between, namely, the free margin of the upper incisors and the posterior margin of the hard palate. The upper or lower surface of the apex of the tongue may be placed with equal facility against the teeth; higher up, or further back, the under surface is more readily used. This difference in the manner and locality of the closure effected by the apex of the tongue gives rise to several varieties of the t, but it is only necessary to mention the more important fact, that the sound of t becomes clearer if the closure is made more forward, and duller if it takes place further back. The same remark applies to the pure formation of t as to p; that as in p the explosive t is necessarily followed by a breathing sound, which, when a vowel is the next sound, intervenes as a hiatus. The occlusive *t*, which may be formed at any of the points of closure for the explosive *t*, is, like the occlusive *p*, a short hard sound of little volume, which, however, and with advantage to its sound, is almost necessarily combined with an explosive *t*, because the apex of the tongue immediately puts an end to the closure in returning to its position of rest.

D is the modification of *t* produced by the addition of tone, to which it stands in exactly the same relations as *b* to *p*. It can be formed both as an explosive and as an occlusive at the points of closure effected by the tongue for *t*. Like *b*, and for the same reasons, it lacks, if explosive, the subsequent breathing sound; and again, like *b*, if occlusive, it only acquires its full sound when followed immediately by the explosive form. As regards combination with vowels, the explosive *d* differs somewhat from the corresponding *b*. The necessary adjustment of the cavity of the mouth for the vowel which follows cannot take place before the formation of *d*, as was the case with *b*, but must be brought about by a rapid change in the position of the tongue after the closure. If tone is formed during the time of closure, an *n* is heard with every variety of *d*; all the points of closure for *t* and *d* being the same as those employed in the formation of the resonant *n*.

S is a fricative noise produced between the apex of the tongue and the points of closure employed for *t*; a pure *s* can, however, only be produced when the upper surface of the tongue serves to form the obstruction; this surface, again, must be hollowed from side to side, so that the current of air flows forward along a more or less narrow path. The different varieties of *s* which can be formed are due partly to the different character of the closure, partly to the width of the path along which the current of air flows upon the dorsum of the tongue. A broad stream gives rise to an impure hissing *s*; a forward closure gives a clearer, a backward a duller *s*. The attempt to form an *s* with the under surface of the tongue only succeeds in producing a hissing or rushing sound, which calls to mind *sch* (*sh* English), from which, however, it is as far removed as from *s*.

If contact by the upper surface of the apex of the tongue is effected in such a manner that it is only brought against the lower margin of the upper incisors, though at the same time the apex of the tongue may protrude beyond the level of the teeth, the English *th* or the modern Greek θ is heard.

There is a sharp, toneless form of *s*, *th*, and θ corresponding to the *f* of the labials, and a soft form with tone which corresponds to the *w* (English *v*) of the labials.

The Gutturals.

k, g; ch.

If contact is formed between the back part of the tongue and the back part of the palate, an explosive sound *k* will be heard. The anterior limit of this region for closure is also the posterior limit of that for *t*, which explains why children, before they are able to form the more difficult guttural closure, employ *t* instead of *k* (*tind, dive*, instead of *kind, give*). Brücke,* however, correctly remarks that the question whether *t* or *k* is formed depends not only upon the situation of the point of closure, but also upon the position of the tongue. Between the distinct space upon the palate for

* Grundzüge der Physiologie und Systematik der Sprachlaute (Wien, 1856), S. 43.

t and the distinct space for *k* lies, namely, a third space, which may be employed at will either for *k* or for *t*. The limits of this space are very clearly marked; we need only remember that in forming *t* the upper surface as well as the lower surface of the apex of the tongue may be employed. If the contact between the dorsum of the tongue and the palate is gradually made further back, a point is at length reached, when the explosive sound corresponding to the closure changes from a *t* to a *k*. If the experiment is made with the lower surface of the apex of the tongue, a point will again be reached, when the explosive sound changes from *t* to *k*; this point will, however, be more backward than when the experiment was made with the dorsum of the tongue. The space between these two points is that intermediate region, which begins, therefore, with the posterior limit of the *t* formed by the dorsum of the tongue, and terminates with the posterior limit of the *t* formed by the lower surface of the tongue. Varieties of *k* as of *t* are formed by altering the locality of the closure, but here the varieties form two distinct classes, that, namely, of the forward *k*, and that of the backward *k*. The cause for this division lies clearly in the different nature of the parts of the palate employed for the closure, the posterior portion of the hard palate being used for the forward *k*, the soft palate, on the contrary, for the backward *k*. These varieties of the explosive *k* are represented by an equal number of varieties of the occlusive *k*; the occlusive *k*, however, even more than the occlusive *t* or *p*, only acquires its full importance when followed by the corresponding explosive sound.

In *g* (hard) we have *k* with tone. To *g*, moreover, applies all that has been said with reference to *k*, both as regards the limits of the region of closure, and the correspondence between the explosive and occlusive forms.

The corresponding fricative noises are those which are expressed in German by *ch*. The difference which has been pointed out between the forward and backward *k* is still more marked in the fricative noise. To the forward *k* (formed with the hard palate) corresponds, namely, the pure, clear, fricative noise which is heard after *i* and *e* (in *Licht*, *Pech*, Germ.); to the backward *k* (formed with the soft palate) corresponds the rougher, deeper fricative noise following *a*, *u*, *o* (in *Dach*, *Wucht*, Germ., *Loch*, Scotch). In the latter we readily notice the addition of a trembling noise produced by the vibration of the soft palate, which to a certain extent assimilates this *ch* to the guttural *r*, as appears, for example, from the name of the river *Aar*, which is the same word as *Ach* in the names of the rivers *Wolfach*, *Gutach*. The difference between the two sounds of *ch* is, however, so great that we seem to be justified in distinguishing them as *chi* and *ach*. The *chi*-form combines more easily with *i* and *e*, and the *ach*-form more easily with *a*, *o*, and *u*, because in the formations of *i* and *e* the tongue is placed more forward, and therefore easily passes to the *chi*-position, while the *ach*-position more resembles the backward position of the tongue for *a*, *o*, and *u*. In proof of the correctness of this assertion we find that the *ach*-sound can only be combined with an *i* or *e* by means of an intermediate *a* (*i*[*a*]*ch*, *Re*[*a*]*chen*, provincialisms for *ich*, *Rechen*). This shows that the tongue, in its transition from the *i*-position to the *ach*-position, must pass through the *a*-position.

The two kinds of guttural fricative noises can also be made with tone, though these sounds are not recognized, at least in the grammars of the German, English, and

Romance languages. They do, however, appear in dialects. The *ch* with tone is heard in the North-German pronunciation of *g* (for instance, in *gut*), which resembles *j*, though it is not *j*, as we shall presently show. The *ach* with tone also appears in the North-German dialect as a peculiar pronunciation of *k* (for instance, in *König*), and again in the Alemannic dialect in the pronunciation of *k* (for instance, in *komm*).

The Marginals.
l, j, sch.

We have already described the peculiarities which are common to the marginal sounds. The three sounds just enumerated all belong to the fricative noises, and though we should also distinguish a marginal explosive, it has not been given with the above, as it can scarcely be employed as a separate sound. We shall, however, presently describe it.

In the formation of the three sounds enumerated above, the apex of the tongue, or a part of the tongue near to the apex, is brought more or less firmly against the anterior portion of the hard palate, and the current of air is thus forced to flow over the sides of the tongue.

In *l* the apex of the tongue touches the posterior surface of the upper incisors, though the point of contact may be either higher or more backward; the entire dorsum of the tongue is at the same time so much depressed that its edges lie rather below the lower margin of the molar teeth. It can also be formed with tone as well as without tone.

In the formation of *j* a somewhat longer portion of the upper surface of the apex of the tongue is brought against the alveolar process of the upper jaw, and the entire dorsum is so raised that its edges lie lightly against the molar teeth. The apex may, however, be placed lower against the posterior surface of the teeth, or further back, against the hard palate, provided the edges of the tongue occupy the position described with regard to the molar teeth. The under surface of the tongue may also be employed in forming contact at any of the points mentioned, but the *j* thus produced will be dull and impure. Thus the formation of *j* is due to the apex of the tongue being placed firmly against the upper jaw and the air then passing through the narrow crevice between the edges of the tongue and the molar teeth. It is clear, therefore, that the similar sound which was described above as the *chi* with tone cannot be identified with it, being produced by a perfect *chi*-position of the tongue. The toneless j is more used in German, as in *jetzt*, the modification with tone more in English, where it is written *y*, as in *year*, *yonder*.

For *sch* the upper surface of the apex of the tongue is brought against the alveolar process of the upper jaw, and the dorsum so raised that its edges lightly press against the inner surface of the molar teeth. While forming this sound the apex of the tongue frequently falls away from the upper jaw, and thus an *s* is mixed with the sound. When uttered as a pure marginal without this admixture, the *sch* has a more hissing sound. The English *sch* (written *sh*) has more this sound than the German, though it also is not without the *s*-sound. The *sch* in general use cannot, therefore, be regarded as a pure marginal sound, but as being *principally* a fricative noise produced by the edges of the tongue, and therefore as belonging to the marginals. *Sch* also may be either toneless (*Asche*) or be pronounced with tone (*schön*, Germ., *jamais*, French).

If the tongue is placed in the position for the formation of *sch*, and a strong current of air suddenly driven through the cavity of the mouth, without removing the apex of the tongue, a hard *tsch* is heard, which may be analyzed into a marginal explosive *t* and a pure marginal *sch*. This double sound appears in the well-known German refrain: *tschin tschin rataplan*.

The Vibrants.

Vibrating noises can be created at all the points of closure suitable for the formation of consonants, and all have the sound of *r*. Thus there is a labial *r*, a dental *r* (formed by the apex of the tongue), a forward guttural *r*, and a backward guttural *r*, a marginal r, and probably a laryngeal *r*.

Of these six, the labial *r* can scarcely be employed as an articulate sound, though this is said to be the case in an island not far from New Guinea.* With this exception it is only used as a kind of interjection, and in some countries as a sign to horses to stop; in both cases it is, however, accompanied by a vibratory noise of the protruded apex of the tongue.

For the dental *r*, also called the lingual *r*, the apex of the tongue is turned upwards and placed behind the teeth; and when driven downwards by the force of the current of air, it springs back again to its former position.

The forward guttural *r* is formed between the raised dorsum of the tongue and the hard palate. As, however, the dorsum of the tongue has little capacity for vibration, there is not much roughness in this *r*, and it can-

---

* Brücke, Grundzüge der Physiologie und Systematik der Sprachlante (Wien, 1856), S. 35.

THE FORMATION OF ARTICULATE SOUNDS. 321

not be pronounced very loudly. Still, it is the form most commonly used in German.

The backward guttural *r* arises from the vibration of the uvula in a groove formed by the depression of the root of the tongue. It is very common in French.

The marginal *r* is caused by the vibration of the edges of the tongue, when the apex is pressed against the most forward part of the palate and the air is thus driven between the molar teeth and the edges of the tongue which lie close to them.

The possibility or probability of a laryngeal *r* has already been discussed.

These varieties of the *r* must be regarded less as different articulate sounds than as different forms of the articulate sound *r*, and thus the choice of one or the other form depends partly upon the combination with other sounds, partly upon individual or national peculiarities.

The Double Consonants.

Any two consonants can be pronounced quickly one after the other, some easily, others with more difficulty. When this association is difficult, either from the character of the sounds or from individual incapacity, a small pause intervenes between the two consonants, which may be merely a breath or silent pause (*hiatus*), or else may take the form of a transitional sound.

The pure hiatus is most frequently met with when two consonants are situated between two vowels, even when the two consonants belong to the same syllable, and are otherwise easily associated: *Ak-se, Achse; Fük-se, Füchse; Kat-se, Katze; Gel-der, Gelder.* This hiatus again invariably appears when the consonants belong to two combined words: *ab-legen, un-genau, all-seitig*.

The hiatus may be filled either by a vowel or a consonant.

This vowel will be an indistinct vowel-sound formed accidentally by the mouth assuming the position for such a vowel in passing from the position for one consonant to that for the other, the current of air flowing continuously. It is generally an *e fermé*, with, however, a sound of *a* or *o*—*Kremel, Dnieper;* a distinct *u*-sound appears if we try to associate *ch* with *p*—*ch(u)p;* a similar sound, though approaching to *o*, is heard if we try to pronounce *fk* with the most backward *k*—*f(o)k*. Individual incapacity is in a great measure the cause of such interpositions; there are persons who find a difficulty in pronouncing successively almost any two consonants, even those which are most easily associated, saying *schár-ef, géleb*, etc., instead of *scharf, gelb*.

It can scarcely be said that the hiatus is actually filled by a consonant, but rather that the transition is facilitated by the interposition of a consonant which is easily connected with one, especially the first of the two other consonants. As a rule, however, a hiatus follows even the interposed consonant; but the duration of the hiatus is so diminished by the interposition of the consonant, that the latter may be said at least to partially fill it: *gelegentlich, Hundsveilchen*.

Many combinations of two consonants are so easily pronounced that in writing they are expressed by one letter (x, z, ψ). This fact gives rise to the question whether among the consonants there are not double sounds similar to those which in the vowels assume the form of diphthongs. Before answering this question, we must have a clear idea as to the conditions which must be fulfilled for any combination of consonants to be regarded as a double consonant (consonant-diphthong). There will be no difficulty in doing this if we consider the consonant-diphthongs from the same point of view as the vowel-diphthongs—regarding, namely, each one as an unit, in which indeed we recognize the constituent elements, but which under any conditions can or must remain a unit. The best way of proving this seems to be to pronounce such a combination of consonants between two vowels. If they are separated by a hiatus it shows that the combination is imperfect, and renders it impossible to regard them as consonant-diphthongs. If now, setting aside the resonants, we try all possible combinations of consonants in this manner, we find that no two can be pronounced between two vowels without a hiatus, though in some instances it may be almost imperceptible. We may consider this a sufficient proof that there are no true consonant-diphthongs.

This, however, should not deter us from investigating those combinations of pure consonants (with the exception of the resonants) which under certain conditions can be pronounced without hiatus, and therefore under these conditions may be regarded as analogues of consonant-diphthongs. These conditions will naturally be (1) when pronounced alone, (2) when employed at the commencement, (3) when employed at the termination of a word.

As the remarks we shall make upon each *tenuis* apply equally to the corresponding *media*, we shall in the following discussion devote our attention to the former, though the *mediae* may sometimes be employed as examples. It will, however, be well first to particularize a few sounds for the sake of brevity, namely—

The k and ch (chi) formed at the anterior part of the soft palate as k^1 and ch^1.

The k and ch (ach) formed at the lower part of the soft palate as k^2 and ch^2.

The four middle r's as r^1 (labial r), r^2 (lingual r, formed by the apex of the tongue), r^3 (palatal r, formed at the hard palate), r^4 (formed at the soft palate).

Let us consider first the combination of an *explosiva* followed by a *continua*. It would seem that such a combination should be very easily accomplished, as the current of air which has been held back for the formation of the *explosiva* would, when the closure is at an end, be well adapted to form a *continua*. This is, in fact, often the case, though there are not many in the number of possible combinations which can be pronounced without hiatus, while others can be formed alone, but are with difficulty attached to other sounds, so that only a few can readily be employed in speech. There is, moreover, an important difference in these combinations according as they are used at the commencement or termination of a word. At the commencement of a word the *explosiva* in question is really an *explosiva* to which the remark made above applies perfectly; at the termination of a word the same sound stands, however, to the preceding sounds in the relation of an *occlusiva*, to which another sound cannot be attached without a distinct hiatus. Such combinations are, however, met with at the ends of words, and must, therefore, be explained by the fact already mentioned, that though a pure *occlusiva* undoubtedly exists both in theory and practice, it is not in actual use; for when the parts which have produced the closure separate to return to a position of rest, an *explosiva* necessarily follows immediately upon the *occlusiva.* Therefore if it is possible to form a combination of this kind at the end of a word, the possibility is given by this explosive element, which, however, being weak, confines the application of these combinations within narrow limits.

The most perfect combination is formed by an *explosiva* and a *stridula* of the same region, as the air which breaks out after the formation of the *explosiva* can be used at the same point for the fricative noise; thus we have the combinations

$$pf, \ ts, \ k^1ch^1, \ k^2ch^2.$$

These can all be formed as double consonants, in the broader sense given above, though the first only can be used as easily at the commencement as at the termination of a word, for there is so much difficulty in combining the two last with other sounds that they can never be generally employed. There is nothing to choose between *pf* and *ts* for the commencement of a word (*Pfund, Zoll*), but in ending a word with *pf* a hiatus can scarcely be avoided, because *f* requires a stronger current of air and a different position of the lips (*Kopf*), while, on the contrary, the current of air which is liberated by *t* is quite sufficient for the formation of *s* (*Platz*). The ease with which *t* combines with *s* in either position has also led to its being represented by the simple sign *z*.

Next in order we have the *stridula* of a more forward region joined to a preceding *explosiva*—

$$tf, \ kf, \ k^1s.$$

The two first can be produced by adjusting the lips for *f* and then forming the *k* or *t* with a strong current of air. An easy succession both at the beginning and ending of words is, however, only afforded by k^1s, to express which, therefore, the simple sign *x* was introduced. The *k* must, however, be the forward k^1, else the current of

326   THE ORGANS OF SPEECH.

air would not immediately reach the teeth; at the commencement of a word k^2 can also be employed, though with some effort (*pax, rex, Klecks, Fuchs, Xaver*).

Thirdly, there is the connection of a *stridula* of a more backward region with a preceding *explosiva*, such as

$$ps,\ pch^1,\ pch^2;\ tch^1,\ tch^2.$$

If, before the formation of the *explosiva*, the narrow outlet necessary for the *stridula* is prepared, the latter will follow immediately upon the outburst of the air. The only combination which can easily be employed both at the beginning and end of words is *ps*, which had, therefore, even in Greek the simple sign ψ (ψιλος, *Psalm, Reps*); tch^1 at the beginning of a word can be heard in the affected pronunciation of "ja" as tch^1a. At the end of words tch^1 and pch^1 are heard in dialects, though not quite without hiatus ($fitch^1$ for *Fittich*, *tepch* for *Teppich*).

The second class of *continuae* to be considered are the *marginals*, and here we have combinations of a preceding *explosive* with a *marginal*.

The combinations with *l* are

$$pl,\ tl,\ k^1l,\ k^2l.$$

These are all formed easily at the commencement of words, if the mouth is adjusted for the *l*-position before the formation of the *explosive*, so that the liberated air in passing over the dorsum of the tongue will produce the sound of *l*. The only difficulty lies in *tl*, for the apex of the tongue, which has been removed from the palate for *t*, has to be instantly replaced for the formation of *l*, and thus a small hiatus can scarcely be avoided; this combination of consonants is almost confined to names derived from the ancient language of Mexico. Whether k^1 or k^2 is to precede *l* depends upon the vowel which follows *l*; those vowels which require a contraction of the anterior part of the cavity necessitating the utterance of k^1; k^2, on the contrary, depending upon the more posterior contraction of the cavity of the mouth—thus showing, from the difference in the *k*, that there is a preparation for the ensuing vowel. It is possible to pronounce *kl* with a *k* not thus decided by the vowel; it is, however, more difficult. *Plan, Tlaskala, Klinge* ($k^1 linge$), *Klotz* ($k^2 lots$). At the end of a word these combinations are always accompanied by a hiatus.

The combinations of *explosives* with *sch* are

psch, tsch, ksch.

Of these *ksch* is the most difficult to form, and is, in German at least, only met with in dialects, and then always as k^1, because the point for the formation of this sound lies nearest to that of *sch*. The cause of this difficulty is that for k^1 the back part of the dorsum of the tongue is raised and the apex depressed, while for *sch* the apex must be elevated and the back part of the dorsum depressed. The change from one position to the other cannot, however, be well performed without a hiatus, though it may be an exceedingly small one. *G'scheid, tü'cksch*. *Psch* is easily pronounced, if the mouth is adjusted before the formation of *p*; still it is only employed, in German at least, in dialects, except for names (*Pschorr, Berlepsch*), and has a strong inclination for a hiatus: *tsch*, on the contrary, is like *ts*, and for similar reasons easy to pronounce; still it is little met with in German, and then only at the end of words (*Klatsch*); it is, however, used in Italian both with and without tone (*cima, giro*), and in English, though written in a great variety of ways (*chain, ginger, jump, patch, pledge*).

The third class of *continuæ* comprises the different forms of *r*, which are joined to *explosives* in the following combinations:—

$pr^2, tr^2, k^1 r^3, k^2 r^4.$

At the end of words these combinations cannot be uttered without hiatus, as the current of air required for r is too strong. The r which combines with the explosive is that which lies nearest to the point at which the former is formed, as may be seen from the above group. K^1r^3, like k^1l, and for the same reason, precedes i and e; k^2r^4, like k^2l, precedes a, o, u. The r^2 in pr^2 and tr^2 is, from this preadjustment for the ensuing vowel, pronounced more forward before i and e than before a, o, u. Prinz, Pracht, Trieb, trocken, Krieg, Kragen.

The relations which characterize the combinations considered in the foregoing remarks, are exactly reversed in those combinations where a *continua* stands first and is followed by a p, t, or k. With a *continua* the latter sounds assume the occlusive character which they retain even when the combination is situated at the end of a word; when, however, it stands at the commencement of a word the impure character of the *occlusive* is very marked, for to the following sound it appears as an *explosive*.

Starting with the *continuae stridulae* we find that the sounds in questions may be grouped as follows:—

fp, ft, fk; sp, st, sk^1, sk^2; $chp, ch^1t, ch^2t, ch^1k, ch^2k$.

Of these, fp, ch^2k^2, and also ch^1k^1 can be uttered alone, but they require such a forcible current of air that they cannot be attached to any other sounds; fk^1, fk^2, sk^2 ch^1p, ch^2p, ch^1k^2, and ch^2k^1 cannot be pronounced without a very considerable hiatus. Of all this series, therefore, which is greatly simplified if we remark that sk is the only sound which distinguishes between the two forms of k, there remain only the six combinations, ft, sp, st, sk, ch^1t, and ch^2t, which can be included amongst the double consonants. In ft the f-stream is suddenly interrupted by closure with the tongue (t); it is found at the beginning of words (though not entirely without hiatus) in Greek (φδορος), at the termination of words in *schuft, cleft*. In the three combinations of *s* the *s*-stream is in the same manner interrupted by an occlusive sound; that k^1 is the only one of the two forms of *k* which can be used for this purpose, is due to the circumstance that in changing from the *s*-position the tongue can only reach the k^1-position, for the *s* must not disappear till the *k* is formed. All three combinations are equally well adapted for commencing and ending words (*speed, Visp*, Germ. *grasp; start, ist*, Germ. *fast; sky, risk*). In English, at the termination of a word after *a*, a more backward impure *s* may be heard combined with k^2, as, for instance, in *ask*. We find *cht* used at the beginning of words in Greek (χδων), and at the end of words we find ch^1t after *i* and *e, Licht, Recht*, and ch^2t after *a, o, u, Nacht, Docht, Wucht*.

Adding the sounds *p, t, k* to the marginals, we have the series

lp, lt, lk^1, lk^2; schp, scht, schk.

Of these sounds those formed with *l* can be pronounced without effort if the second sound appears as a true *occlusive* before *l* is silent; this also applies to the two forms of *k*, if when the combination is with k^2 the *l* is formed a little further back. This combination can therefore only be used without hiatus at the end of words: lk^1 follows *i* and *e*, lk^2 *a, o, u* (*help, gelb, hilt, Bild, milk, Schalk*); *schp* and *scht* can, like *sp* and *st*, and for the same reason, be formed without difficulty and used both at the beginning and end of words. They may be heard in ordinary German at the beginning of words written *sp, st* (*Spiel, Stein, Stand, Vischp* (in dialects), *Gischt*); *schk* is not difficult to form with *k*, but seems to have no application.

With the vibrants we have the series
$$r^2p, \ r^2t, \ r^3k, \ r^4k^2,$$
all four of which are easily formed as terminations to words. If while r is still vibrating the second sound is formed as a pure *occlusive*, r^3k^1 follows i and e, r^4k^2 a, o, u (*sharp, hart, Werk, stark, shark*). They cannot be formed at the beginning of words without a hiatus.

We have shown the relation which springs from the attachment of an *explosiva* or *occlusiva* to a preceding *stridula*; it now remains to discuss the relation produced by annexing other *continuae* to the latter.

A succession of two *stridulae* gives the series
fs, fch; sf, sch; chf, chs.
None of these combinations can be formed without hiatus, though if the tongue is protruded while *ch* is still sounding a ch^1s or ch^2s may be produced almost without hiatus, for instance, in the genitive form of Schlich and Dach, *Schlichs, Dachs*, which, however, from the difficulty of the double sound generally have the sound of *Schliches, Daches*.

A *marginal* joined to a *stridula* gives
fl, sl, chl; fsch, ssch, chsch.
Of these combinations those with an *sch* in the second place cannot, on account of the great change in the position of the tongue, be pronounced without a hiatus. Those with l in the second place are, on the other hand, possible at the beginning of words, if, before the first sound is ended, such preparation is made for l by the position of the tongue that the apex only has to be brought against the palate to produce the l. Example: *Floh, slave*, ch^1li (Alemannic for klein), ch^1loyd (the right pronunciation of the name Lloyd, which for this reason is always spelt *Floyd* by the unlettered housekeeper in " Humphry Clinker."

The combinations between *vibrants* and *stridulae* are
$$fr^2,\ sr^2,\ ch^1r^3,\ ch^2r^4,$$
all of which can be pronounced if the tongue is placed for the *stridula* in the proper position for the corresponding r; thus when the *stridula* is s in the position for r^2, when ch^1 in the position for r^3, and when ch^2 in the position for r^4, a slight expiratory effort then gives rise to the *stridula* and if gradually increased develops from it the r. With f the tongue must be placed in the position for r^2, as r^1 cannot be used as an articulate sound. These combinations, again, can only be used at the beginning of words, and that to a limited extent; they can scarcely be pronounced without hiatus at the end of words, for the difficulty which they offer when pronounced alone is increased when they follow immediately upon a vowel. The most difficult form, sr, is scarcely ever heard; fr^2 is in very common use; the r which follows the f may, however, be either r^3 or r^4, according to the succeeding vowel, though the change is not absolutely necessary, as, for instance, *fragen* can be as easily pronounced with r^2 as with r^3 or r^4 (*frisch, frech, froh, Frucht*). *Chr* is found at the commencement of words in Greek, χρη, χρονος, when, according to the rule we have found to hold good in so many cases, the χρ in χρη must be ch^1r^3, and in χρονος ch^2r^4, because in the first case η follows, and in the second ο.

The relations between *marginals* and *explosives*, or, as the case may be, *occlusives*, have already been discussed, and also those when they are connected as a second sound with a *stridula* as a first sound. We have now, therefore, to consider their properties as a first sound connected with *stridulae and vibrants*.

With the *stridulae* the following combinations can be formed:—

lf, ls, lch; schf, schs, schch.

Of these combinations those which have l as a first sound stand in the same relation as *tf, ts, tch*, the tongue in both cases being brought against the palate. For instance, *lf* and *lch* can be produced if the lips are protruded while l is sounding, the current of air being increased in force for the former combination, and for the latter the dorsum of the tongue being raised; the only *ch* which can be used is ch^1. For *ls* it is sufficient to remove, while l is sounding, the apex of the tongue from its position of contact and to raise its edges; this combination is, therefore, more often met with than the others. All three can only be formed at the end of words, because if placed at the beginning the combination is broken up by the closer connection between the second sound and the succeeding vowel. (*Elf, Hals, Kelch.*) Passing to the combinations with *sch*, we find that *schf* and *schch* can be formed, though not without care and some difficulty; *schs* is, however, easier when placed at the end of a word, for if the apex of the tongue is depressed and the edges raised, the transition can be made from *sch* to *s*. (*Fischs* genitive of *Fisch.*)

Two combinations are possible with the *vibrants*

lr, schr,

the first of which (*lr*) can only be pronounced with difficulty, the formation of the l being interrupted by the vibration of the extreme tip of the tongue; it has, therefore, no value as an articulate sound: *sch*, on the contrary, can, if the dorsum of the tongue is raised, be easily connected with an r^3, and sometimes, as an individual peculiarity or in a dialect, with an r^2; this combination, however, like all those with r as a second sound, can only be used at the beginning of words. If i or e follows, the r^3 is formed a little more forward;

THE FORMATION OF ARTICULATE SOUNDS. 333

if *a, o,* or *u,* more backward (*Schrift, Schreck, Schramme, Schrot, Schrunde*).

Lastly, we have the combinations between *vibrants* in the first place and *stridulae* and *marginals* in the second ; and, as we found with *rp, rt, rk*, these combinations cannot be employed at the beginning of words.

The combinations with *stridulae* are

rf, rs, rch.

The character of the *r* is regulated by the preceding vowel, though it is always a little more forward for *f* and *s* than with the same vowel for *ch*. It is, however, in our power to form, though not always without effort, these combinations with any of the forms of *r*, of course excepting r^1. The *ch* following *r* is always ch^1, because the formation of ch^2 resembles that of r^2 too closely for the two sounds to be separated. (*Dürf-en, scharf; Birs, iners, ars, Werch* [*Werg*], *Sarch* [*Sarg*].)

The combinations with the marginals are

rl, rsch.

Both are formed without difficulty, if during the utterance of r^2 or r^3 the tongue is gradually advanced to the *l* or, as the case may be, to the *sch* position. Here, again, the r^3 or r^2 is forward after *i* or *e*, and the r^3 more backward after *a, o, u*. In grammars we find the use of *rl* confined within very narrow limits (*Quirl*, Germ. *gnarl*, Eng.), though in the Austrian dialects it is widely distributed as a diminutive (*Ganserl*). The two following examples will suffice for *rsch* :—*Hirsch, marsch.*

CONSONANTS AND RESONANTS.

Having now discussed the question whether double consonants do not exist in the same sense as double vowels, and having found that certain combinations of consonants, under the condition that they are not placed between two vowels, can be formed with more or less ease without a hiatus, and therefore may be regarded as analogues of double vowels, it remains to see whether similar relations do not exist between the resonants themselves or between resonants and consonants.

The resonants depend, as we know, upon a closure at three different points: at the lips for *m*, the teeth and tongue for *n*, the tongue and soft palate for *ng*. In the closure for *ng* the entire cavity of the mouth in front of the soft palate is open; in that for *n*, the cavity of the lips. As in the closure for *m* the cavity of the mouth is completely closed to the front, the tongue may assume any position, and though for a full-sounding *m* it should be depressed, yet it may be raised and the apex placed against the upper incisors. If, when in this position, a deep tone is sounded, a pure *m* is heard; if a higher tone, an intermediate sound, which is neither *m* nor *n*, but bears some resemblance to both, and thus stands towards the two sounds in the position of *ae* to *a* and *e*. We have already shown, when describing the resonants, that a similar intermediary sound exists between the region of closure for *n* and that for *ng*. Intermediary sounds similar to the intermediary vowel-sounds are, therefore, met with among the resonants.

It is possible, moreover, to pass or glide from one resonant into another, if the position of the closure is gradually either advanced or removed further back. Thus if *ng* is uttered the closure may be gradually advanced along the entire palate to the anterior end of the *n*-region at the teeth, and then by closing the lips pass into *m*. Then, again, if the apex of the tongue is placed behind the teeth and *m* is uttered, when the lips are opened *n* will be heard, and if the closure is gradually moved backwards along the palate, the whole series of resonants can be formed backwards in an unbroken succession. The Greek initial sound μν (μνημα) can, therefore, be pronounced without hiatus. This peculiarity more resembles those of vowels, as, for instance, the transition from *a* to *o*, than the relation between consonants.

Among consonants the explosive sounds only can be immediately connected with the resonants, and, moreover, the combination can only take place between a resonant and the explosive corresponding to its point of closure; the only combinations are, therefore, *mp, nt, ngk*. The combination *nk* is, indeed, written, but as *k* must be preceded by a closure at the soft palate, *ng* must of necessity be formed (*Lump, Rand, trink, schrank*). As an explosive is due to the opening of a closure, it is often more or less distinctly heard as an after sound at the end of a word or before a vowel; formerly, indeed, it was written (*Irrthumb*), and is now in some languages retained, in others lost in the same word both as written and spoken (*Zimmer, limber; kin, Kind; numerus, nombre*). The *explosive* is heard even more distinctly when the resonant is followed by a consonant, and here, again, it is written in some cases and not in others. *Rumpf, Triumf; Gans, gants* (*ganz*); *Drangs* (genitive), *beengt* (pronounced *Drangks, beengkt*).

L AND N MOUILLÉ.

By the term *mouillé* is meant a manner of pronouncing *l* and also *n* when a *j* is annexed to these sounds. This pronunciation is generally heard between two vowels, but not unfrequently at the beginning of words, and sometimes at the end, as, for instance, in the French *detail*.

Before attempting to assign to this phenomenon its proper place we must consider it in connection with other phenomena, and especially the relation between *u* and sounds to which it is annexed.

The close connection between *i* and *j*, and between *u* and *w*, was alluded to in the remarks upon iambic diphthongs with *i* or *u* as a first sound, and it was then shown that the two consonants in question can be developed from the corresponding vowel in two ways, namely, (1) if while the tone is sounding the force of the current is so increased that a fricative noise is produced, when the vowel is *u* by the protruded lips, and when *i* by the apex and the edges of the tongue over which the stronger current of air is driven towards either side; (2) if in passing to another sound the tongue, or, as the case may be, the lips, are rapidly drawn back, thus producing a fricative noise. Both causes have the same effect—an *i* spoken quickly and strongly before another vowel, turning it into a *j* (*je, ja*)—and under the same conditions a sound beginning as *u* becoming *w*, as in the English *w* (double ju).

Besides appearing in several other iambic diphthongs, we often find *u* after *k*, and followed by another vowel. The *u* in such words appears to be nothing more than the transition from one vowel to the other—so, at least, the fact would seem to show; that it is present in many Italian words (*guanto, guerra*), and absent, or, if written, not pronounced, in the corresponding French words (*gant, guerre*). We find further, in connection with this peculiarity, that this *u* follows *k* less frequently before *o* than before other vowels, especially when the *k* is the *k*-sound with tone, namely, *g*, the explanation of which lies in the manner in which the intervening *u*-sound is produced. For the formation of *k* the tongue is drawn very far back, and its anterior portion lies, therefore, both backward and low; this is, however, the position of the tongue for *u*. The lips, it is true, need not necessarily be in the position ascribed for a full, round *u*, but this, as we showed when speaking of the vowels, is not of primary importance. Now when, after the formation of the *explosive k*, the current of air is released, this position of the tongue gives rise to an *u* during the short time which elapses before the tongue can be adjusted for the following vowel. The position of the tongue for *o* so closely resembles that for *u* that there is little need for *u* before *o*, for it will either be imperceptible in the rapid change of position which the tongue can here make, or else the *o*-position will have been assumed before the formation of *k*.

It may, however, be asked, why, if the above is true, an *u* is not heard after every *k* followed by a vowel, it being possible to pronounce *kahn*, *kehren*. This objection may be answered at once as follows: If *k* is uttered independently, and the tongue afterwards adjusted for the following vowel, the *u*-sound will result from the position of the tongue for *k* being the same as that for *u*; this can be, however, and is prevented by placing the tongue either exactly or approximately in the position for the succeeding vowel, before *k* is allowed to break out. This will at once be seen from the following experiment: Let *k* be pronounced alone; it will be followed by an indistinct *u*; if then *k-elle* is pronounced, it will be distinctly heard as *Quelle*; if, however, *Kelle* is pronounced, we shall observe that the tongue is raised before the formation of *k*, and thus is prepared for *e*.

Thus *u* constitutes a kind of hiatus between the full deep *k* and the following vowel.

There is another point of interest in connection with the above-mentioned relation between *u* and *w*, namely, the difference in the sound of this intervening *u* after *k* and after *g*. If the first sound is *k* with tone, namely, *g*, after the explosion the current of air will be quiet and sonant, and the *u* will then, however quickly uttered, have a distinct *u*-sound (*guanto, guerra, guida*). If, however, the hard toneless *k* is uttered, the current of air which breaks out is more forcible, and at first toneless; the following *u* will then have more or less decidedly the sound of *w* (*Quelle* is pronounced *Kwelle*, and also *quadra, questo, quinta, quota, cuore*). In the first case the *u* is rather attached to the following vowel, forming a kind of iambic diphthong; in the second to *k*, whence this combination is particularized in our alphabet as *qu*.

Other consonants are in Italian and Spanish followed by a similar *u*, in words, namely, which in Latin have an *o* after the consonant in question, which *o* remains *o* in Italian but becomes *e* in Spanish. Example:—

LATIN.	ITALIAN.	SPANISH.
bonus	*buono*	*bueno*
porta	(*porta*)	*puerta*
domus, donum	*duomo*	*duena*
tonus	*tuono*	(*tono*)
tortus		*tuerto*
focus	*fuogo*	*fuego*
locus	*luogo*	*luego*
mors	(*morte*)	*muerte*
movere	*muovere*	*él mueve*
novus	*nuovo*	*nuevo*
rota	*ruota*	*rueda*
solus	*suolo*	*suelo*
vola-re	(*volo*)	*vuelo*.

The words which do not exhibit this change are pronounced with a cramped feeling. The reason for these exceptions cannot be discussed here. It will be sufficient to show from these examples that *u* is inserted after every consonant, if not in both, yet at least in one of the two languages. We may infer from this fact that the insertion is here due less to the consonant than to the succeeding vowel, a view which is supported by the same insertion taking place in words which do not begin with a consonant (*ovum, uovo, huevo; homo, uomo, hombre*). It would seem, therefore, as if this *u* were merely employed to lead up to *o* or *e*, just as we often hear *j* led to by *n* (*n*-ja), or as in Italian *s* is preceded by *i* (*scopus, iscopo*), or *w* by *g* (*Welfe, Guelfo*), or, again, in French and Spanish *s* by *e* (*sperare, espérer, esperanza; spiritus, esprit, espíritu*). The cause of this insertion is, however, of little importance to our present purpose, for which it is sufficient to note the fact of its existence, and that the *u* is pronounced so rapidly that it forms a single syllable with the following vowel. It is, however, of interest in the question before us that this *u* sounds more as *u* or *w*, according to the consonant by which it is preceded (*ruota, swolo*). It is also worthy of remark that, for the same reason as that given above for *u* sounding more after *g* and *w* after *k*, a difference of pronunciation is to be observed after *d* and *t* (*duomo, twono*).

Before examining the entirely similar relation maintained by *i*, we must first draw attention to the fact that *j* may arise in three different ways, namely, (1) voluntarily as *j*, (2) in the above-mentioned manner after a short *i* (*Bavaria, fiore*), and (3) after a *g* formed very far forward and with an imperfect closure. (Latin: *cingere, plangere, jungere*. Italian: *cignere, lagnare, giugnere*; pronounced *tschinjere, lanjare, dschuniere*.)

The relation in which *u* stands to *k* is the same as that in which *i* stands to *l* and *n*, both of which consonants are formed by closure at the teeth. We should rather have expected, from the relation of *u* to *k*, that *i* would have been connected with *t*. The reason why this is not the case is that *s* or *sch* is much more easily joined to *t*, both, particularly *sch*, being very audible fricative noises, and capable of being produced by the same current of air as that with which *t* breaks out, so that if any after-sound is heard after *t*, it will naturally be *s* or *sch*. Analogy would, after this explanation, lead us to expect *ch* to be the after-sound for *k*. In the first place, however, *ch* does not readily join with *k*; and secondly, it is not a very audible sound, so that *u* follows at once upon *k* without any perceptible *ch*. The following examples will show that *t* really is modified by an after-sound of *s* or *sch*.

LATIN.	ITALIAN.	SPANISH.
turma	*ciurma*	*chusma*
ob-turator	*turaggio*	
attactus (French *attaque*)	*acciacco*	
lucta	*lutta*	*lucha*
gutta	*goccia*	
diurnus	*giorno*	
sedecula	*seggiola*	
lac, lactis	*latte*	*leche*
dictus	*detto, ditto*	*dicho*
pectus	*petto*	*pecho*

To the same cause is due the general pronunciation of *tio, tia, tius* as *tsio, tsia, tsius*, while in French and Spanish even the primary sound is omitted (*natus, natio, nation, nacion*); in English also the *t* is omitted, an *sch*, however, taking the place of *s* (*nation*). In the same manner *tio* is changed to *tscho*, *tsch*, *sch* (*viator* [*viatio*], *viaggio*, *voyage* [English], *voyage* [French]); *ovatio*, *omaggio*, *homage* (English), *homage* (French).

The two sounds *l* and *n* are formed by the tongue being advanced, and laid gently against the teeth, or the margin of the teeth. If the tongue is drawn back from this position, it will be in the position for *i*. When, therefore, *l* or *n* is to be followed by a vowel, the tongue, in order to reach the desired position, must pass through the *i*-position, and this transition is often made perceptible by the sound of *i* being heard. From the slight contact required for *l* and *n*, and the rapidity with which it can be broken, this *i*-sound becomes *j*, just as the *u* after *k* becomes *w*; and just as the intimate relation between *k* and *w* is represented specially by *qu*, so the intimate relation between *j* and *l* and *n* is recognized, and these sounds, when pronounced in this manner, are specially termed *l mouillé* and *n mouillé*; and, again, *lj* is expressed orthographically by *gl* or *ll*, and *nj* by *gn* or *ñ* (Spanish). That, however, these sounds are not peculiar in this respect will appear from the following remarks. Examples show that *l* and *n* may be thus softened before all the vowels, even before *i*, when the softening *j* marks the transition to the position necessary for a clear, true *i*, and thus is in a measure only the impure commencement of *i*.

ITALIAN.	SPANISH.	FRENCH.
figlia	*llano*	*billard*
moglie	*lleno*	*vieillesse*
gli	*cuchillito*	*bouillir*
	llover	*billon*
luglio	*lluvia*	*caillou*
campagna	*dueña*	*Armagnac*

Italian.	Spanish.	French.
ingegnere	*niñera*	*regner*
ogni	*niñita*	*Ligny*
sogno	*sueño*	*vignoble*
ignudo	*pañuelo*	

In the same manner as we saw an *u* intervene before *o* and *e* in words which in Latin have an *o*, and that this *u* is more *u* or *w* according to the consonant which precedes, so also we find in words, which in Latin begin with a consonant followed by *e*, an *i* intervening after the consonant. To this we may apply the same explanation as that given to the corresponding *u*, namely, that it serves merely to facilitate the transition, and to lead up to the *u*. As the words in question in the Italian and Spanish languages cannot, like those containing *uo* and *ue*, be chosen from the same Latin examples so as to give a full series of initial consonants in both languages, a separate list has been taken for each, which mutually complete each other.

Latin.	Italian.	Latin.	Spanish.
		bene	*bien*
pes	*piede*	*pellis*	*piel*
coecus	*cieco*	*coelum*	*cielo*
decem	*dieci*	*dens*	*diente*
tepidus	*tiepido*	*tempus*	*tiempo*
gelare	*gielare*		
levis	*lieve*	*lepus*	*liebre*
mel	*miel*	*membrum*	*miembro*
redire	*riedere*	*graecus*	*griego*
seps	*siepe*	*semper*	*siempre*
vetare	*vietare*	*ventus*	*viento*

We shall readily allow that, in this series also, a difference similar to that which was noticed with regard to *u* may be observed in *i*; that, namely, after certain consonants the *i*-sound will predominate, after others the *j*— for instance, in *miel* the *i*, in *siepe* the *j*. Again, as was the case with *u*, after the consonants with tone (soft) more of the *i* will be heard (*bien, dieci, diente*); after the toneless (hard consonants), on the contrary, more of the *j* (*piede, piel, tiepido, tiempo*).

There is, moreover, a third kind of *i*, which appears as the first sound of iambic diphthongs, and, as it thus bears some resemblance to the interjected *i* under discussion, it must be examined a little more closely. The *i* here alluded to is that which seems to have arisen from an *l* after *f*, *p* (*b*), or *k* (*g*) (*fiamma, fiore, fiume; piacere, piega, pieno, piombo, piu; bianco, biondo* (blond); *chiamare, chiericale, chiostra; ghiaccio, ghiottone* [glouton]). It would almost seem as if this *i*, which sometimes sounds more as *i* (*ghiaccio*), sometimes more as *j* (*pieno*), were nothing more than a weak and carelessly uttered *l*, the tongue not being sufficiently elevated or brought properly into contact; and, indeed, in this manner an *i* or *j* may be obtained as an abortive *l*. If, however, we compare the corresponding Spanish words in which the *i* is present and the *l* nevertheless retained (*clamare, chiamare, llamar; clavis, chiave, llave; plaga, piaga, llaga; plenus, pieno, lleno; flamma, fiamma, llama; piovere, llover*), we shall rather draw the conclusion, that this *i* was originally inserted as an *i* of the former class after *l*, so that forms have existed like *cliamare, plieno*, etc., and that the *l* in Italian and the *p*, *c*, etc., in Spanish was subsequently dropped. We shall accept this view with the less hesitation when we observe how readily the Romance languages, and particularly the Italian, set aside everything which offers any difficulty in pronunciation. The following examples will show the truth of this remark :—*pomeridiano* (*postmeridianus*), *lena* (*halena*), *strano* (*extraneus*), *spiacere* (*displacere*), *scendere* (*descendere*), *sonno* (*somnus*), *sintoma* (*symptoma*), *dittongo* (*diphthongus*), *granaio* (*granarium*), *saëtta* (*sagitta*), *tisico* (*phthisicus*), *síquico*, Span. (*psychicus*), etc.

Upon comparing the facts brought forward in the preceding pages, the conclusion is forced upon us that the *l* and the *n* "mouillé" are not special phenomena, but merely an example of the insertion of a vowel so frequently met with; and the distinct *j*-sound resulting from this softening is explained by the intimate relation between the short *i* and *l* and *n*, the same connection being also observed in other consonants. The softening at the end of a word (*détail*, *grille*) must, however, be regarded as a supplementary sound, resembling the explosive after-sound of the occlusives (" topp-*e* "), which arises from the return of the tongue to its position of rest, and is only pronounced more consciously from habit. Further, we must remember that the *e*, *a*, or *o* which in many dialects follow upon *u* or *i* are to be explained in the same manner (*Liab*, *Muotta*).

INDEX.

a, 279
Abdominal muscles, 23
Adam's apple, 43
Air-current, 5
—— in superior cavity of larynx, 69
—— in the pharynx, 78, 276
——, modifications of, 165
——, regulation of, in speech, 166
——, strength of, in speech, 198, 213
—— strengthening of, 17
Air-passage in restricted sense, 27
—— above the tongue, 263
—— below the tongue, 263
—— for formation of nasal vowels, 299
—— for formation of pure vowels, 276
—— through cavity of mouth, 243
—— through the pharynx, 247
Air-passages, 9
——, motor-nerves of, 167
——, nerves, 164
——, relation to alimentary canal, 28, 67
——, sensory nerves of, 169
——, survey of, 24
Alæ of the nose, 94
Alto, 202
Alphabet, 252
——, general division of, 253
Anterior nares, 85
Antrum, 108
Articulate sounds, 251
——————, compound, 255
——————, elements of, 255

Articulate sounds, physiological division of, 254
Articulation, points of, 309
Arytenoid cartilage, 47
—— ——, mechanism of, 49

b, 311
Bass, 202
"Blowing the nose," 231
Brachycephalous skulls, 117

Cartilage, arytenoid, 47
——, cricoid, 40
——, thyroid, 42
—— of Santorini, 67
—— of Wrisberg, 67
Cavity of the cheeks, 120, 241
—— —— mouth, 120, 241
—— —— thorax, 14
Catalani's compass, 192
ch, 317
chf, 330
Chest-notes, 210
chk, 328
chl, 330
Chords, vocal, 42
chp, 328
chr, 331
chs, 330
chsch, 330
cht, 328
Clicking noise, 185
Consonants, 201, 271, 305
——, dental, 312
——, double, 321
——, guttural, 315
——, hard and soft, 271

INDEX.

Consonants, labial, 310
——, laryngeal, 310
——, marginal, 318
——, tenues and mediæ, 271
Corset, 21
Coughing, 178
Cribriform plate, 81
Crico-thyroid membrane, 43

d, 314
Dentals, 313
Diaphragm, 14
Diphthongs, 291
——, division of, 293
——, iambic, with *i* and *u*, 297
——, trochaic, with *i*, 293
—— with *e fermé*, 294, 343
—— with *u*, *a*, and *o*, 294
Dolicocephalous skulls, 117
Double consonants, 321

e, 284
e as commencement of word, 339
e fermé, 285
Epiglottis, 30
——, structure of, 66
Ethmoidal cells, 90
—— sinus, 108
Expiration, 8, 15
——, altered forms of, 177
—— strengthened, 23

f, 312
Falsetto, 210
fch, 330
Fischer's compass, 201
fk, 328
fl, 330
fp, 328
fr, 331
Frontal sinus, 108
Frenum linguæ, 130
fs, 330
fsch, 330
ft, 328

g, 315
g as commencement of word, 339
Glosso-epiglottic ligament, 130
Glottis, 41, 190
——, adjustment of, 48, 194
——, elevation and depression of, 55

Glottis respiratoria, 49, 64
—— ——, closure of, 197
——, structure of, 46
—— vocalis, 49
Groaning, 184
Gums, 120
Gutturals, 315

h, 307
Head-notes, 210
Hiatus, 321
—— filled by consonants, 322
—— filled by vowels, 322
Hiccough, 174
Hissing, 188
Hyoid bone, 62

i, 282, 336
i as commencement of word, 339
i interjected, 341
Inspiration, 8, 15
——, altered forms of, 174
—— strengthened, 23
Isthmus of fauces, 120

j, 297, 318, 336, 339
Jaw, lower, structure, 124
——, ——, mechanism, 124
Jaws, movement of, 123

k, 315
kch, 325
kf, 325
kl, 326
kr, 327
ks, 325
ksch, 327
ku, 337

l, 318
l and *n* mouillé, 335
l changed to *i*, 343
Labials, 310
Lachrymal canal, 109
Larynx, 26, 32
——, artificial, 38
——, depression of, 148
——, elevation of, 148
——, noise produced in, 264
——, relation to production of tone, 37, 190
——, structure of, 32

INDEX. 347

Larynx, superior cavity of, 34, 61, 64, 247
—— tone produced by, 189
Laughing, 178
lch, 331
lf, 331
Ligament, glosso-epiglottic, 130
Ligamenta interannularia, 35
Lips, 129
——, cavity of, 242
——, muscles of, 130
——, noise produced by, 269
lk, 329
Loop-muscles, 152
lp, 329
lr, 332
ls, 331
lt, 329
Lungs, 8, 10, 17
——, air-cells of, 11
——, development of, 26
——, root of, 11

m, 303, 334
Marginals, 318
Masseter muscles, 128
mn, 334
Morgagni, ventricles of, 70, 191, 248
Mouillé, 335
Mouth, cavity of, 119
——, depression of floor, 145
——, diaphragmatic closure, 144
——, division of, 241
——, elevation of floor, 144
——, inner, 241
——, isolation from pharynx, 228
——, mechanical movements, 121
——, noises peculiar to, 265
——, orifice of, 120
——, posterior, 242
——, restricted sense, 120, 241
mp, 335
Muscle, aryteno-epiglottideus, 68
——, arytenoid, oblique, 68
—— ——, transverse, 59, 64
——, buccinator, 130
——, chondro-pharyngeus, 150
——, compressor narium, 97
——, constrictores pharyngis, 153
——, crico-arytenoid, anterior, 56
——, ——, posterior, 57

Muscle, crico-pharyngeus, 154
——, crico-thyroid, 45
——, depressor alæ nasi, 97, 136
——, depressor anguli oris, 134
——, depressor cartilaginis arytenoidis, 68
——, depressor labii inferioris, 133
——, depressor septi mobilis, 98
——, digastric, 145
——, genio-hyo-glossus, 139
——, genio-hyoid, 147
——, hyo-glossus, 139
——, incisivi, 136
——, intercostal, 23, 24
——, kerato-pharyngeus, 154
——, levator alæ nasi, 97
——, levator anguli oris, 134
——, levatores costarum, 23
——, levator labii superioris, 133
——, levator menti, 137
——, levator uvulæ, 162
——, levator veli, 162
——, lingualis longitudinalis, 146
——, lingualis transversus, 140
——, mylo-hyoid, 145
——, mylo-pharyngeus, 154
——, orbicularis oris, 136
——, risorius Santorini, 134
——, omo-hyoid, 147
——, palato-pharyngeus, 158
——, pterygoid, external, 127
——, pterygo-pharyngeus, 154
——, pyramidalis nasi, 98
——, salpingo-pharyngeus, 161
——, scaleni, 23
——, serratus posterior et superior, 23
——, sterno-hyoid, 147
——, stomato-pharyngeus, 155
——, stylo-glossus, 139
——, stylo-hyoid, 147
——, stylo-pharyngeus, 161
——, tensor palati, 162
——, thyro-arytenoid, 54
——, thyro-epiglotticus, 68
——, thyro-hyoid, 63
——, thyro-pharyngeus, 154
——, triangularis menti, 134
——, zygomatic, 134

n, 303, 334
n, as intonation, 339

INDEX.

Nasal bone, 87
—— cavity, 27
—— ——, air-passage of, 87
—— ——, bony framework of, 83
—— ——, cartilage of, 92
—— ——, division of, 81
—— ——, horizontal section, 104
—— ——, imperfect isolation of, 238
—— ——, individual variations, 115
—— ——, isolation from cavity of mouth, 223
—— ——, meatuses, 106
—— ——, noises of, 231
—— ——, resonance of, 233
—— ——, septum, 100
—— ——, stoppage of, 237
—— ——, turbinated bone, inferior, 102
—— ——, turbinated bone, middle, 102
—— ——, turbinated bone, superior, 106
—— ——, walls of, 100
"Nasal twang," 236
—— vowels, 298
ng, 304
ngk, 335
Noise, 256
——, burring, 259
——, clapping, 260
——, clicking, 260
——, explosive, 260
——, fricative, 258
——, hissing, 259
——, rattling, 259
Nose, alæ of, 94
——, external, 92
——, lateral cartilage of, 95
——, moveable septum of, 94
——, muscles of, 96
——, side chambers of, 107
—— ——, their importance, 109
Nostrils, 82
nt, 335

o, 285
Olfactory nerve, 87
Organ of smell, 81

p, 310
Palate, hard, 29
——, soft, 29
pch, 326
pf, 325
Pharynx, 26, 73, 152
——, constrictor muscle of, 122, 153
——, division, 79
——, form of the cavity, 74
——, walls of, 75
pl, 326
pr, 327
ps (ψ), 322, 326
$psch$, 327

qu, 338

r, 307, 320
rch, 333
Reed-instruments, 138
Reeds, membranous, 191
——, vibration of, 192
Resonance, 256
Resonants, 257, 300
——, combination with consonants, 333
Respiration, mechanism of, 14
——, unusual forms of, 173
Respiratory noises, 181
—— organs, 6
—— process, 6.
rf, 333
Ribs, 19
——, mechanism of, 21
rk, 330
rl, 333
rp, 330
rs, 333
$rsch$, 333
rt, 330
Rudimentary skull, 93

s, 314
s interjected after t, 340
Santorini's cartilage, 67
sch, 320
sch interjected after t, 340
$schch$, 331
$schf$, 331
$schk$, 329
$schp$, 329
$schr$, 332

schs, 331
scht, 329
Scream, 207
Sessi, compass of, 201
sf, 330
Singers, respiratory process of, 21
Sighing, 178
sk, 328
sl, 330
Sneezing, 178
Snoring, 191
Snorting, 191
Soprano, 202
sp, 328
Speech, 33, 217
———, audible, 33
Spheno-ethmoidal recess, 111
Sphenoidal sinus, 108
sr, 331
ssch, 330
st, 328
Staccato, 167
Stammering, 176
Strepitus avulsivus, 267
——— continuus, 267
——— explosivus, 268
——— occlusivus, 268
——— repentinus, 269
——— spirans, 266
——— stridulus, 267
——— vibrans, 267
Stuttering, 177
Swallowing, 149, 160

t, 312
t changed into *s* and *sch*, 340
t marginal, 320
tch, 326
Teeth, 120
Tenor, 202
tf, 325
th (English), 315
Thorax, 19
Thyro-hyoid membrane, 63
Thyroid cartilage, 42
Tight lacing, 21
tl, 326
Tone, conditions for pitch, 203
———, crescendo and decrescendo, 213
——— distinguished from noise, 2??
———, intensity, 213

Tone, production of, in air passages, 187
Tongue, 26, 122, 137
———, alteration of form, 140
———, dorsum, 138
———, muscles, 146
———, root of, 138
———, tip of, 138
Tonsils, 159
tr, 327
ts, 325, 340
tsch, 327, 340
Tympanum, 109

u, 283, 336
u, interjected, 338
Uvula, 159

Velum palati, 26, 30, 122, 156
——— ———, adjustment of, 158, 220
——— ———, division of, 222
Ventricles of Morgagni, 70
Vibrants, 320
Vocal apparatus, 35
——— chords, 33, 42, 190
——— ———, division, 48
——— ———, superior, 249
——— ———, tension, 204
Vocal plates, 60, 190
——— ———, material of, 191
Voice, 33, 216
———, compass of, 194, 202
———, quality of, 212
Vowels, 274
———, cause of difference between, 276
———, closure of nasal cavity, 225
———, mixed, 289
———, nasal, 257, 298
———, pure, 257, 275
———, summary, 286
———, varieties, 288

w, 297, 312, 336
Whispering, 272
Windpipe, 12
———, structure of, 35
Whistling, 189
Wrisberg, cartilage of, 67

x, 325

PRINTED BY WILLIAM CLOWES AND SONS, LIMITED,
LONDON AND BECCLES.

www.ingramcontent.com/pod-product-compliance
Lightning Source LLC
Chambersburg PA
CBHW030252240426
43673CB00040B/949